U·F·O·l·o·g·y™

tynion iv · yuenkel · fox · metcalfe

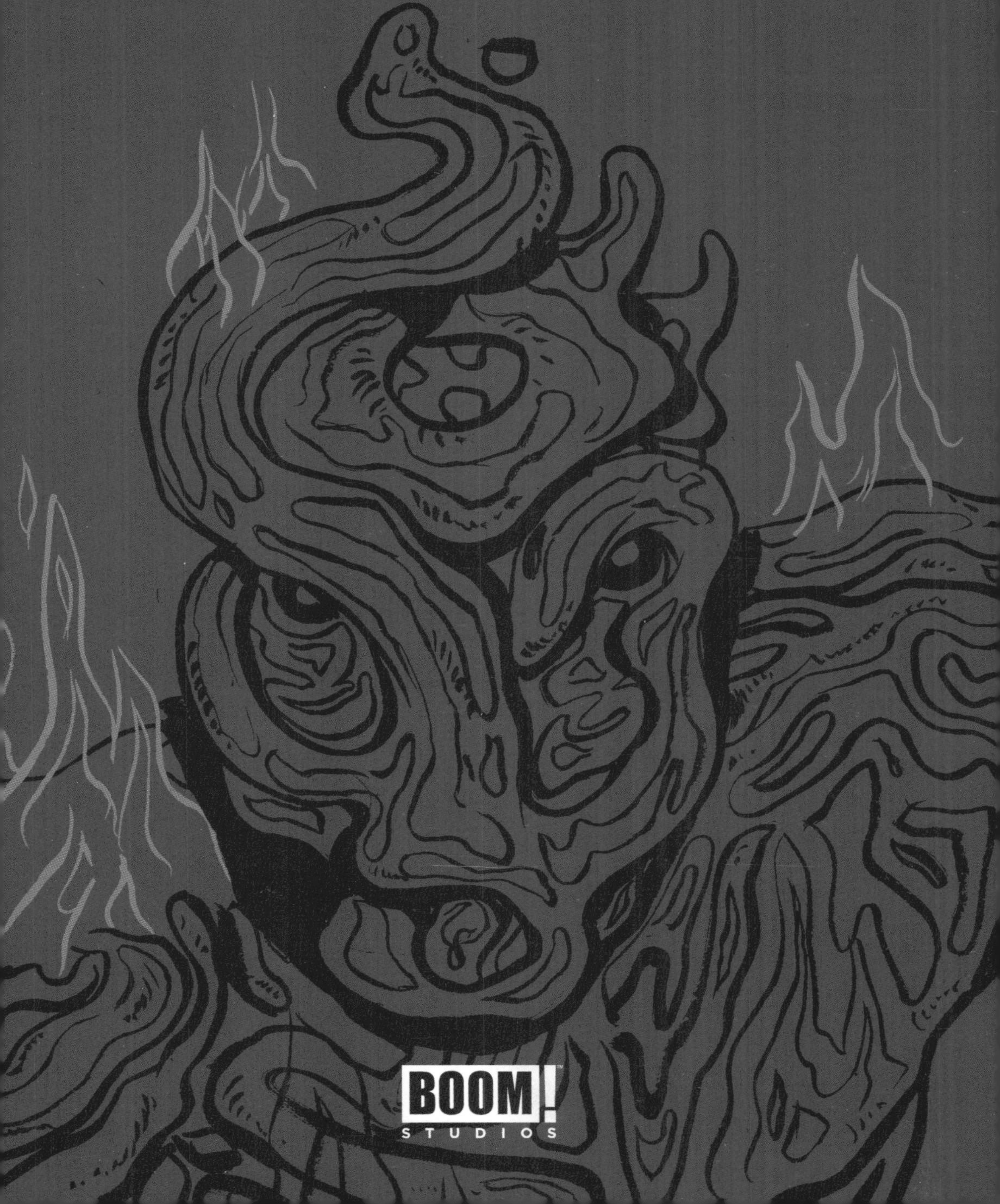

BOOM! STUDIOS

ROSS RICHIE...CEO & Founder
MATT GAGNON ....Editor-in-Chief
FILIP SABLIK ....President of Publishing & Marketing
STEPHEN CHRISTY.................President of Development
LANCE KREITER........... VP of Licensing & Merchandising
PHIL BARBARO .... VP of Finance
BRYCE CARLSON ....Managing Editor
MEL CAYLO.. Marketing Manager
SCOTT NEWMAN ....Production Design Manager
IRENE BRADISH ....Operations Manager
CHRISTINE DINH........Brand Communications Manager
SIERRA HAHN..Senior Editor
DAFNA PLEBAN ....Editor
SHANNON WATTERS....................................Editor
ERIC HARBURN ....Editor
WHITNEY LEOPARD .... Associate Editor
JASMINE AMIRI.. Associate Editor
CHRIS ROSA .... Associate Editor
ALEX GALER.. Assistant Editor
CAMERON CHITTOCK.......................... Assistant Editor
MARY GUMPORT .... Assistant Editor
KELSEY DIETERICH ....Production Designer
JILLIAN CRAB ....Production Designer
KARA LEOPARD.......................................Production Designer
MICHELLE ANKLEY..............Production Design Assistant
AARON FERRARA...........................Operations Coordinator
ELIZABETH LOUGHRIDGE ....Accounting Coordinator
JOSÉ MEZA .... Sales Assistant
JAMES ARRIOLA .... Mailroom Assistant
STEPHANIE HOCUTT .... Marketing Assistant
SAM KUSEK ....Direct Market Representative
HILLARY LEVI.. Executive Assistant
KATE ALBIN...................................Administrative Assistant

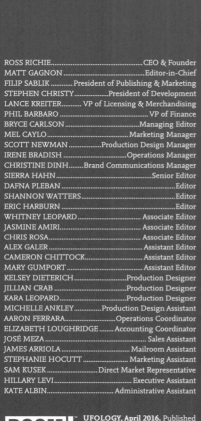

UFOLOGY, April 2016. Published by BOOM! Studios, a division of Boom Entertainment, Inc. Ufology is ™ & © 2016 James Tynion IV & Noah J. Yuenkel. Originally published in single magazine form as Ufology No. 1-6. ™ & © 2015 James Tynion IV & Noah J. Yuenkel. All rights reserved. BOOM! Studios™ and the BOOM! Studios logo are trademarks of Boom Entertainment, Inc., registered in various countries and categories. All characters, events, and institutions depicted herein are fictional. Any similarity between any of the names, characters, persons, events, and/or institutions in this publication to actual names, characters, and persons, whether living or dead, events, and/or institutions is unintended and purely coincidental. BOOM! Studios does not read or accept unsolicited submissions of ideas, stories, or artwork.

A catalog record of this book is available from OCLC and from the BOOM! Studios website, www.boom-studios.com, on the Librarians page.

BOOM! Studios, 5670 Wilshire Boulevard, Suite 450, Los Angeles, CA 90036-5679. Printed in China. First Printing.

ISBN: 978-1-60886-821-6, eISBN: 978-1-61398-492-5

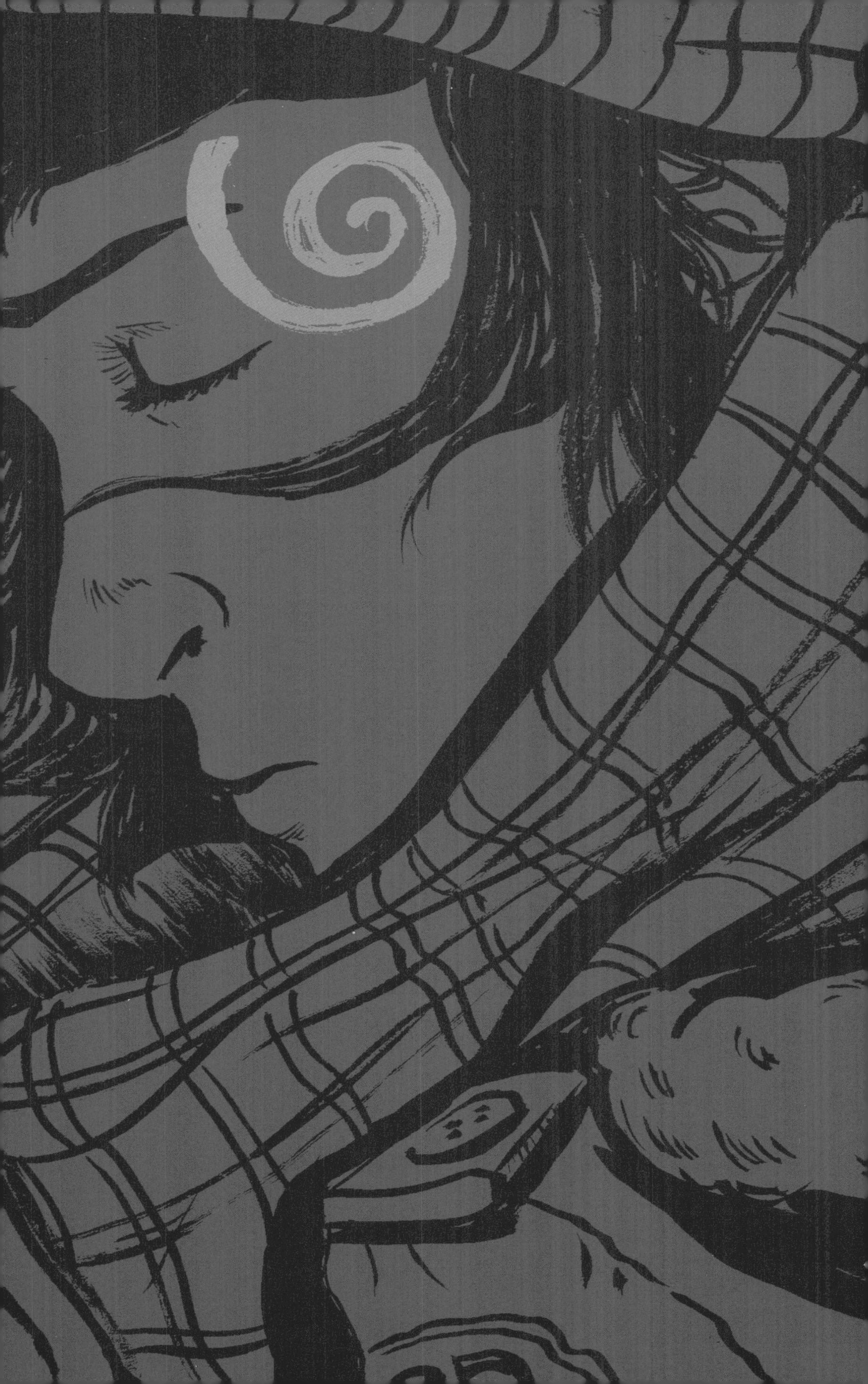

created and written by
james tynion iv & noah j. yuenkel

U·F·O·

colors by
adam metcalfe

letters by
colin bell

cover by
matthew fox

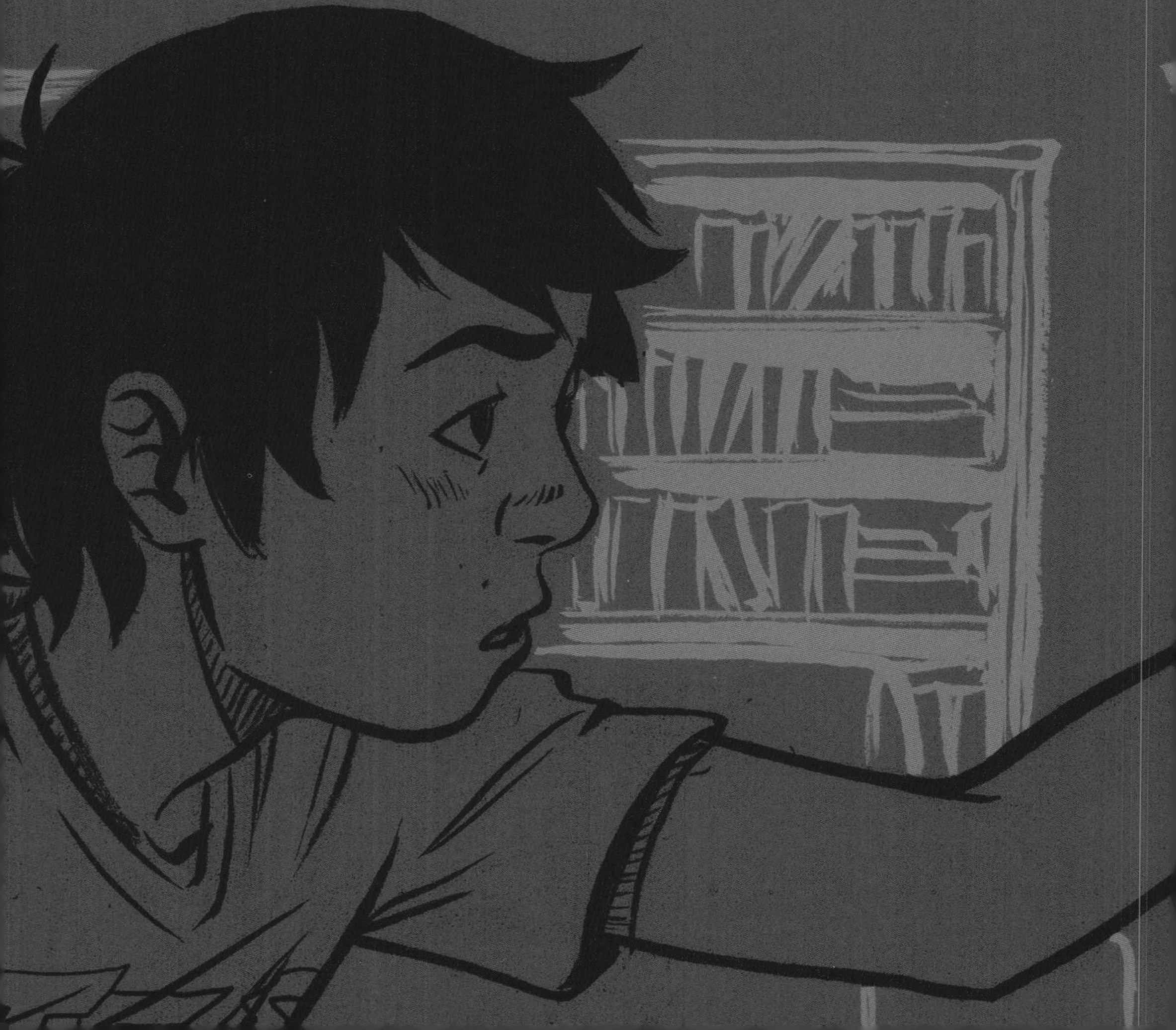

illustrated by
matthew fox

·o·g·y™

designer
jillian crab

associate editor
jasmine amiri

editor
eric harburn

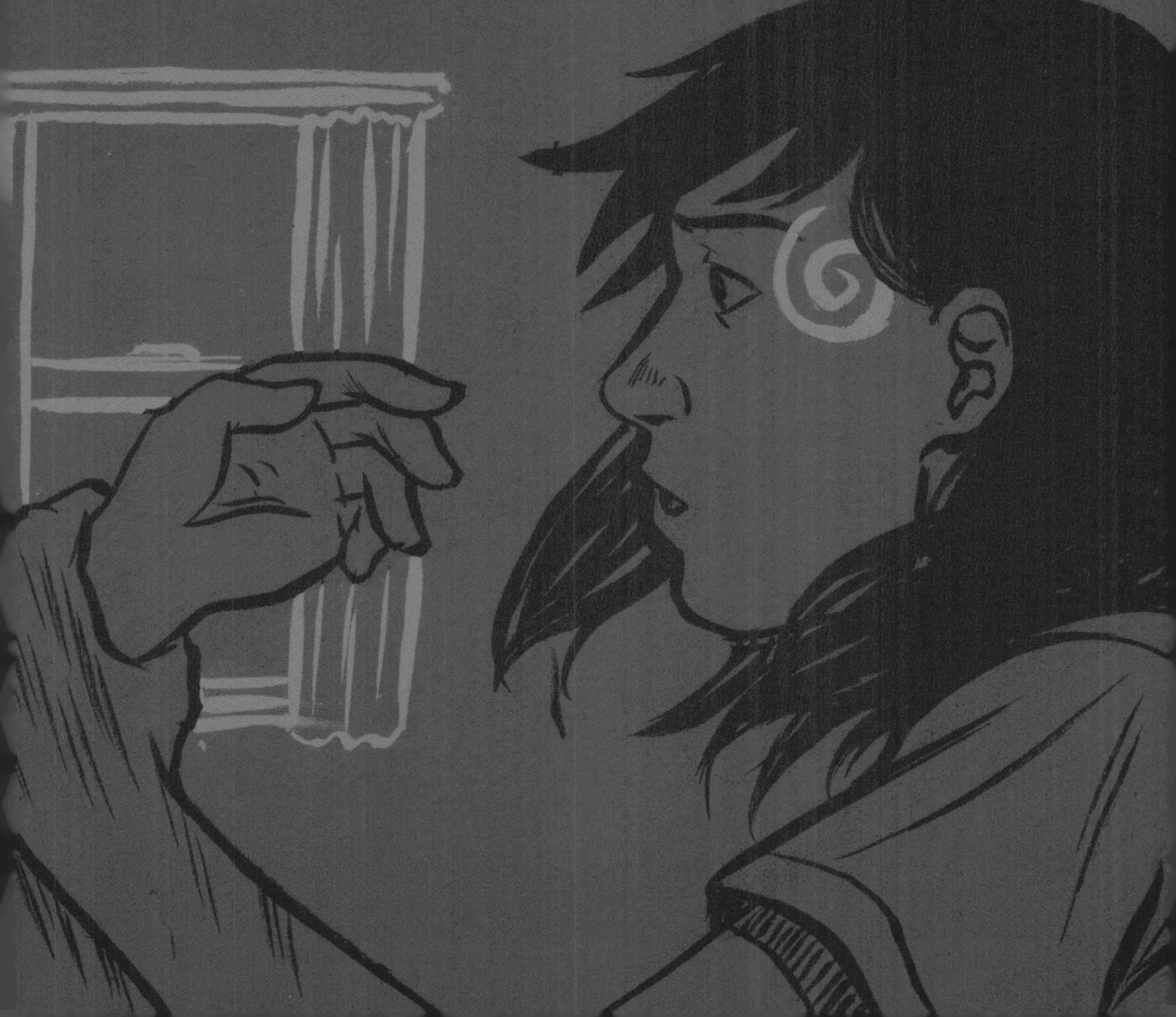

o·n·e

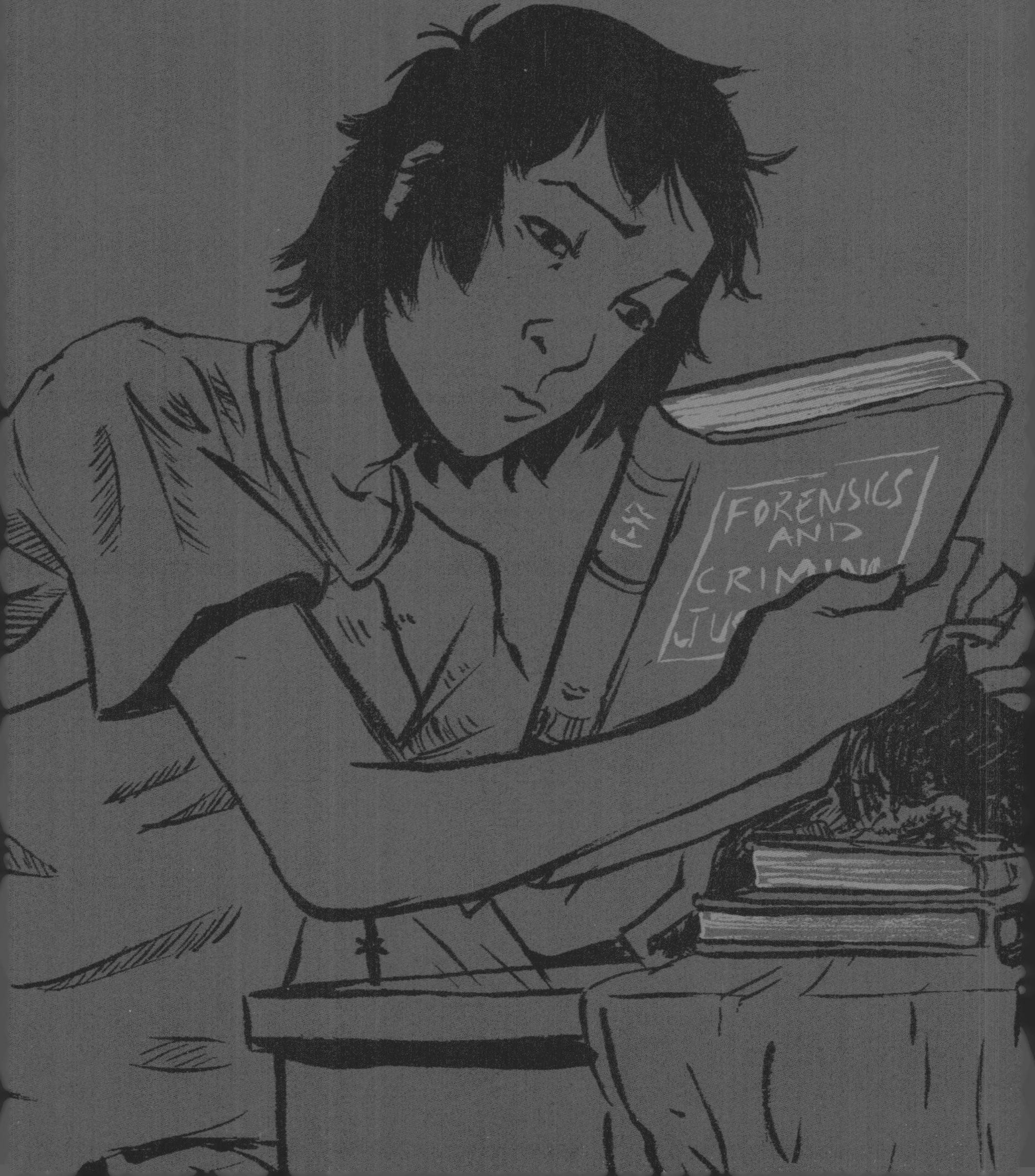
FORENSICS
AND

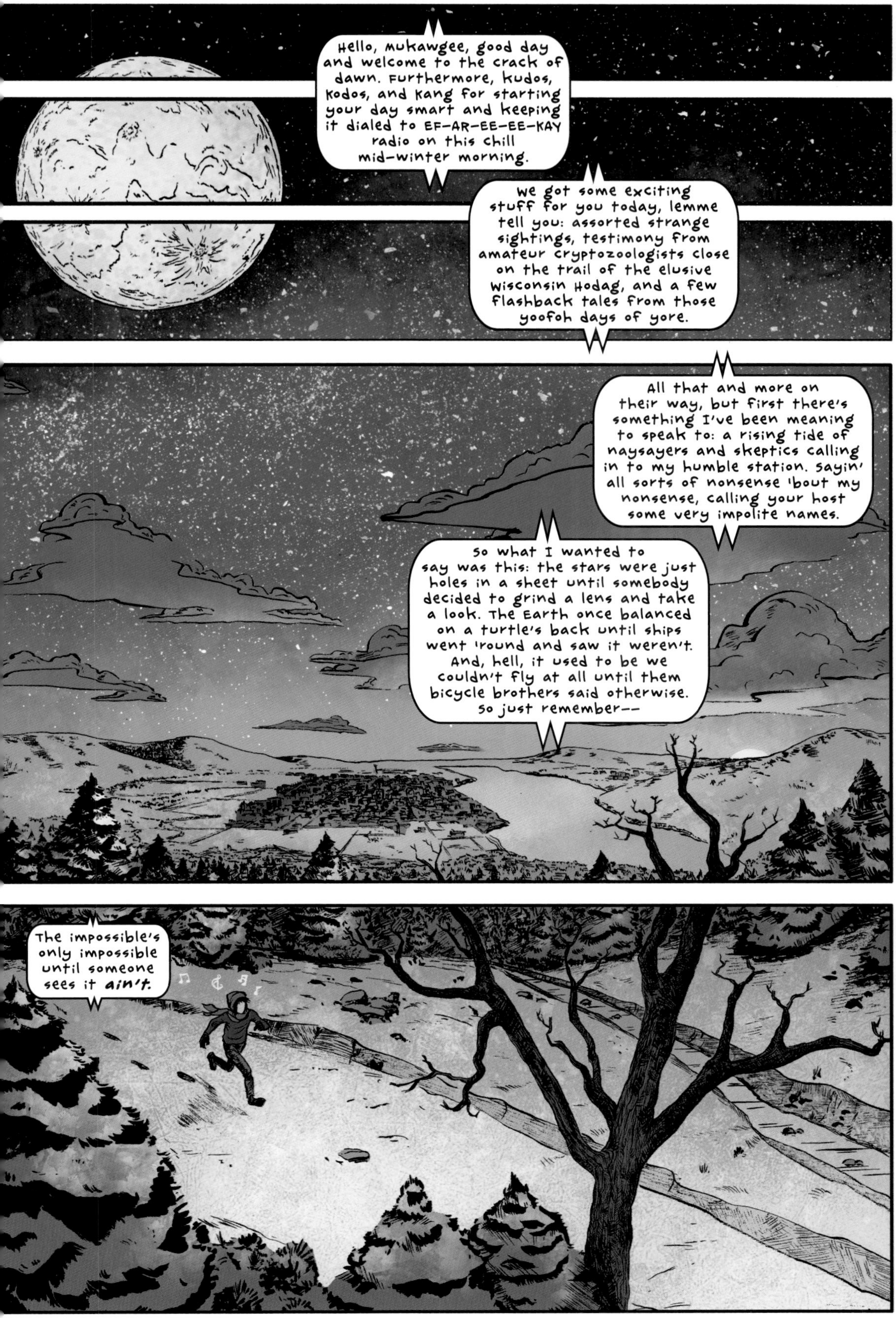
Hello, Mukawgee, good day and welcome to the crack of dawn. Furthermore, kudos, Kodos, and Kang for starting your day smart and keeping it dialed to EF-AR-EE-EE-KAY radio on this chill mid-winter morning.
We got some exciting stuff for you today, lemme tell you: assorted strange sightings, testimony from amateur cryptozoologists close on the trail of the elusive Wisconsin Hodag, and a few flashback tales from those yoofoh days of yore.
All that and more on their way, but first there's something I've been meaning to speak to: a rising tide of naysayers and skeptics calling in to my humble station. Sayin' all sorts of nonsense 'bout my nonsense, calling your host some very impolite names.
So what I wanted to say was this: the stars were just holes in a sheet until somebody decided to grind a lens and take a look. The Earth once balanced on a turtle's back until ships went 'round and saw it weren't. And, hell, it used to be we couldn't fly at all until them bicycle brothers said otherwise. So just remember--
The impossible's only impossible until someone sees it *ain't*.

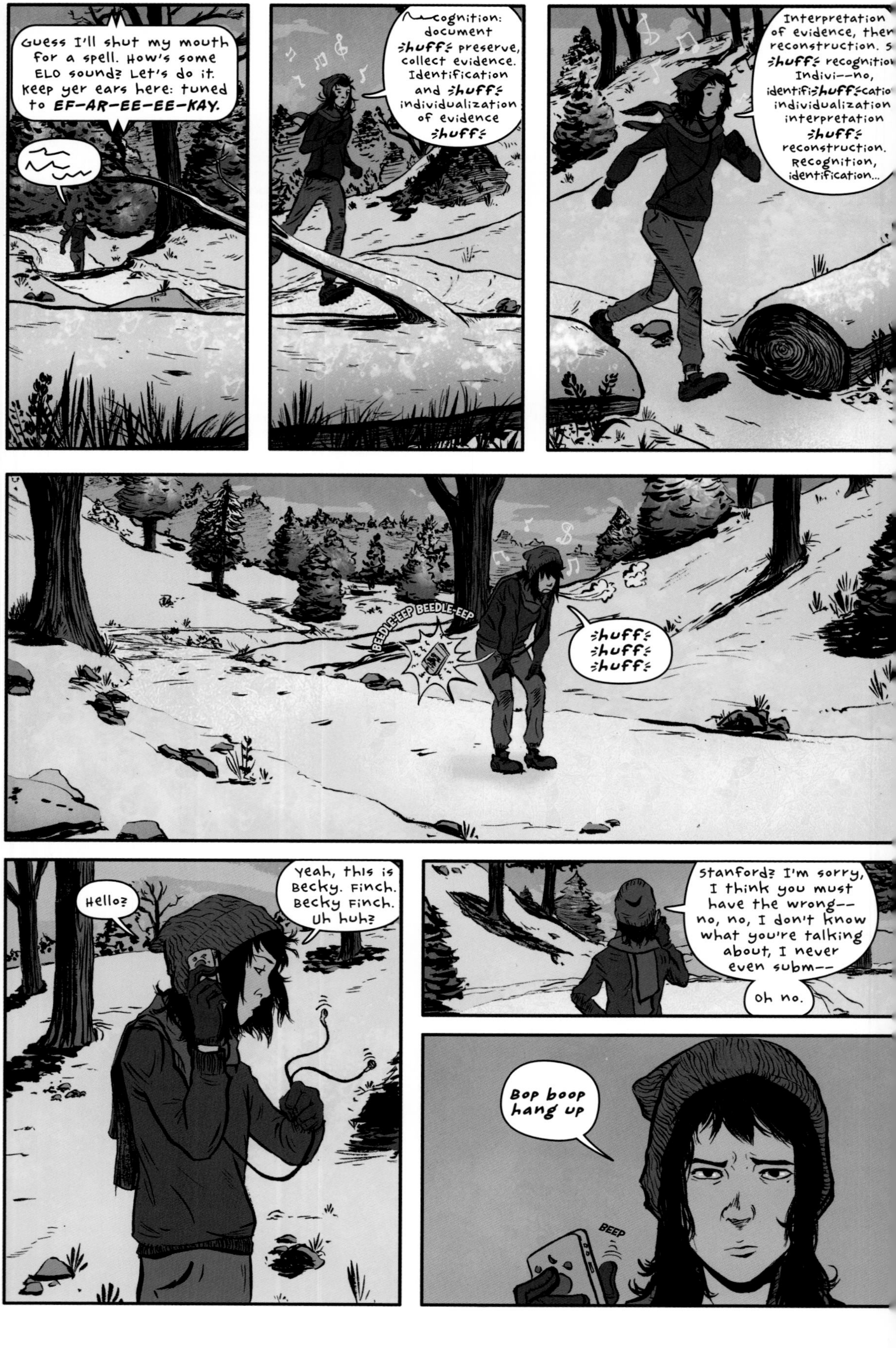

Guess I'll shut my mouth for a spell. How's some ELO sound? Let's do it. Keep yer ears here: tuned to EF-AR-EE-EE-KAY.
cognition: document *huff* preserve, collect evidence. Identification and *huff* individualization of evidence *huff*
Interpretation of evidence, then reconstruction. *huff* recognition Indivi--no, identifi*huff*cation individualization interpretation *huff* reconstruction. Recognition, identification...
BEEDLE-EEP BEEDLE-EEP
huff *huff* *huff*
Hello?
Yeah, this is Becky. Finch. Becky Finch. Uh huh?
Stanford? I'm sorry, I think you must have the wrong-- no, no, I don't know what you're talking about, I never even subm--
Oh no.
Bop boop hang up
BEEP

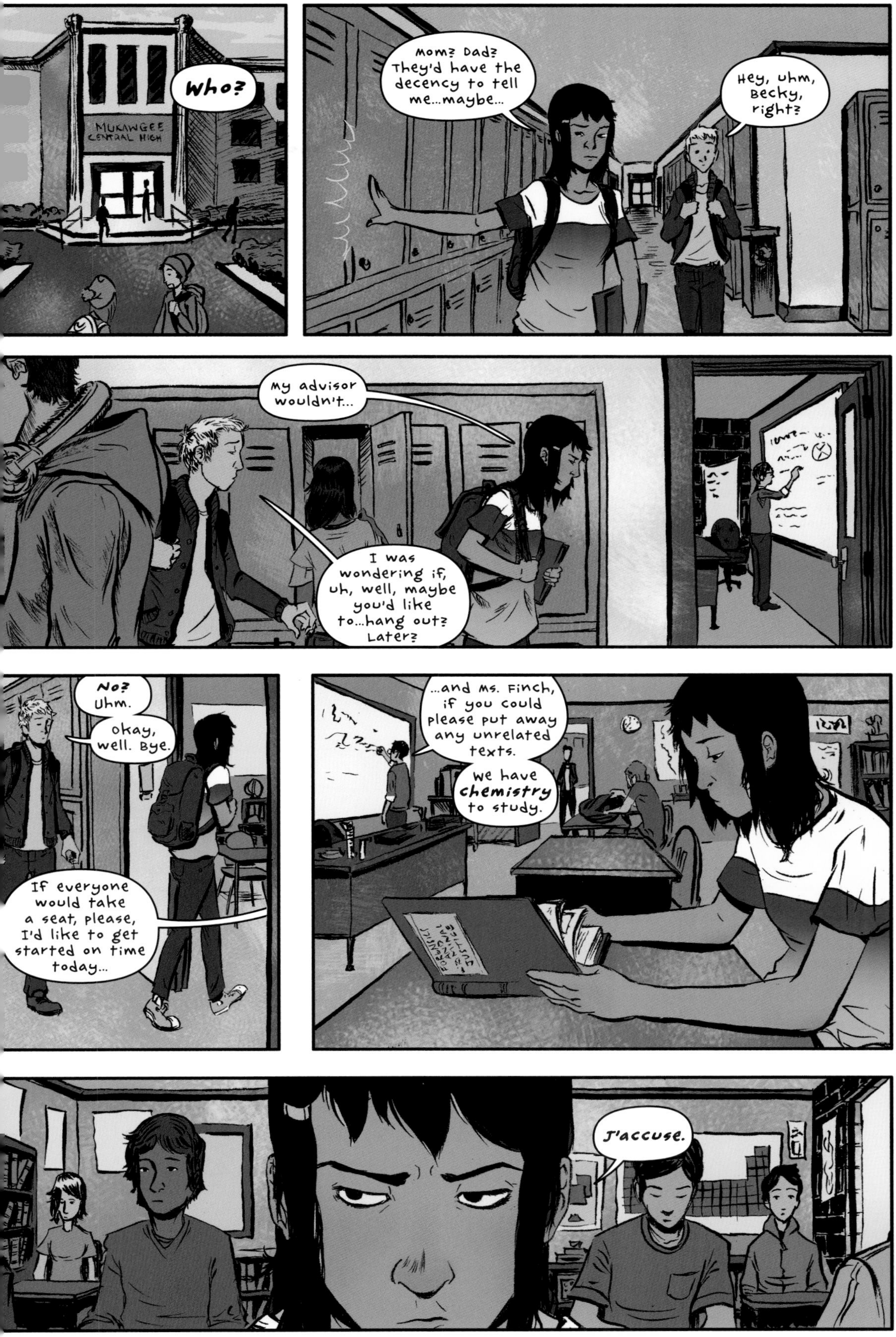

MUKAWGEE CENTRAL HIGH
Who?
Mom? Dad? They'd have the decency to tell me...maybe...
Hey, uhm, Becky, right?
My advisor wouldn't...
I was wondering if, uh, well, maybe you'd like to...hang out? Later?
No? Uhm.
okay, well. Bye.
If everyone would take a seat, please, I'd like to get started on time today...
...and Ms. Finch, if you could please put away any unrelated texts.
We have **chemistry** to study.
J'accuse.

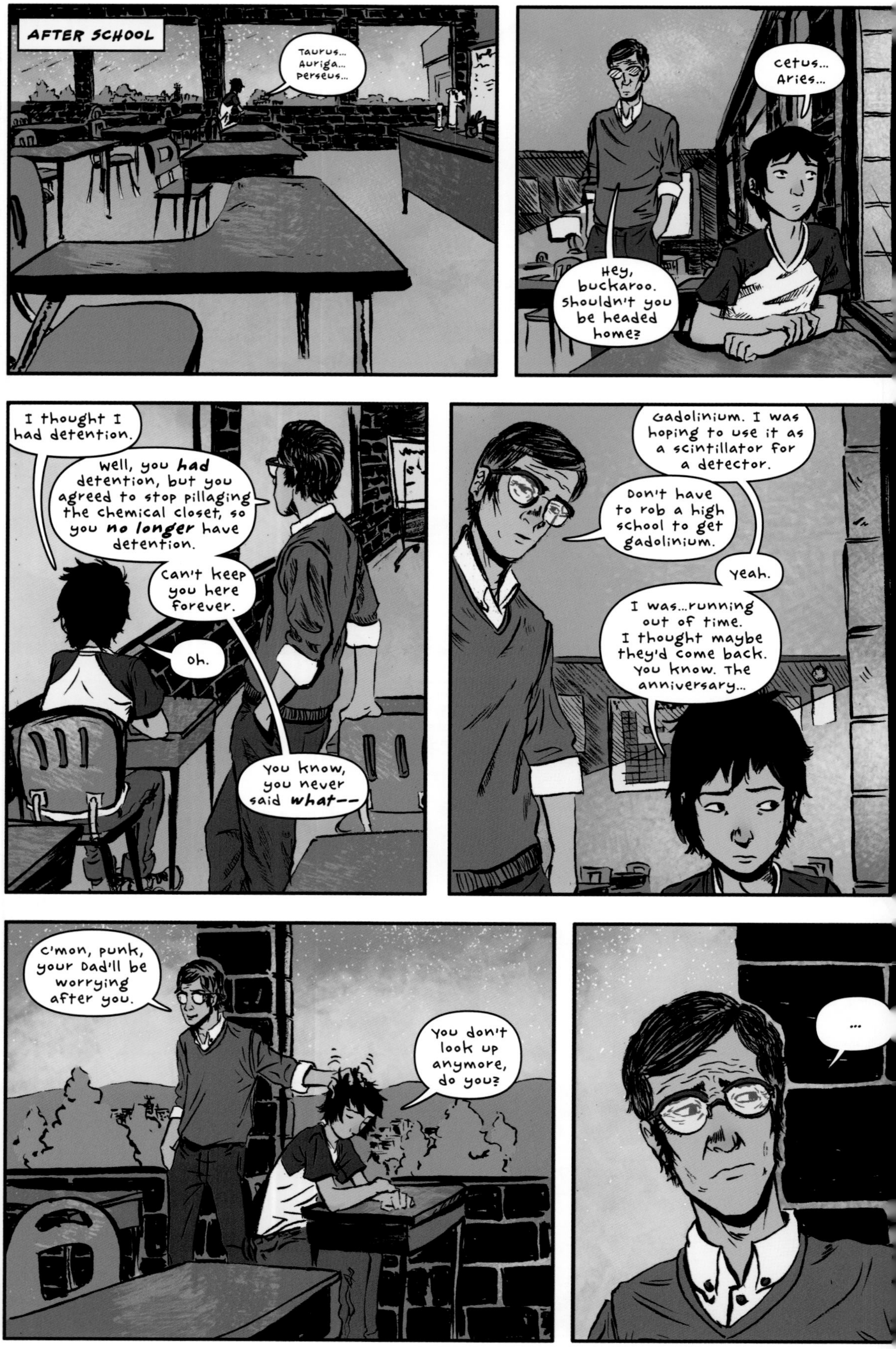
AFTER SCHOOL
Taurus... Auriga... Perseus...
Cetus... Aries...
Hey, buckaroo. Shouldn't you be headed home?
I thought I had detention.
Well, you *had* detention, but you agreed to stop pillaging the chemical closet, so you *no longer* have detention.
Can't keep you here forever.
Oh.
You know, you never said *what*--
Gadolinium. I was hoping to use it as a scintillator for a detector.
Don't have to rob a high school to get gadolinium.
Yeah.
I was...running out of time. I thought maybe they'd come back. You know. The anniversary...
C'mon, punk, your Dad'll be worrying after you.
You don't look up anymore, do you?
...

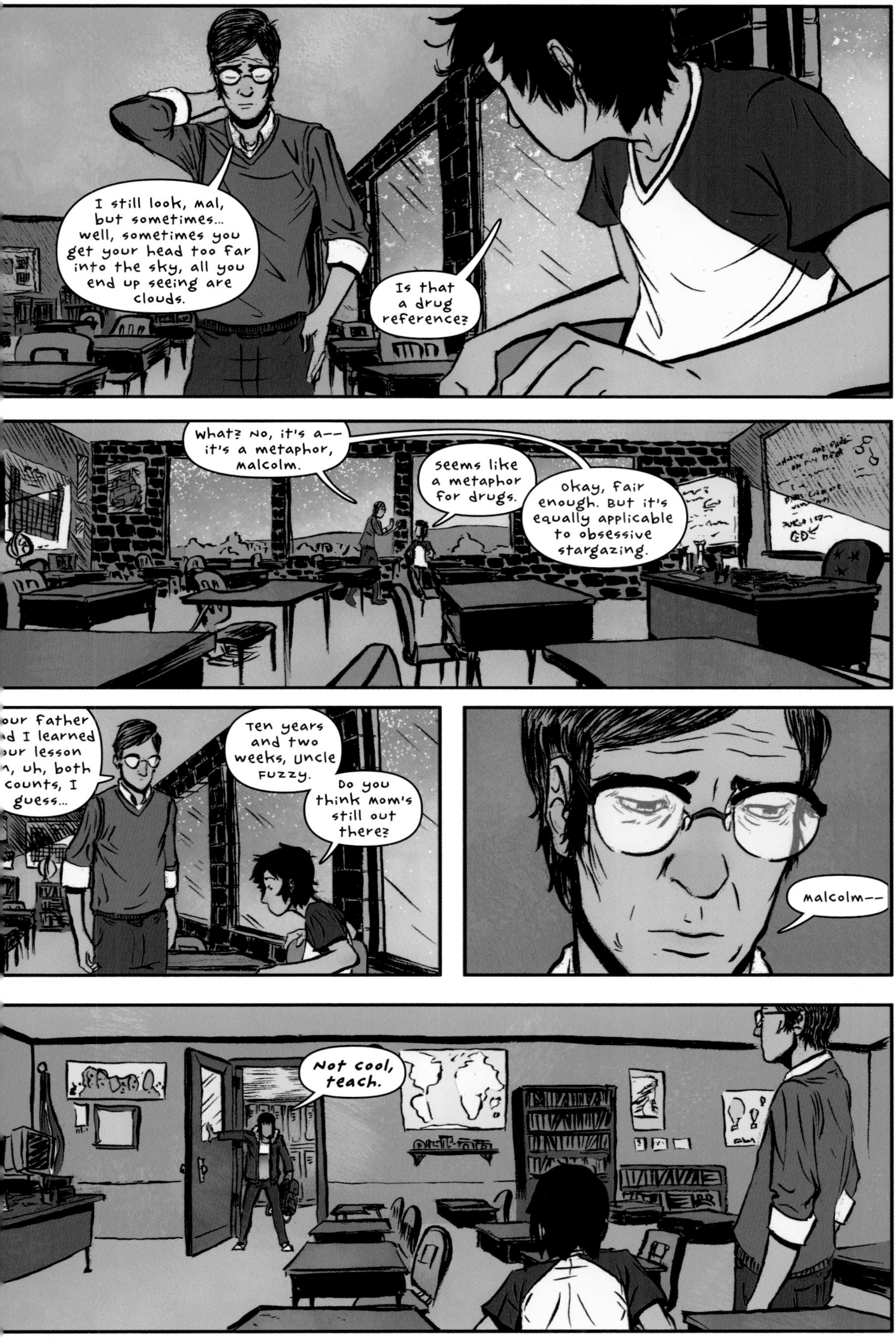
I still look, mal, but sometimes... well, sometimes you get your head too far into the sky, all you end up seeing are clouds.
Is that a drug reference?
What? No, it's a-- it's a metaphor, malcolm.
seems like a metaphor for drugs.
okay, fair enough. But it's equally applicable to obsessive stargazing.
our father d I learned our lesson n, uh, both counts, I guess...
Ten years and two weeks, uncle Fuzzy.
Do you think mom's still out there?
malcolm--
Not cool, teach.

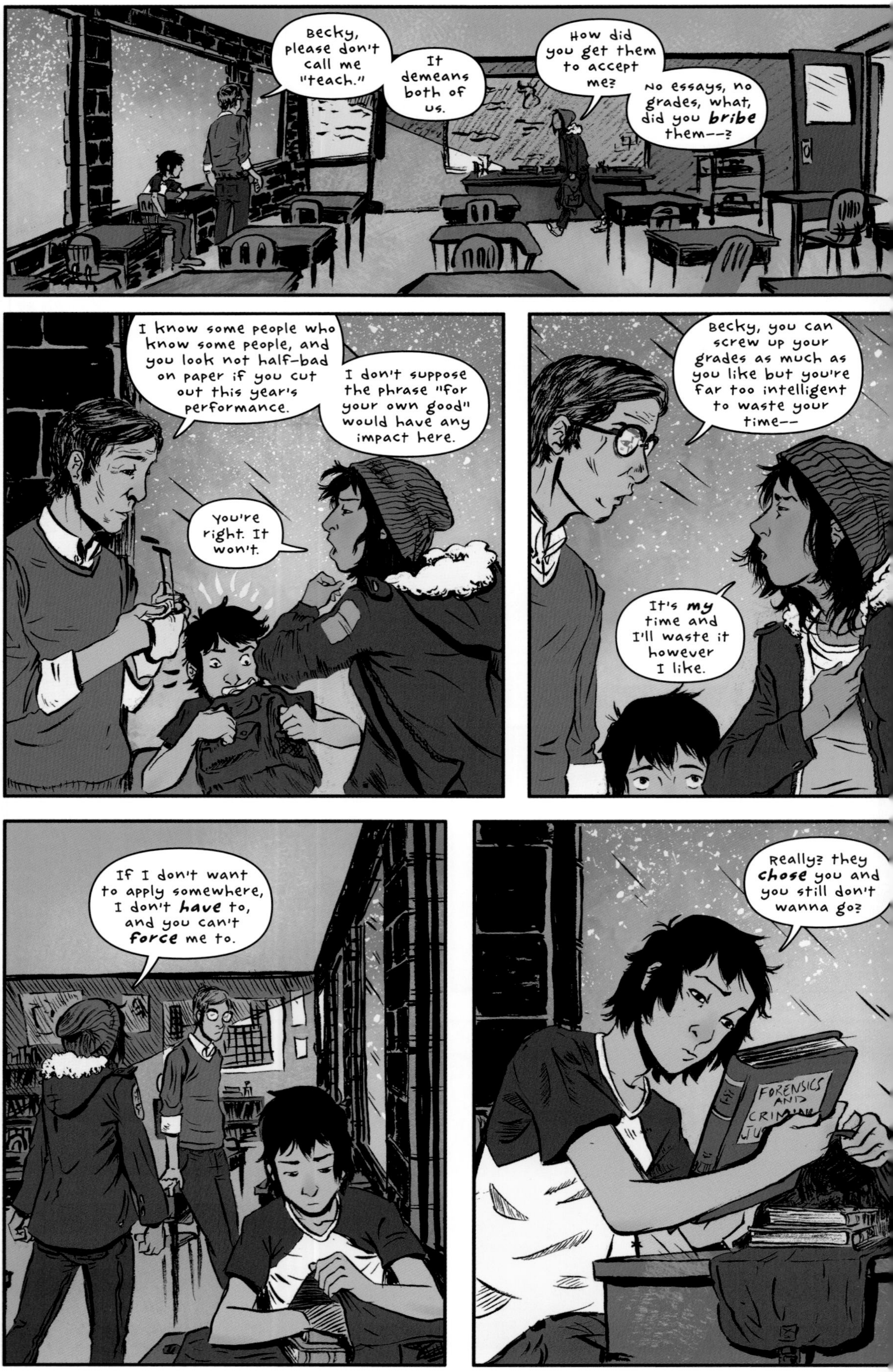
Becky, please don't call me "teach."
It demeans both of us.
How did you get them to accept me?
No essays, no grades, what, did you bribe them--?
I know some people who know some people, and you look not half-bad on paper if you cut out this year's performance.
I don't suppose the phrase "for your own good" would have any impact here.
You're right. It won't.
Becky, you can screw up your grades as much as you like but you're far too intelligent to waste your time--
It's my time and I'll waste it however I like.
If I don't want to apply somewhere, I don't have to, and you can't force me to.
Really? They chose you and you still don't wanna go?
FORENSICS AND

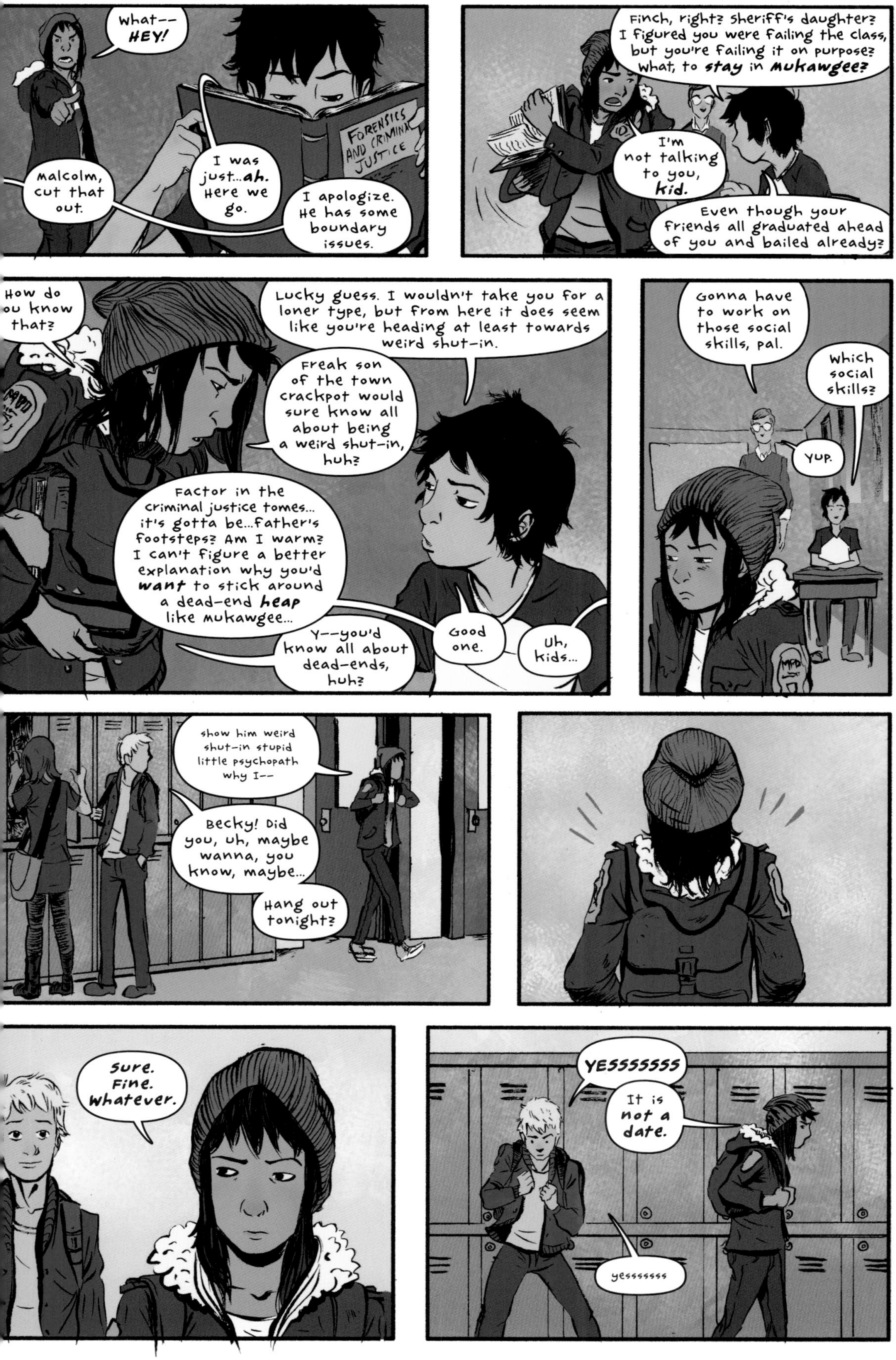
What-- HEY!
I was just...ah. Here we go.
Malcolm, cut that out.
I apologize. He has some boundary issues.
FORENSICS AND CRIMINAL JUSTICE
Finch, right? Sheriff's daughter? I figured you were failing the class, but you're failing it on purpose? What, to stay in Mukawgee?
I'm not talking to you, kid.
Even though your friends all graduated ahead of you and bailed already?
How do you know that?
Lucky guess. I wouldn't take you for a loner type, but from here it does seem like you're heading at least towards weird shut-in.
Freak son of the town crackpot would sure know all about being a weird shut-in, huh?
Factor in the criminal justice tomes... it's gotta be...father's footsteps? Am I warm? I can't figure a better explanation why you'd want to stick around a dead-end heap like Mukawgee...
Y--you'd know all about dead-ends, huh?
Good one.
Uh, kids...
Gonna have to work on those social skills, pal.
Which social skills?
Yup.
show him weird shut-in stupid little psychopath why I--
Becky! Did you, uh, maybe wanna, you know, maybe...
Hang out tonight?
Sure. Fine. Whatever.
YESSSSSSS
It is not a date.
yessssssss

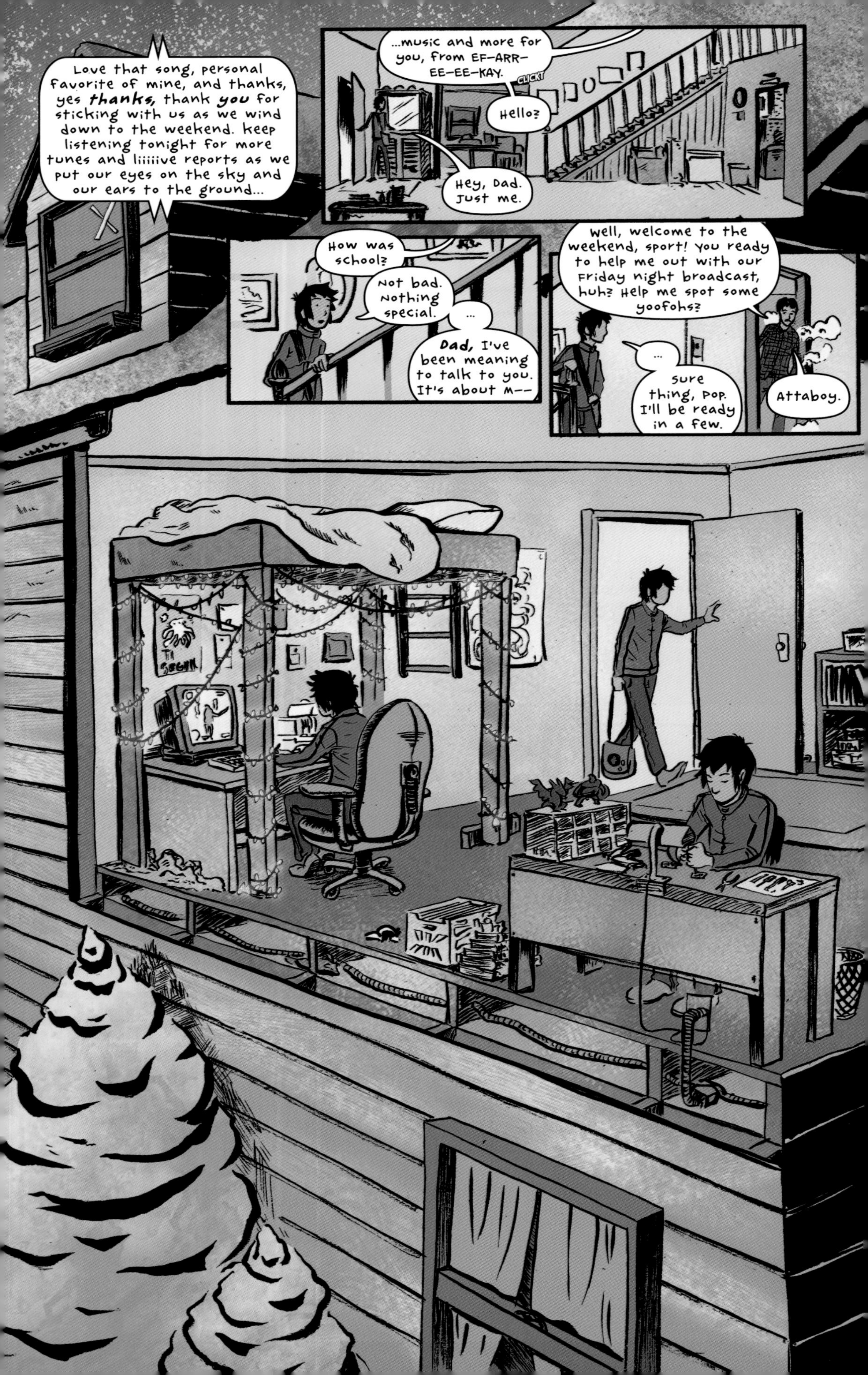
Love that song, personal favorite of mine, and thanks, yes thanks, thank you for sticking with us as we wind down to the weekend. keep listening tonight for more tunes and liiiiive reports as we put our eyes on the sky and our ears to the ground...
...music and more for you, from EF-ARR-EE-EE-KAY.
CLICK!
Hello?
Hey, Dad. Just me.
How was school?
Not bad. Nothing special.
...
Dad, I've been meaning to talk to you. It's about M--
well, welcome to the weekend, sport! You ready to help me out with our Friday night broadcast, huh? Help me spot some yoofohs?
...
Sure thing, Pop. I'll be ready in a few.
Attaboy.

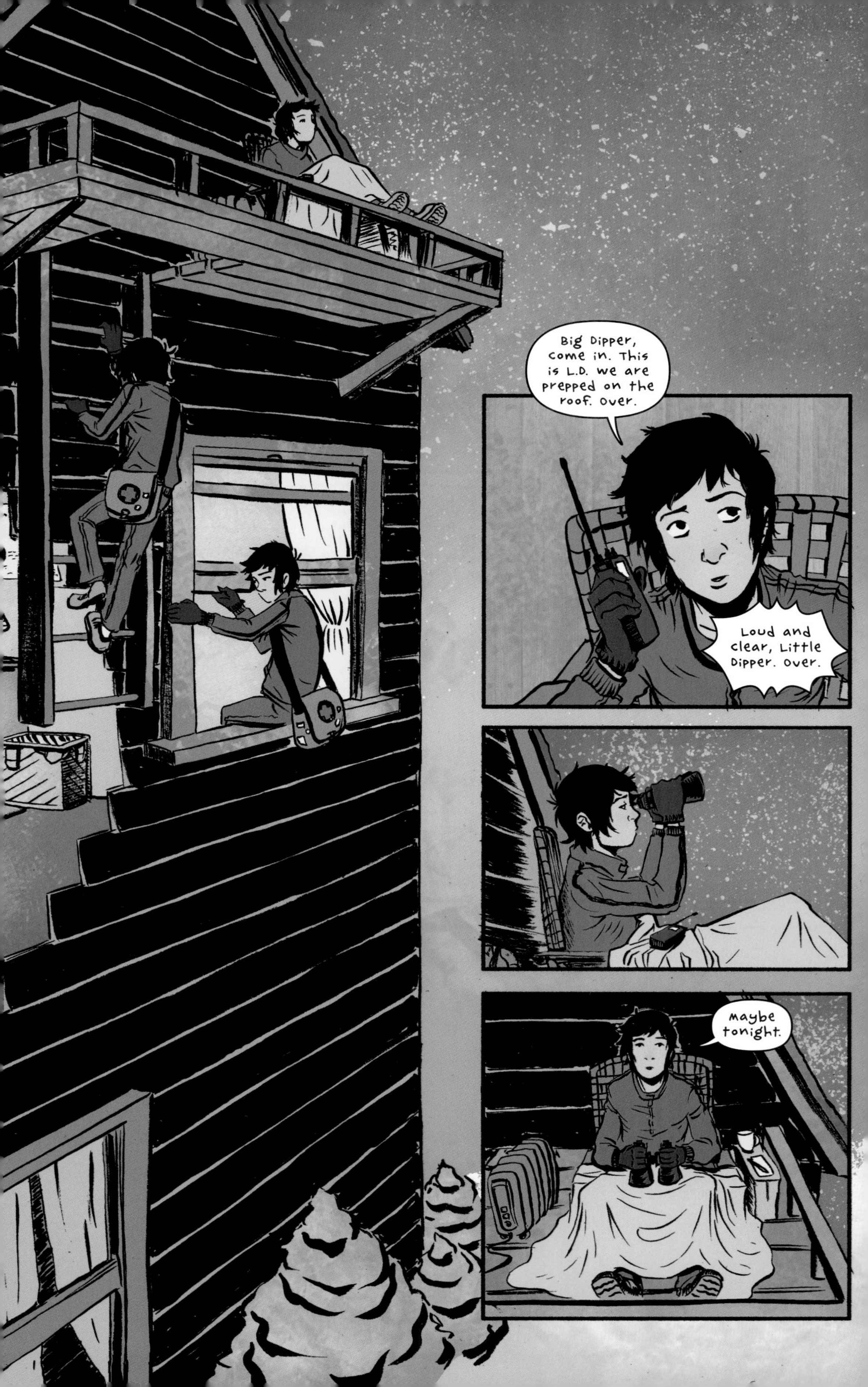
Big Dipper, come in. This is L.D. we are prepped on the roof. over.
Loud and clear, Little Dipper. over.
Maybe tonight.

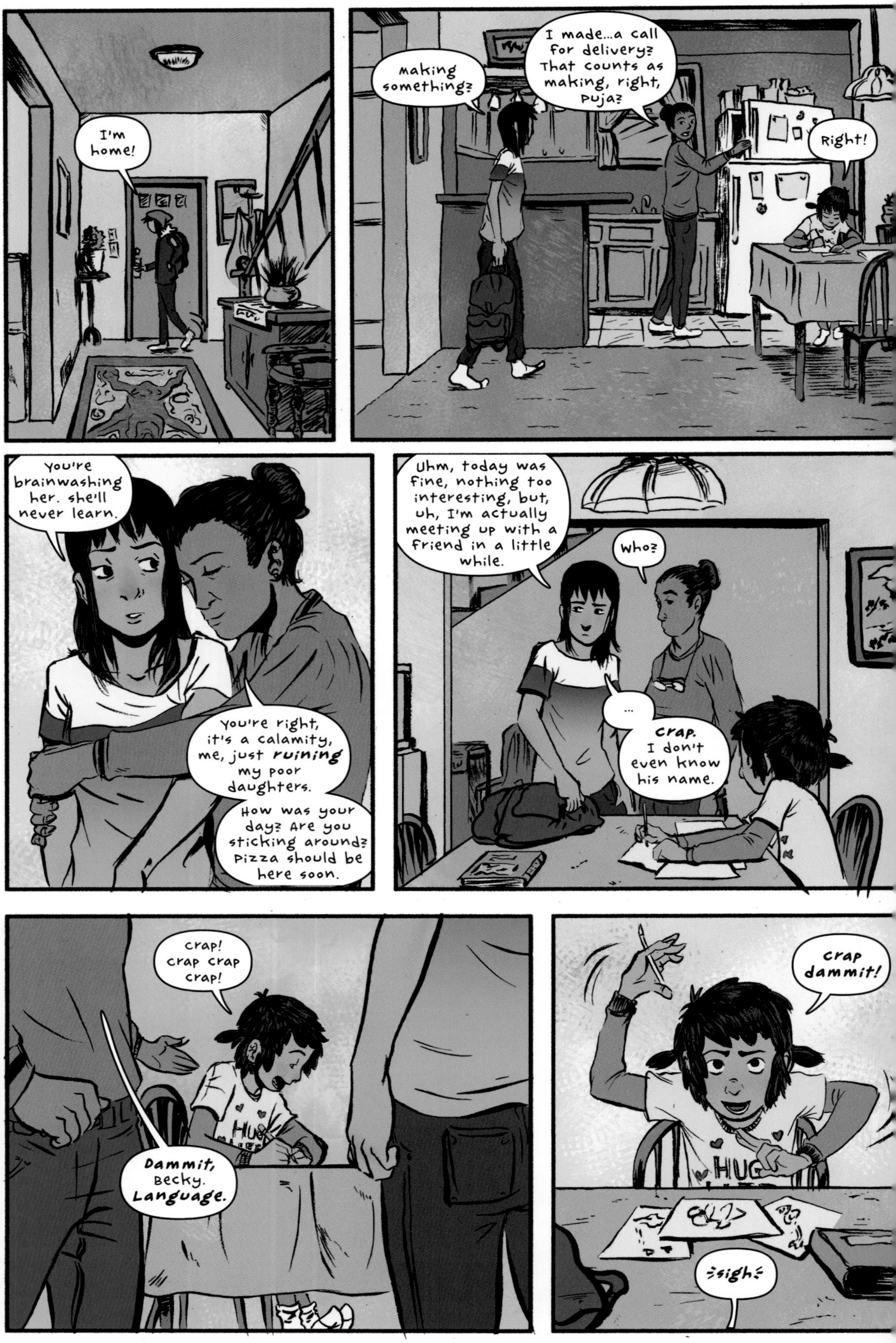
I'm home!
Making something?
I made...a call for delivery? That counts as making, right, Puja?
Right!
You're brainwashing her. She'll never learn.
You're right, it's a calamity, me, just ruining my poor daughters.
How was your day? Are you sticking around? Pizza should be here soon.
Uhm, today was fine, nothing too interesting, but, uh, I'm actually meeting up with a friend in a little while.
Who?
...
Crap. I don't even know his name.
Crap! Crap crap crap!
Dammit, Becky. Language.
Crap dammit!
sigh

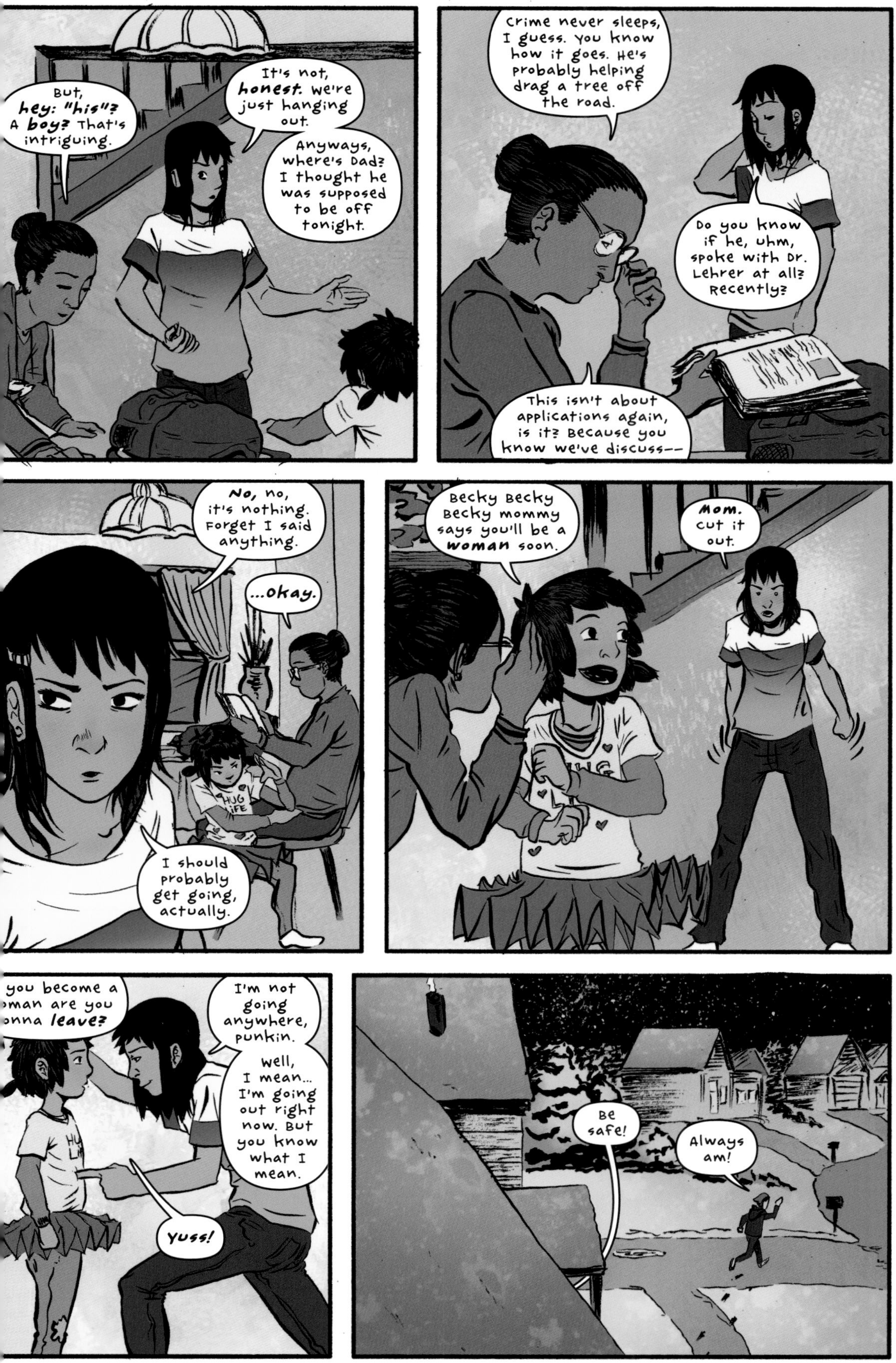
But, hey: "his"? A boy? That's intriguing.
It's not, honest. We're just hanging out.
Anyways, where's Dad? I thought he was supposed to be off tonight.
Crime never sleeps, I guess. You know how it goes. He's probably helping drag a tree off the road.
Do you know if he, uhm, spoke with Dr. Lehrer at all? Recently?
This isn't about applications again, is it? Because you know we've discuss--
No, no, it's nothing. Forget I said anything.
...okay.
I should probably get going, actually.
Becky Becky Becky mommy says you'll be a woman soon.
Mom. Cut it out.
you become a oman are you onna leave?
I'm not going anywhere, punkin.
Well, I mean... I'm going out right now. But you know what I mean.
Yuss!
Be safe!
Always am!

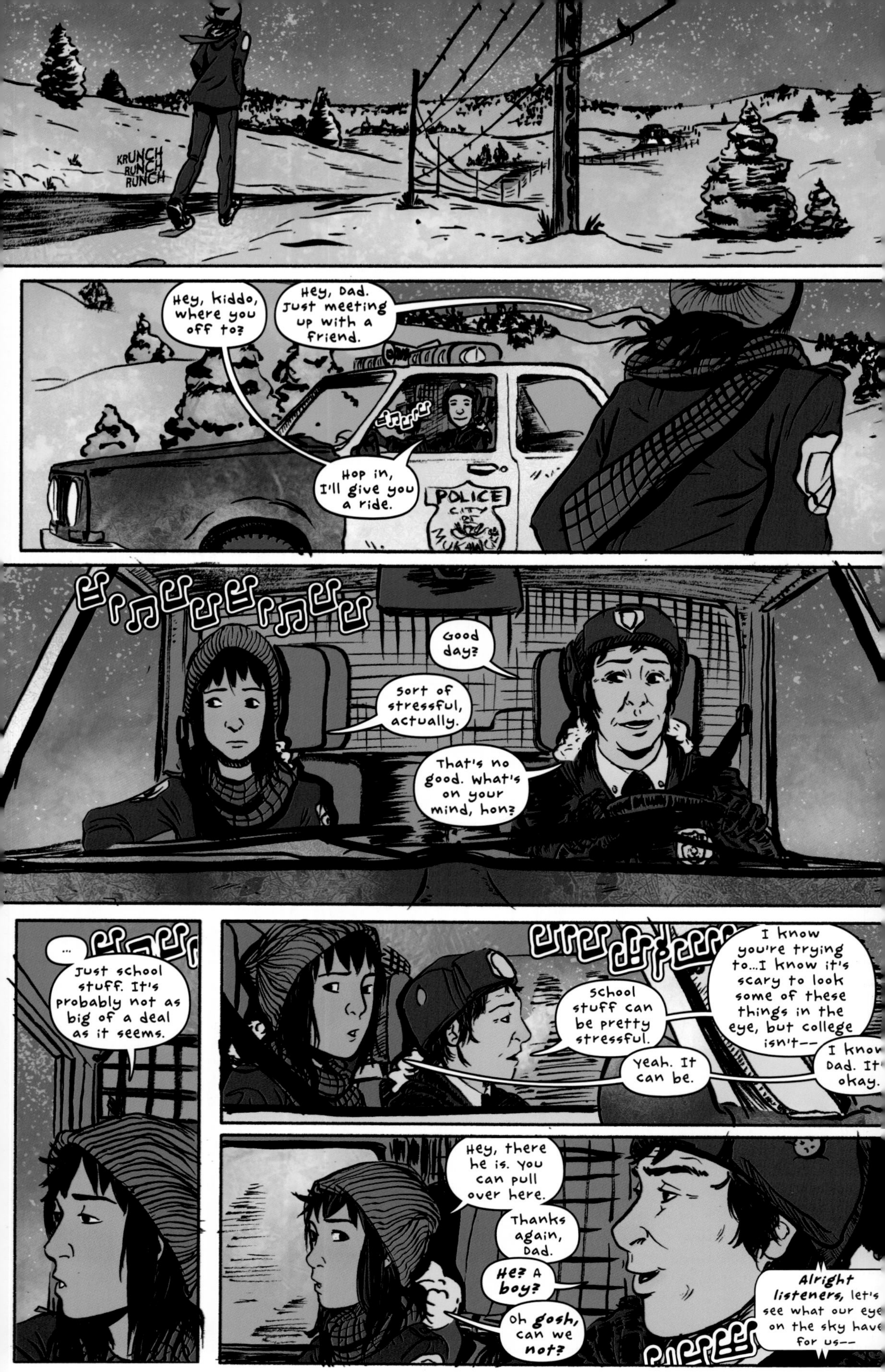
KRUNCH
RUNCH
RUNCH
Hey, kiddo, where you off to?
Hey, Dad. Just meeting up with a friend.
Hop in, I'll give you a ride.
POLICE
CITY OF
Good day?
Sort of stressful, actually.
That's no good. What's on your mind, hon?
...
Just school stuff. It's probably not as big of a deal as it seems.
School stuff can be pretty stressful.
Yeah. It can be.
I know you're trying to...I know it's scary to look some of these things in the eye, but college isn't--
I know Dad. It okay.
Hey, there he is. You can pull over here.
Thanks again, Dad.
He? A *boy?*
Oh *gosh,* can we *not?*
Alright listeners, let's see what our eye on the sky have for us--

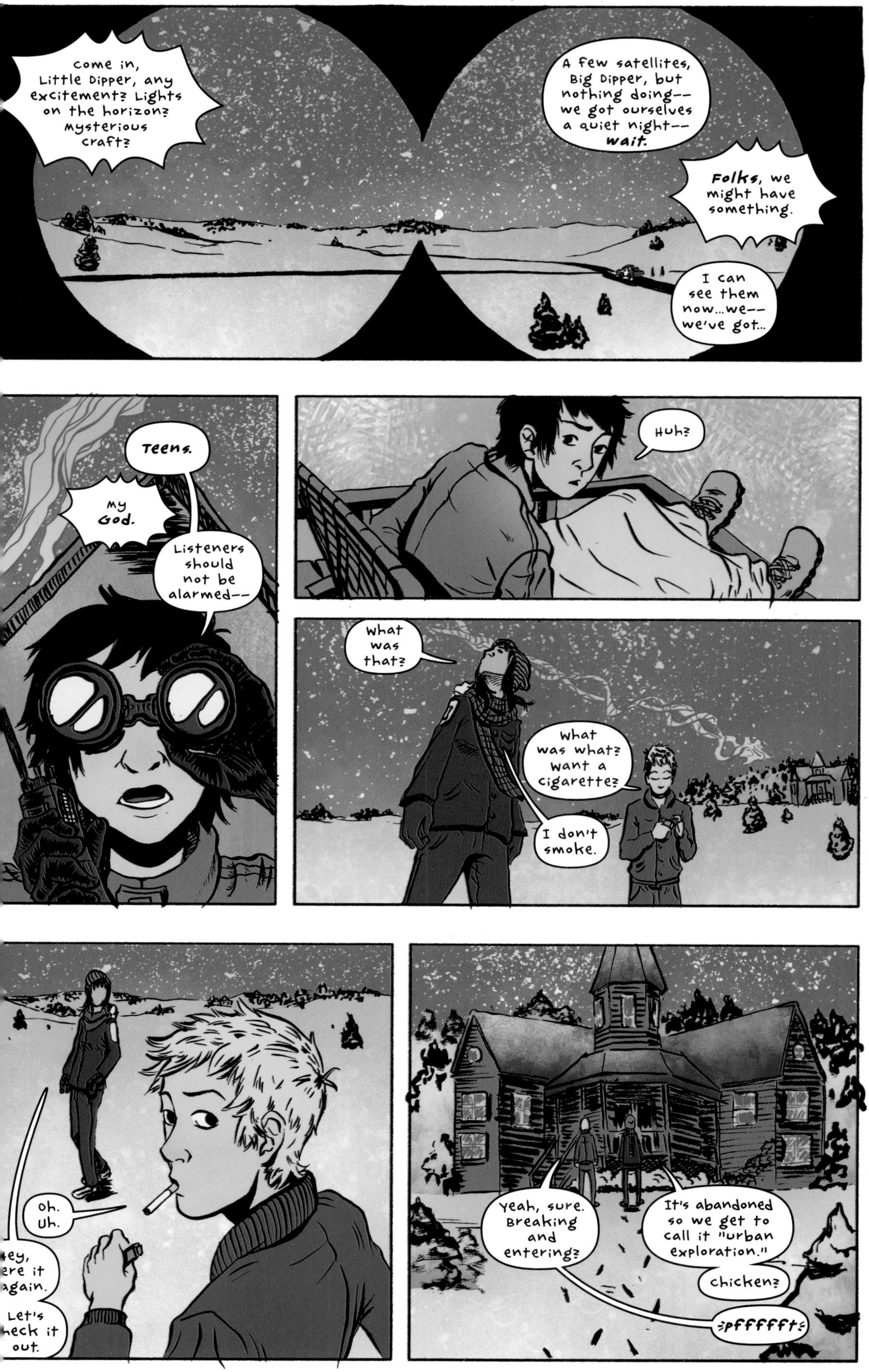
Come in, Little Dipper, any excitement? Lights on the horizon? Mysterious craft?
A few satellites, Big Dipper, but nothing doing-- we got ourselves a quiet night-- *wait.*
Folks, we might have something.
I can see them now...we-- we've got...
Teens.
My **God.**
Listeners should not be alarmed--
Huh?
What was that?
What was what? Want a cigarette?
I don't smoke.
Oh. Uh.
ey, ere it again.
Let's heck it out.
Yeah, sure. Breaking and entering?
It's abandoned so we get to call it "urban exploration."
Chicken?
pffffft

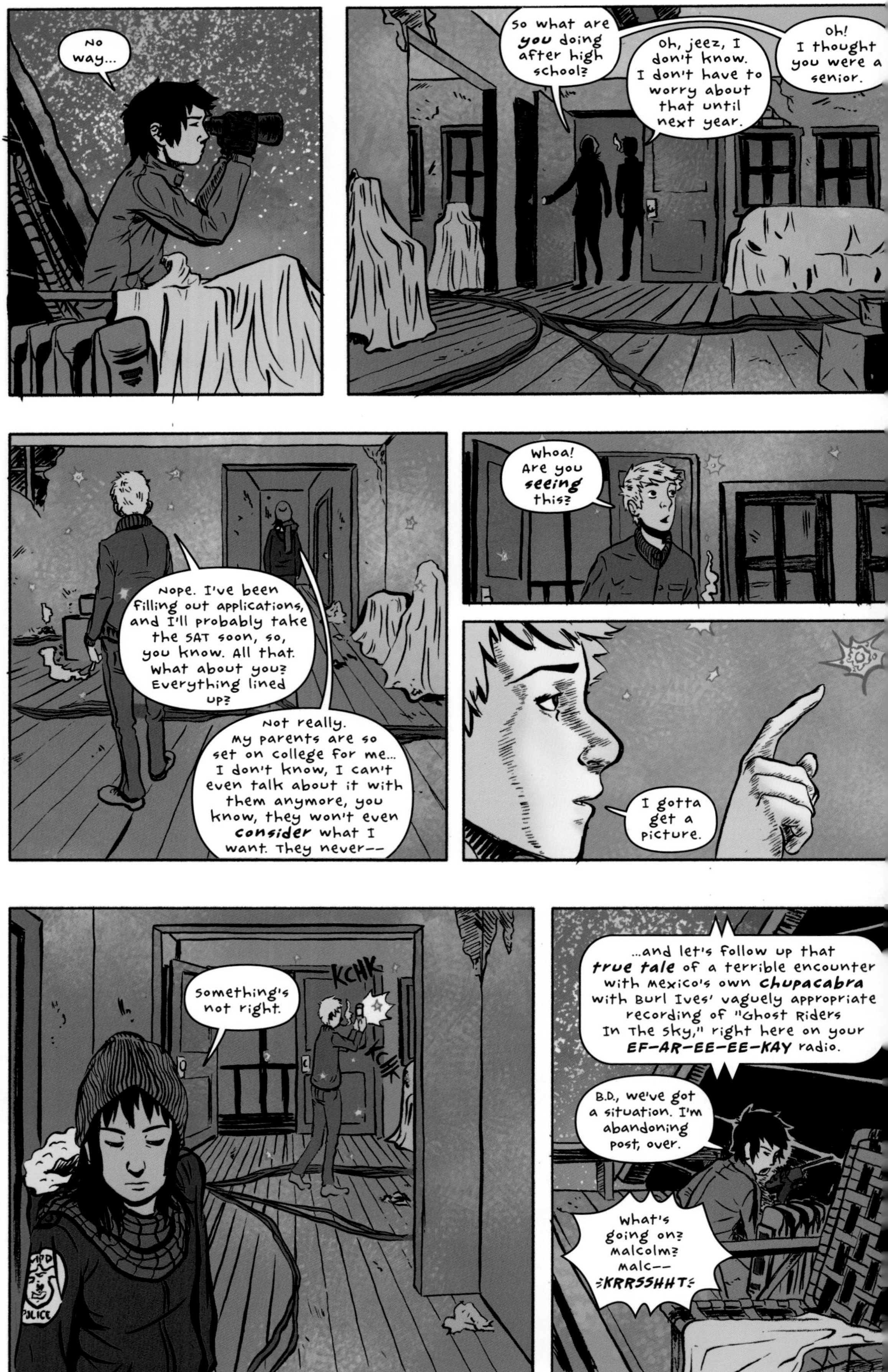
No way...
So what are you doing after high school?
Oh, jeez, I don't know. I don't have to worry about that until next year.
Oh! I thought you were a senior.
Nope. I've been filling out applications, and I'll probably take the SAT soon, so, you know. All that. What about you? Everything lined up?
Not really. My parents are so set on college for me... I don't know, I can't even talk about it with them anymore, you know, they won't even consider what I want. They never--
Whoa! Are you seeing this?
I gotta get a picture.
Something's not right.
KCHK
KCHK
...and let's follow up that true tale of a terrible encounter with Mexico's own chupacabra with Burl Ives' vaguely appropriate recording of "Ghost Riders In The Sky," right here on your EF-AR-EE-EE-KAY radio.
B.D., we've got a situation. I'm abandoning post, over.
What's going on? Malcolm? Malc-- KRRSSHHT

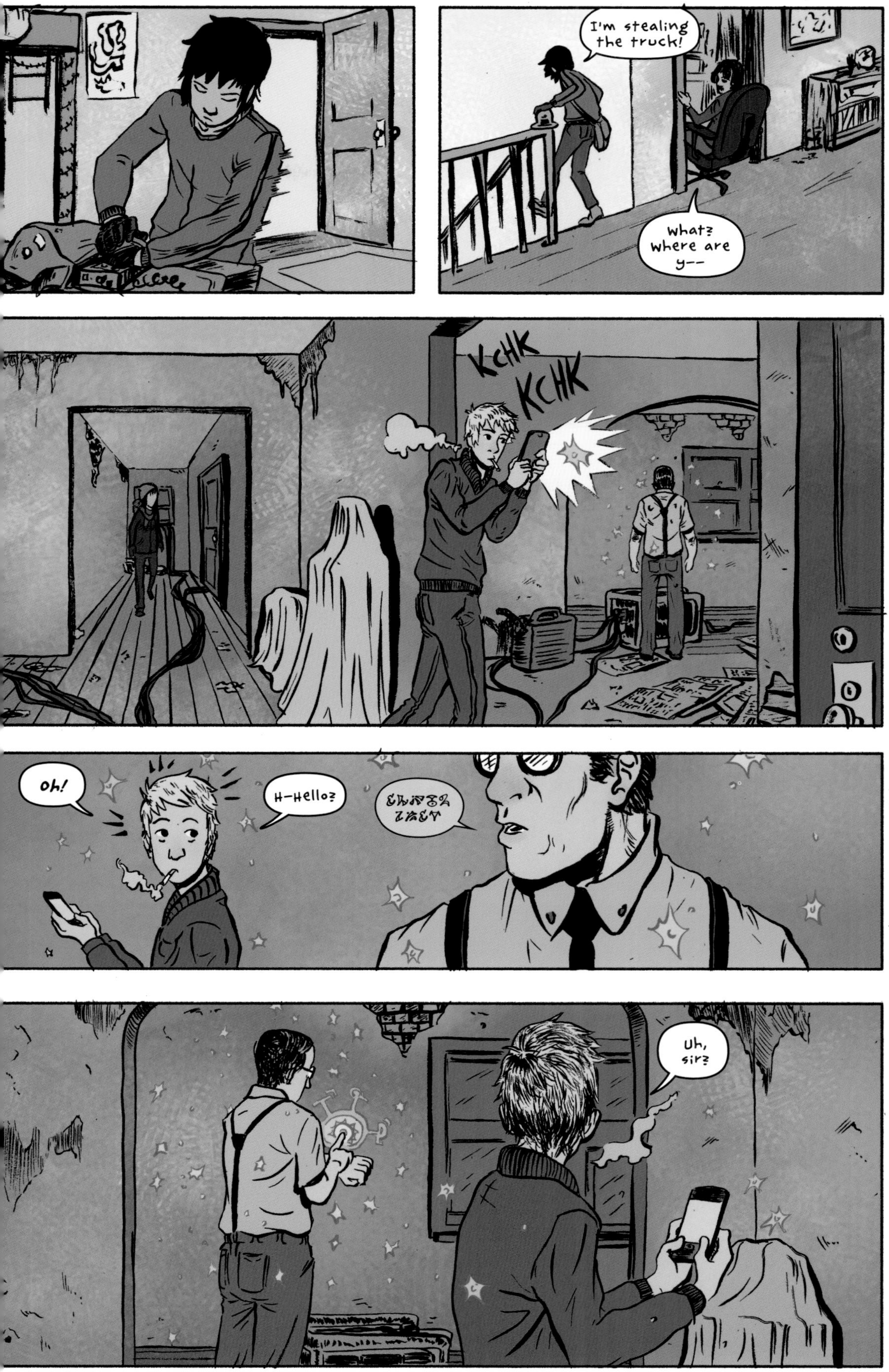
I'm stealing the truck!
What? Where are y--
KCHK
KCHK
Oh!
H-Hello?
Uh, sir?

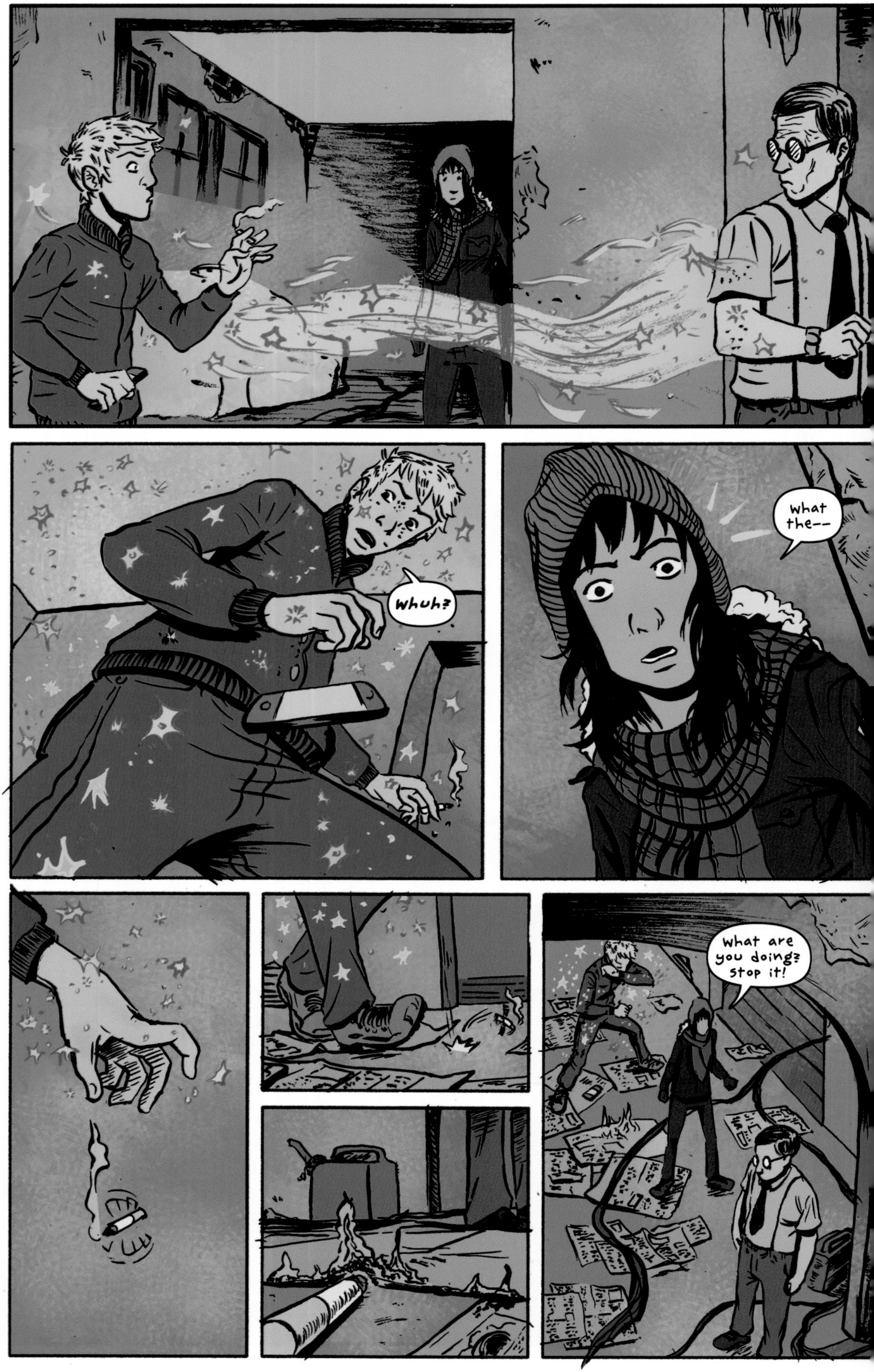
whuh?
what the--
what are you doing? stop it!

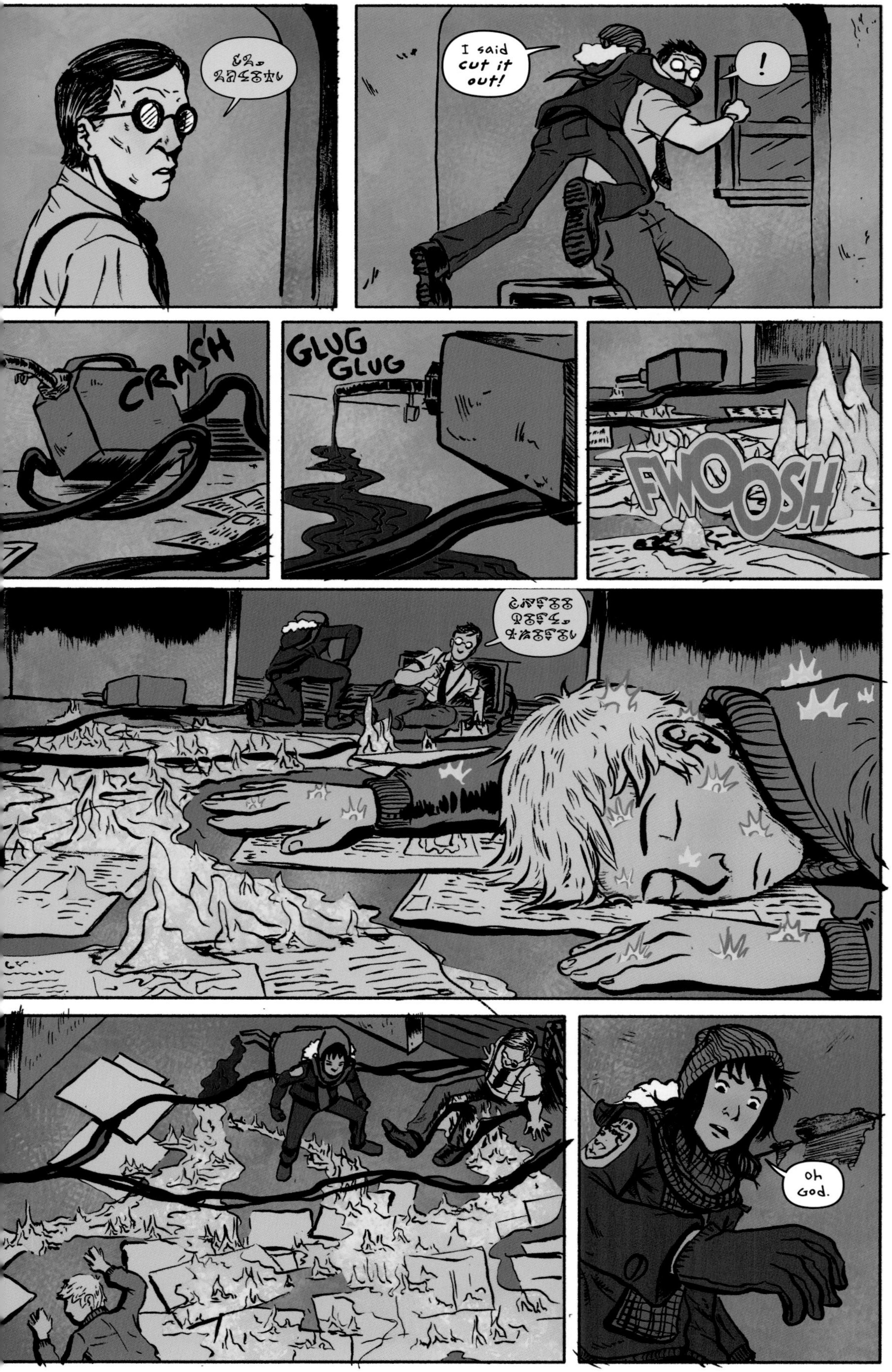
I said cut it out!
!
CRASH
GLUG GLUG
FWOOSH
Oh God.

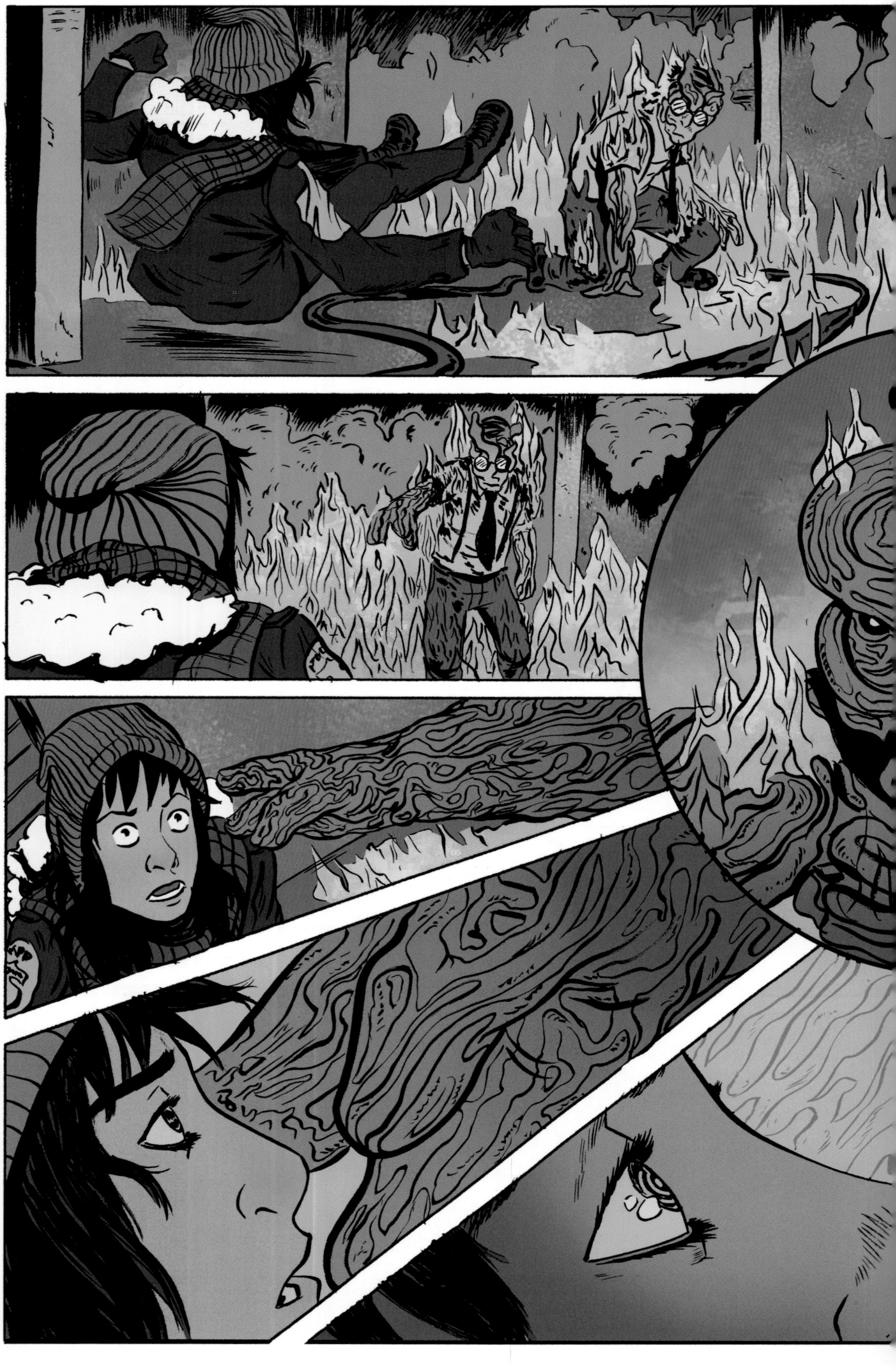

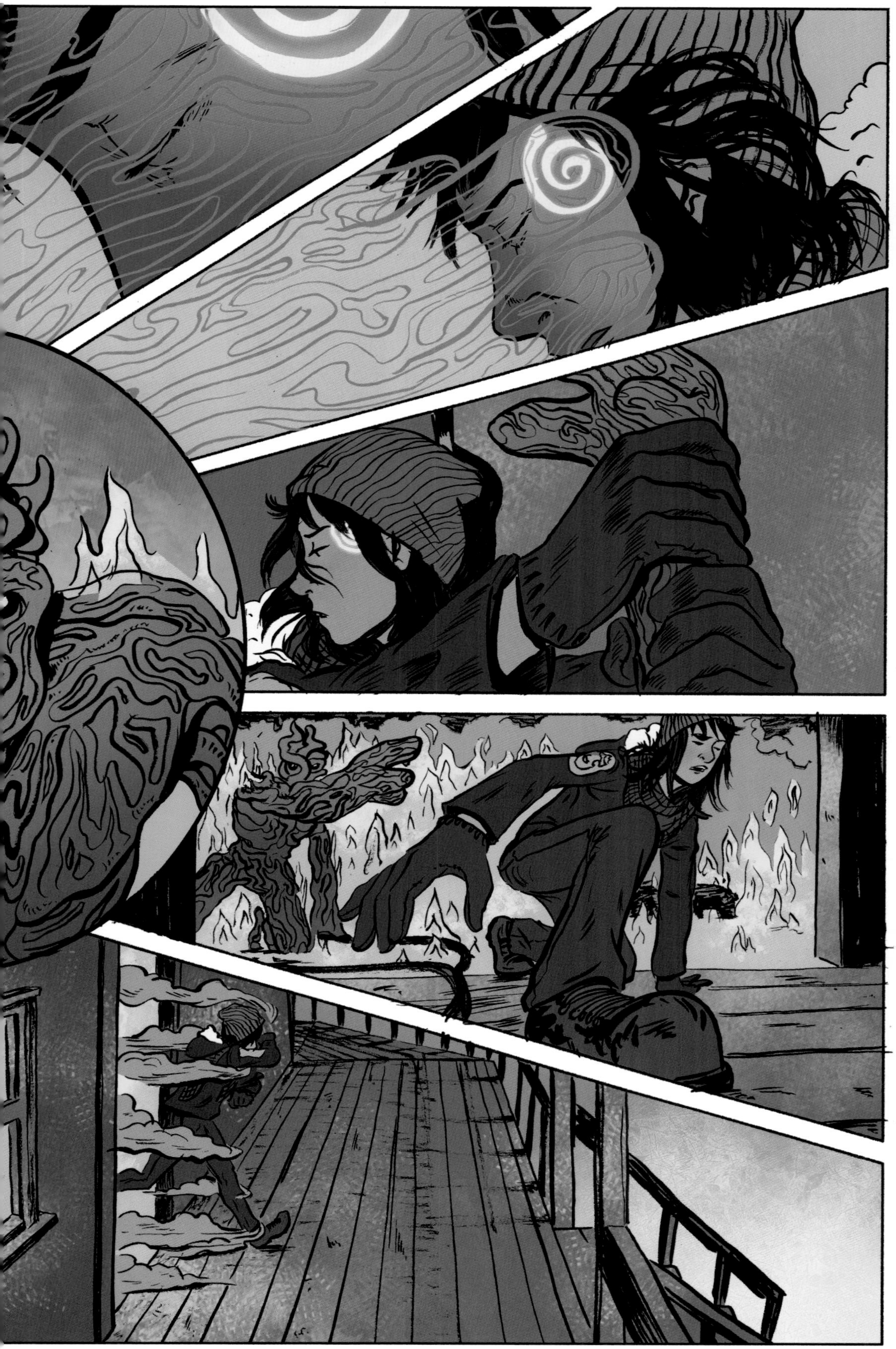

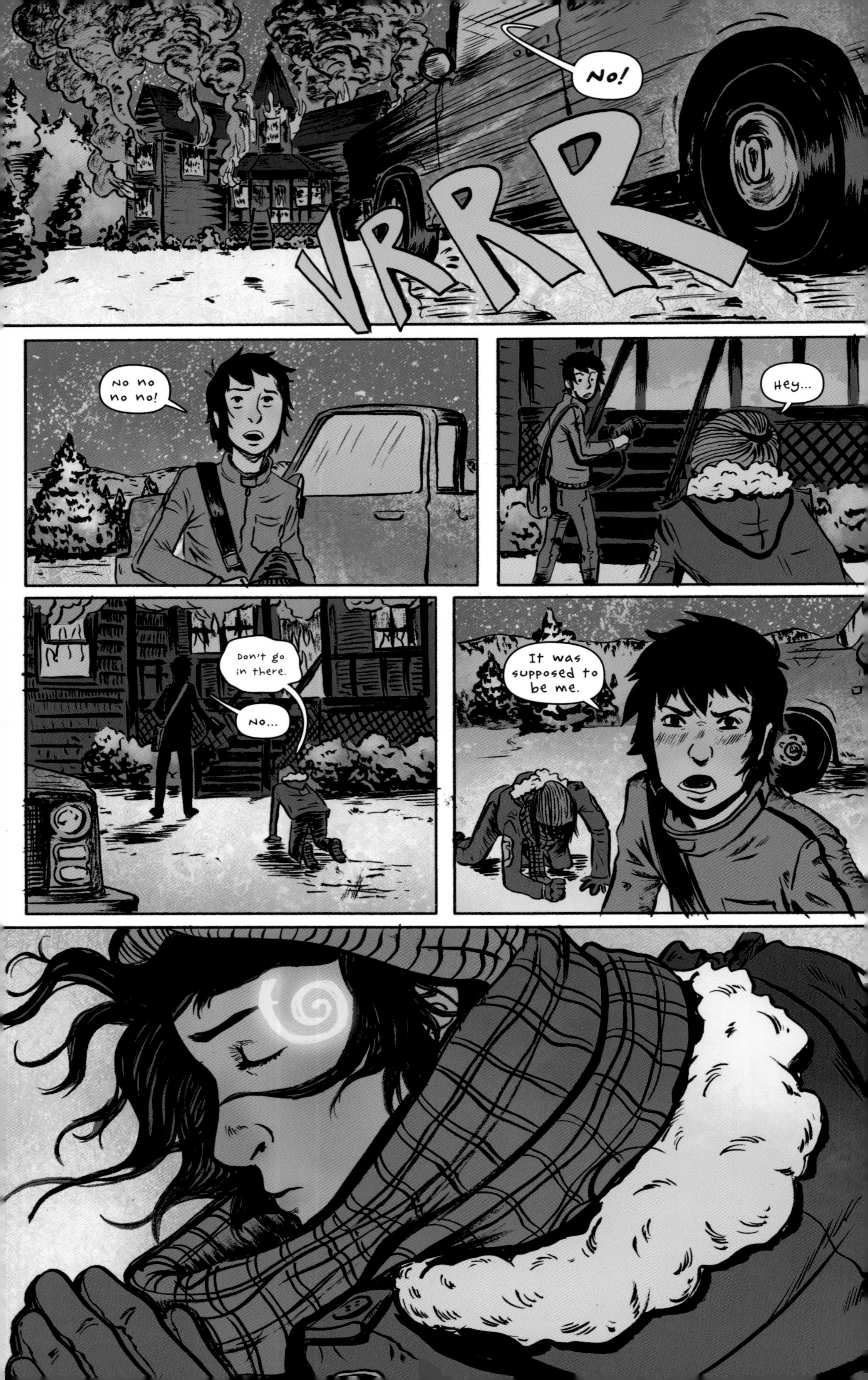
No!
VRRR
No no no no!
Hey...
Don't go in there.
No...
It was supposed to be me.

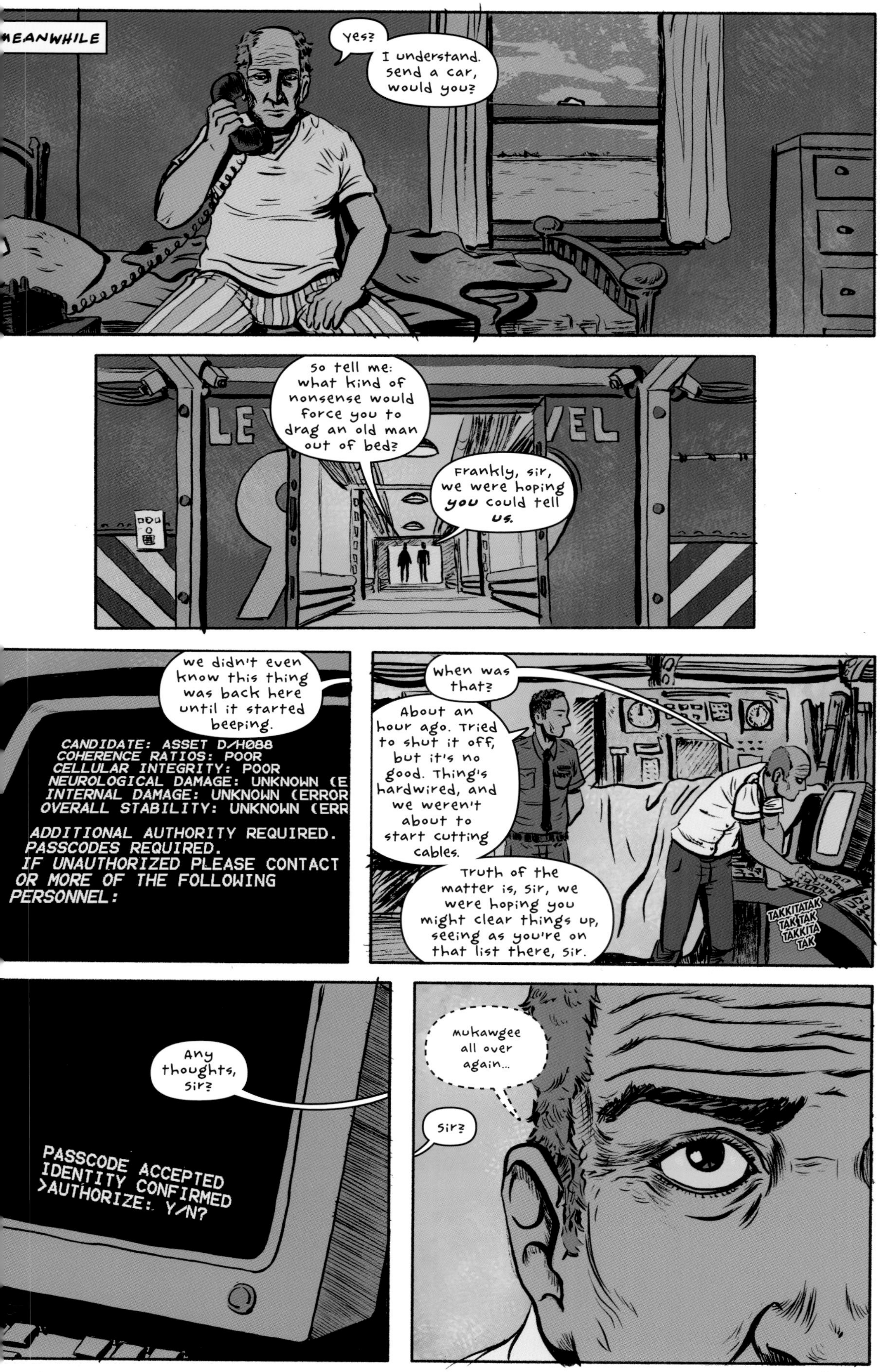
MEANWHILE
Yes?
I understand. Send a car, would you?
So tell me: what kind of nonsense would force you to drag an old man out of bed?
Frankly, sir, we were hoping *you* could tell *us*.
We didn't even know this thing was back here until it started beeping.
CANDIDATE: ASSET D/H088
COHERENCE RATIOS: POOR
CELLULAR INTEGRITY: POOR
NEUROLOGICAL DAMAGE: UNKNOWN (E
INTERNAL DAMAGE: UNKNOWN (ERROR
OVERALL STABILITY: UNKNOWN (ERR
ADDITIONAL AUTHORITY REQUIRED.
PASSCODES REQUIRED.
IF UNAUTHORIZED PLEASE CONTACT
OR MORE OF THE FOLLOWING
PERSONNEL:
When was that?
About an hour ago. Tried to shut it off, but it's no good. Thing's hardwired, and we weren't about to start cutting cables.
Truth of the matter is, sir, we were hoping you might clear things up, seeing as you're on that list there, sir.
TAKKITATAK TAK TAK TAKKITA TAK
Any thoughts, sir?
PASSCODE ACCEPTED
IDENTITY CONFIRMED
>AUTHORIZE: Y/N?
Mukawgee all over again...
Sir?

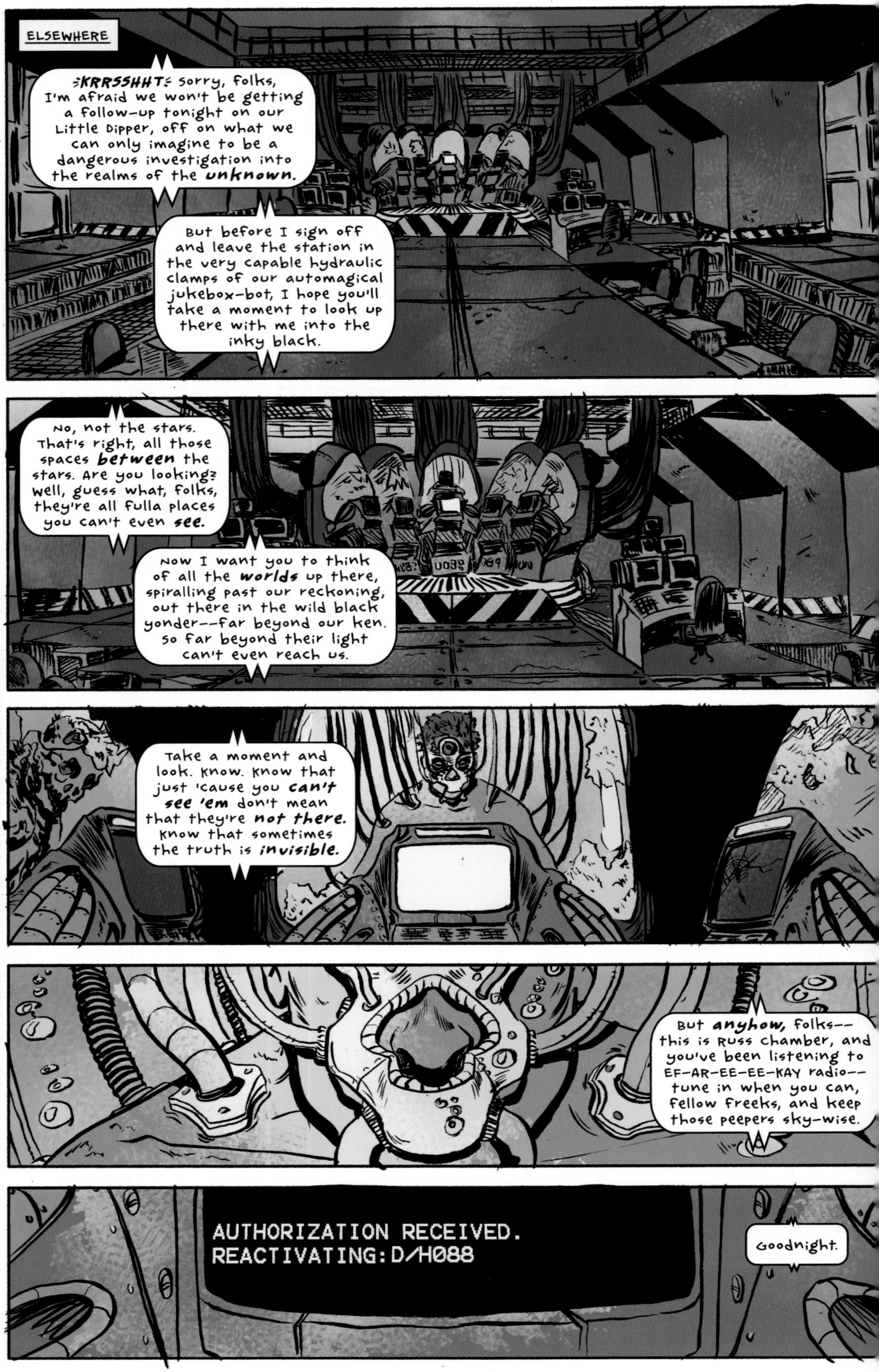
ELSEWHERE
:KRRSSHHT: sorry, folks, I'm afraid we won't be getting a follow-up tonight on our Little Dipper, off on what we can only imagine to be a dangerous investigation into the realms of the unknown.
But before I sign off and leave the station in the very capable hydraulic clamps of our automagical jukebox-bot, I hope you'll take a moment to look up there with me into the inky black.
No, not the stars. That's right, all those spaces between the stars. Are you looking? Well, guess what, folks, they're all fulla places you can't even see.
Now I want you to think of all the worlds up there, spiralling past our reckoning, out there in the wild black yonder--far beyond our ken. So far beyond their light can't even reach us.
Take a moment and look. Know. Know that just 'cause you can't see 'em don't mean that they're not there. Know that sometimes the truth is invisible.
But anyhow, folks--this is Russ Chamber, and you've been listening to EF-AR-EE-EE-KAY radio--tune in when you can, fellow freeks, and keep those peepers sky-wise.
AUTHORIZATION RECEIVED.
REACTIVATING:D/H088
Goodnight.

t·w·o

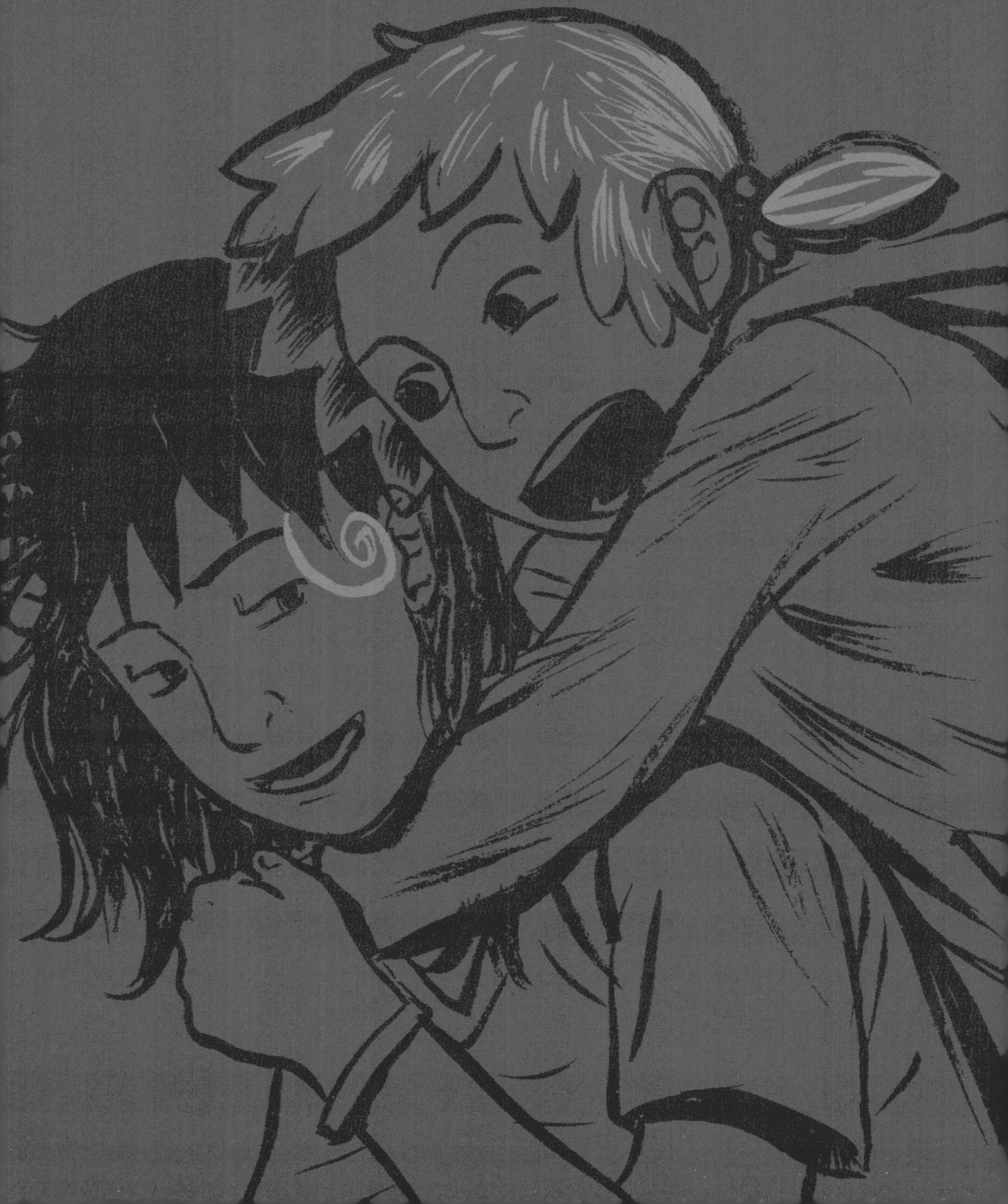

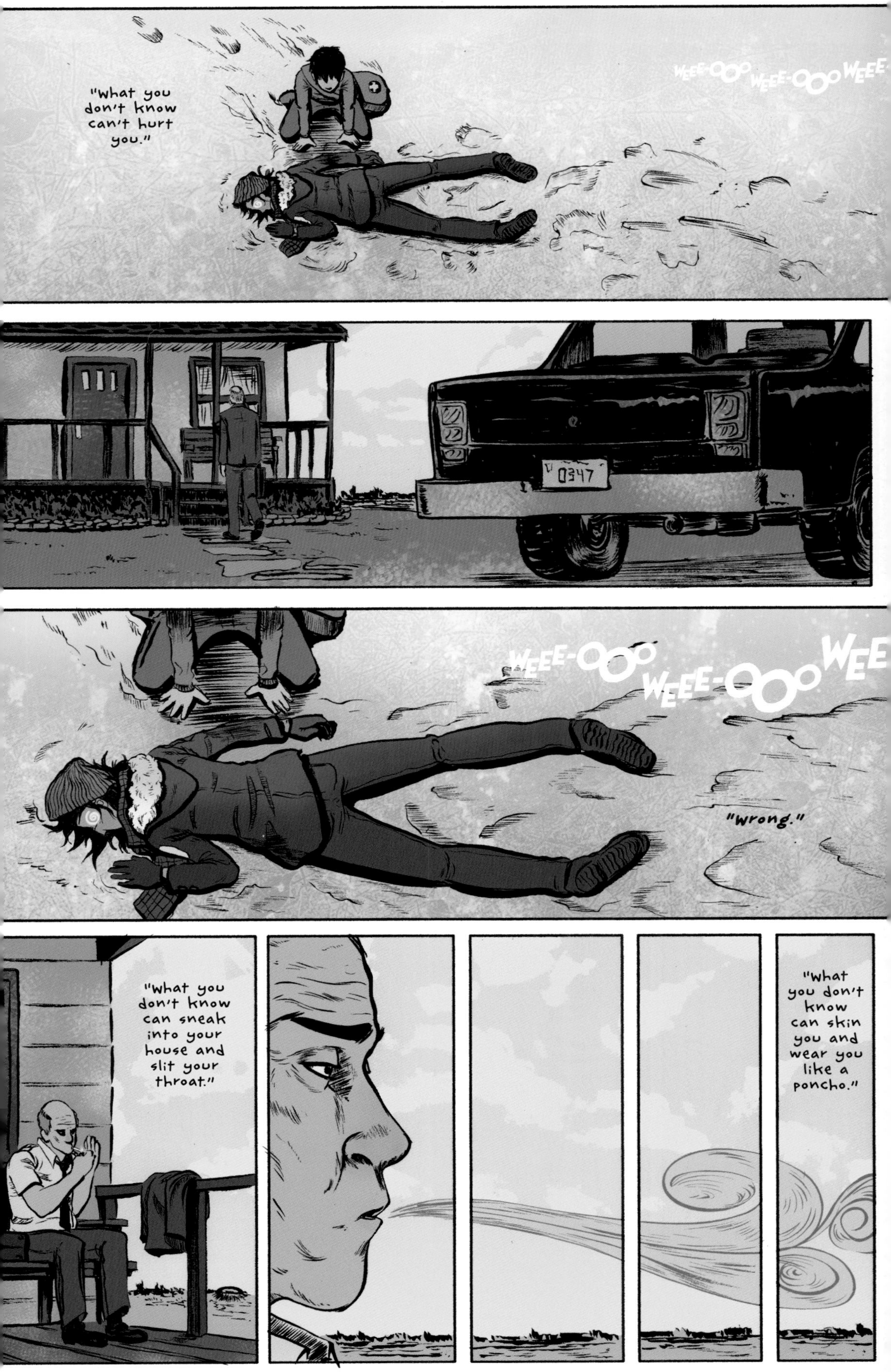
"What you don't know can't hurt you."
WEEE-OOO WEEE-OOO WEEE-
0347
WEEE-OOO WEEE-OOO WEE
"Wrong."
"What you don't know can sneak into your house and slit your throat."
"What you don't know can skin you and wear you like a poncho."

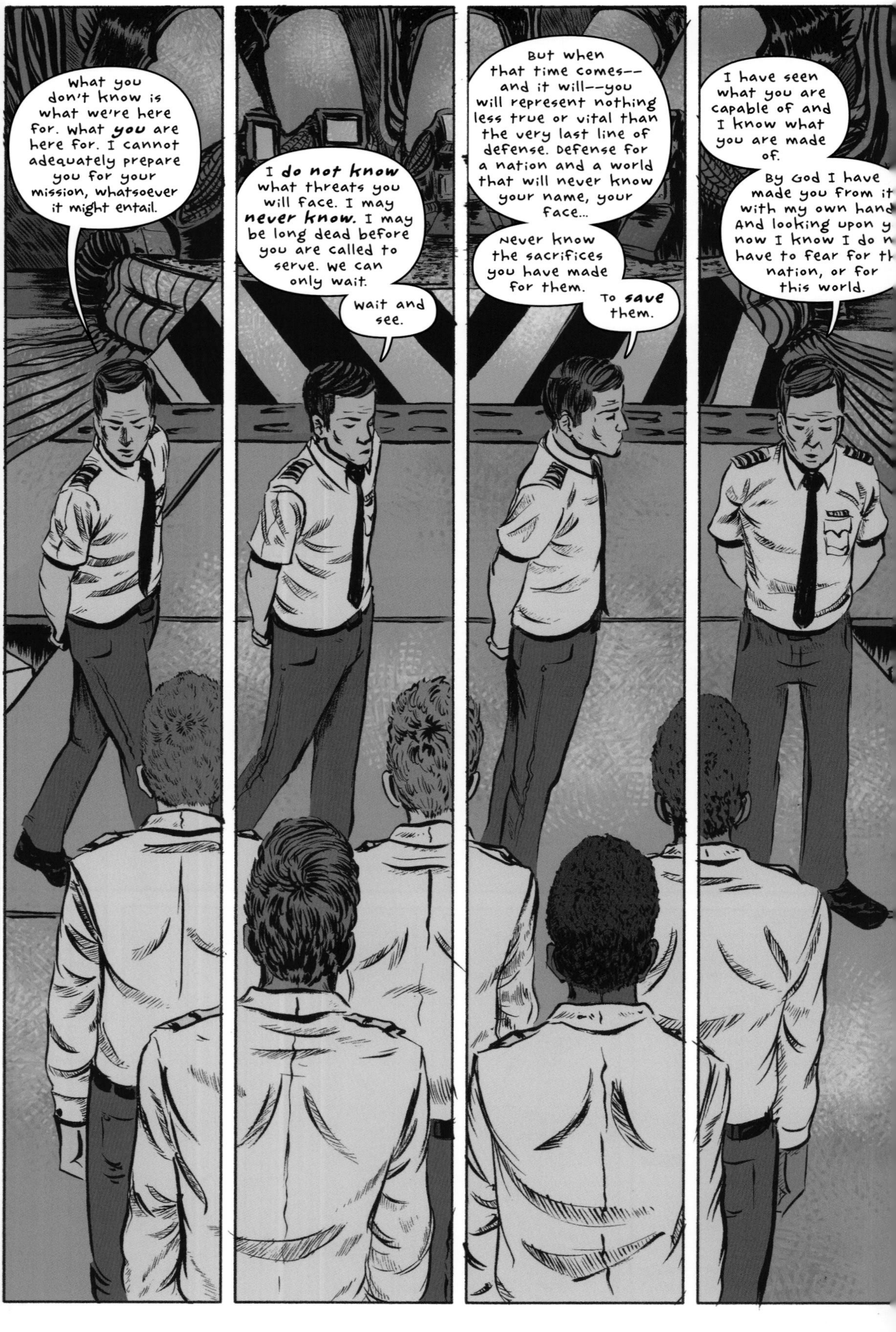
What you don't know is what we're here for. What *you* are here for. I cannot adequately prepare you for your mission, whatsoever it might entail.
I *do not know* what threats you will face. I may *never know.* I may be long dead before you are called to serve. We can only wait.
Wait and see.
But when that time comes-- and it will--you will represent nothing less true or vital than the very last line of defense. Defense for a nation and a world that will never know your name, your face...
Never know the sacrifices you have made for them.
To *save* them.
I have seen what you are capable of and I know what you are made of.
By God I have made you from it with my own hand And looking upon y now I know I do n have to fear for th nation, or for this world.

"I look at you and I know, at long last, there is hope for a future untroubled by nightmares."

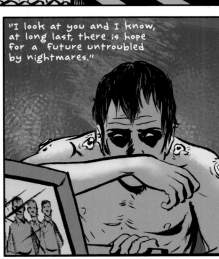

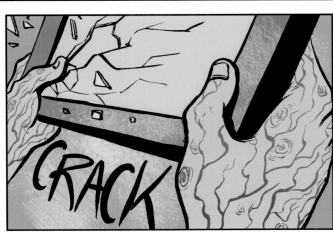

CRACK

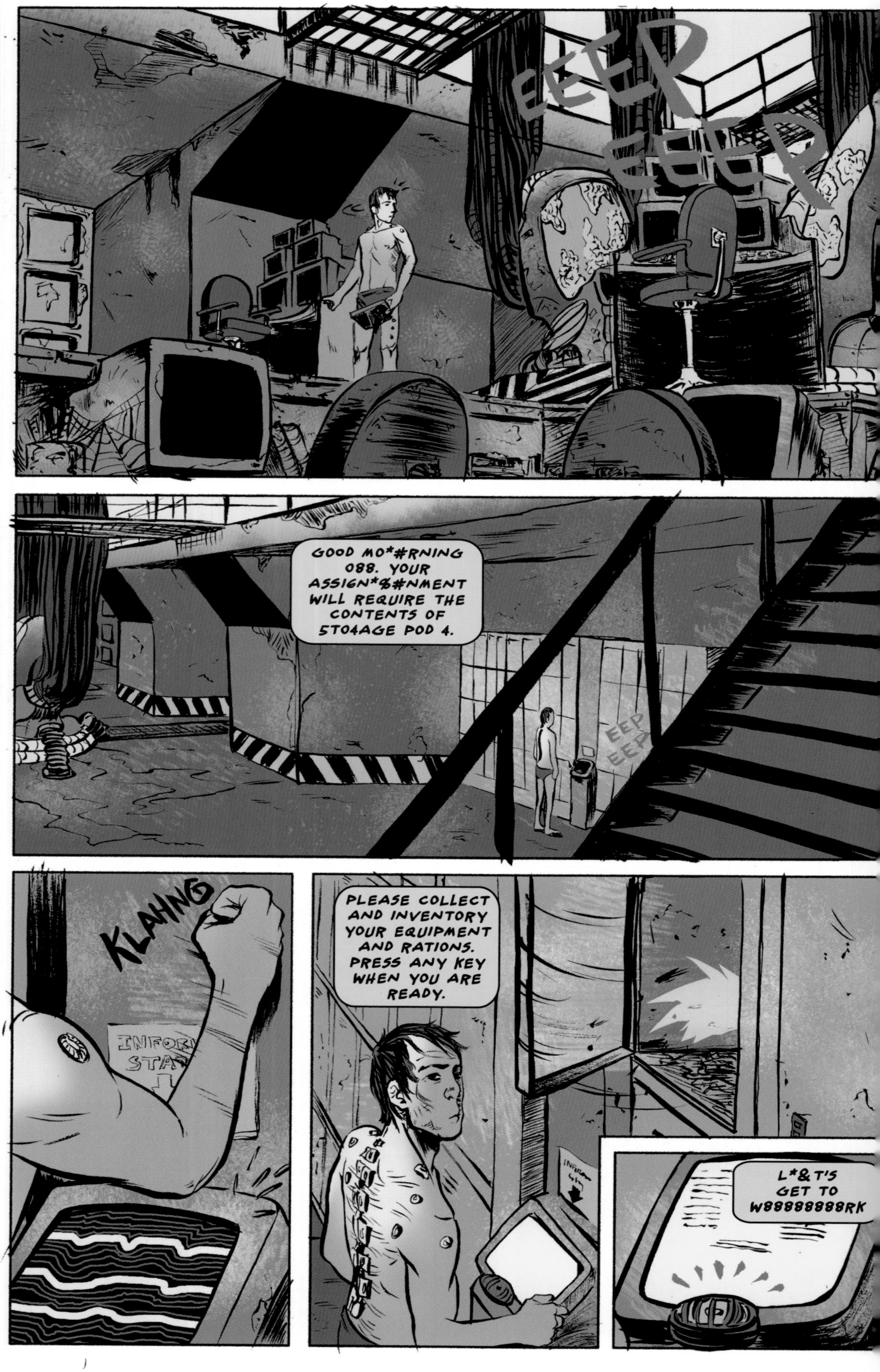
EEEP EEEP
GOOD MO*#RNING 088. YOUR ASSIGN*$#NMENT WILL REQUIRE THE CONTENTS OF 5TO4AGE POD 4.
EEP EEP
KLAHNG
PLEASE COLLECT AND INVENTORY YOUR EQUIPMENT AND RATIONS. PRESS ANY KEY WHEN YOU ARE READY.
L*&T'S GET TO W88888888RK

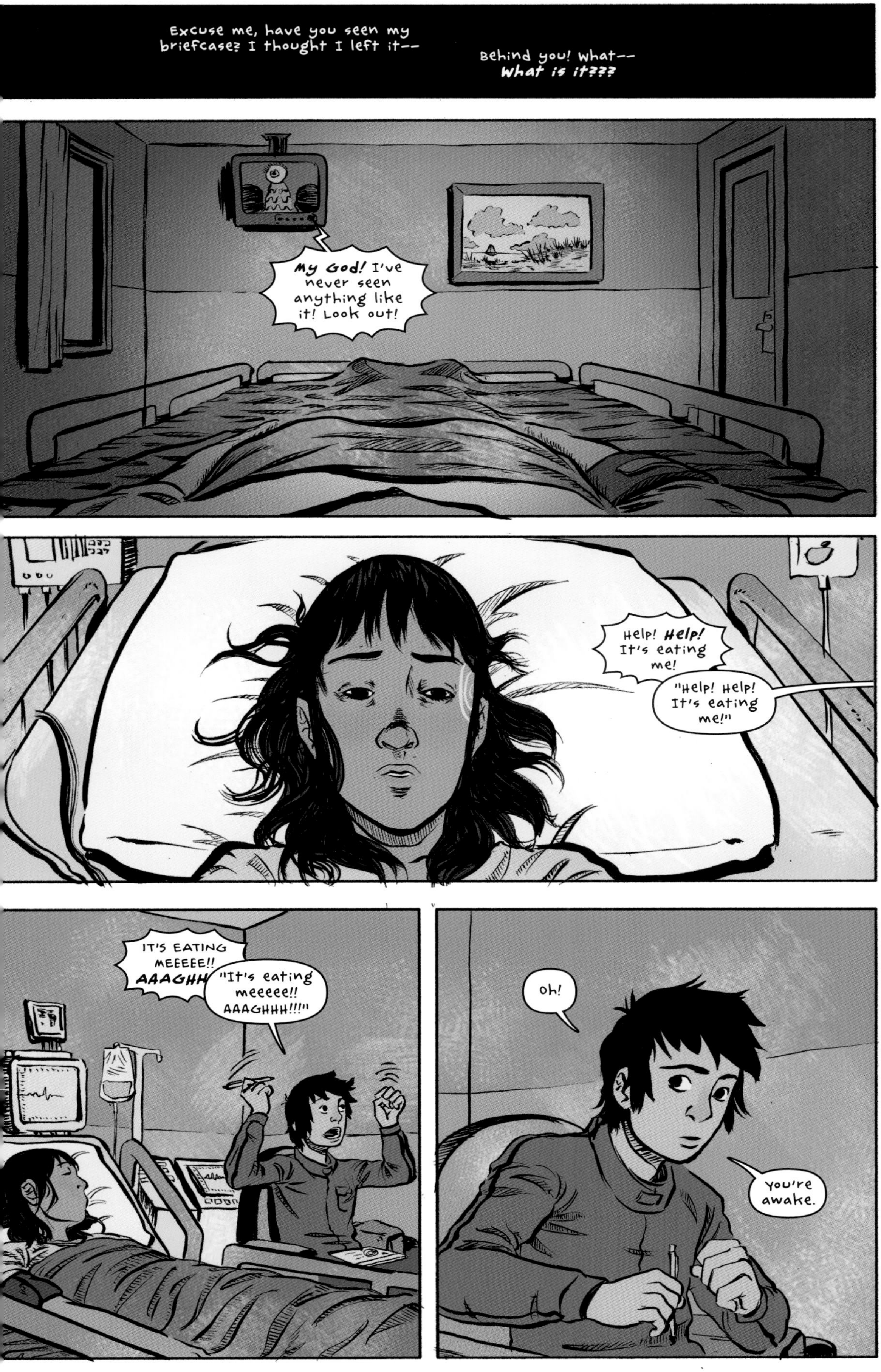
Excuse me, have you seen my briefcase? I thought I left it--
Behind you! What--
What is it???
My God! I've never seen anything like it! Look out!
Help! Help! It's eating me!
"Help! Help! It's eating me!"
IT'S EATING MEEEEE!! AAAGHH
"It's eating meeeee!! AAAGHHH!!!"
Oh!
You're awake.

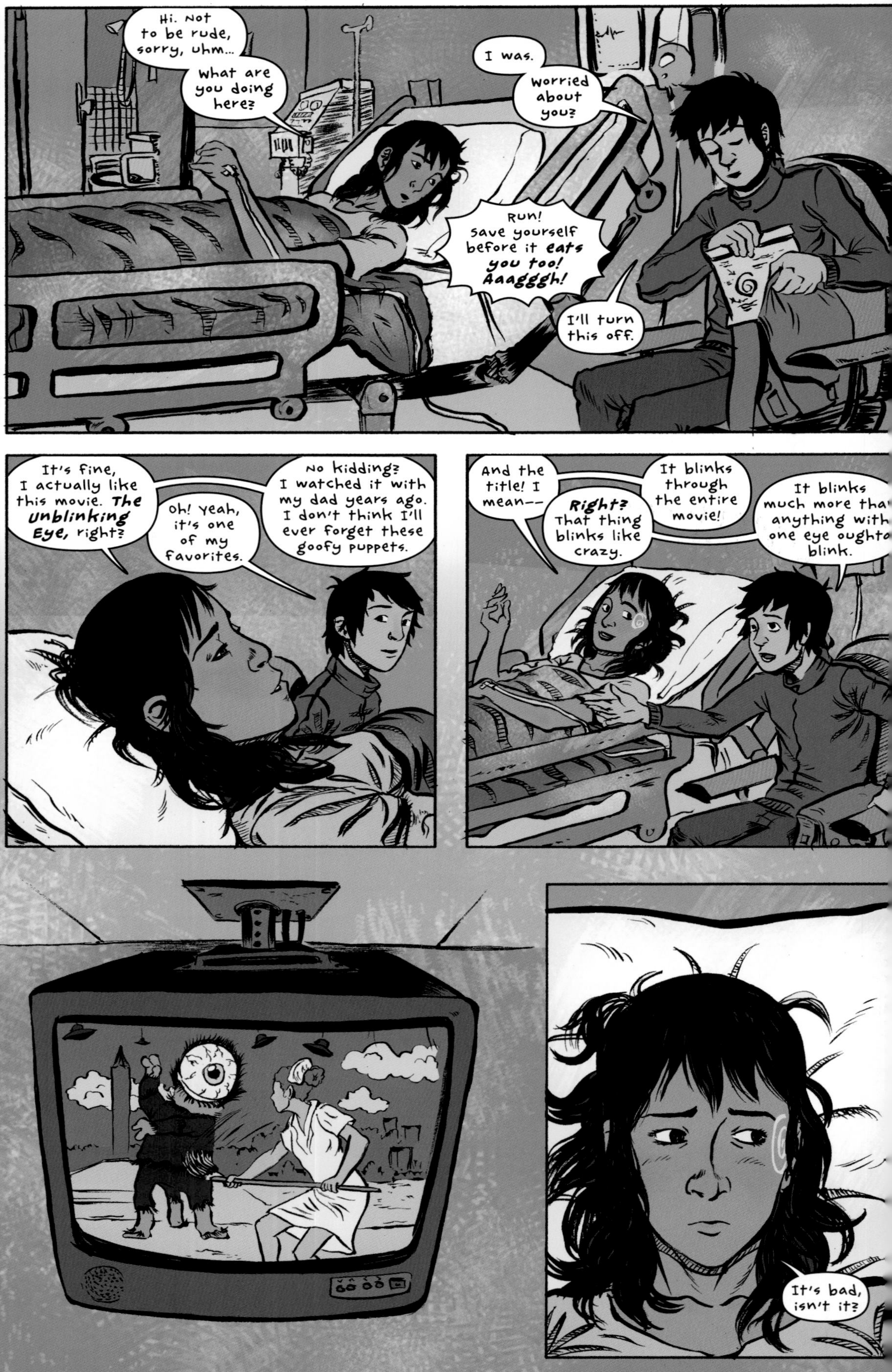
Hi. Not to be rude, sorry, uhm...
What are you doing here?
I was.
Worried about you?
Run! Save yourself before it eats you too! Aaagggh!
I'll turn this off.
It's fine, I actually like this movie. The Unblinking Eye, right?
Oh! Yeah, it's one of my favorites.
No kidding? I watched it with my dad years ago. I don't think I'll ever forget these goofy puppets.
And the title! I mean--
Right? That thing blinks like crazy.
It blinks through the entire movie!
It blinks much more tha anything with one eye oughta blink.
It's bad, isn't it?

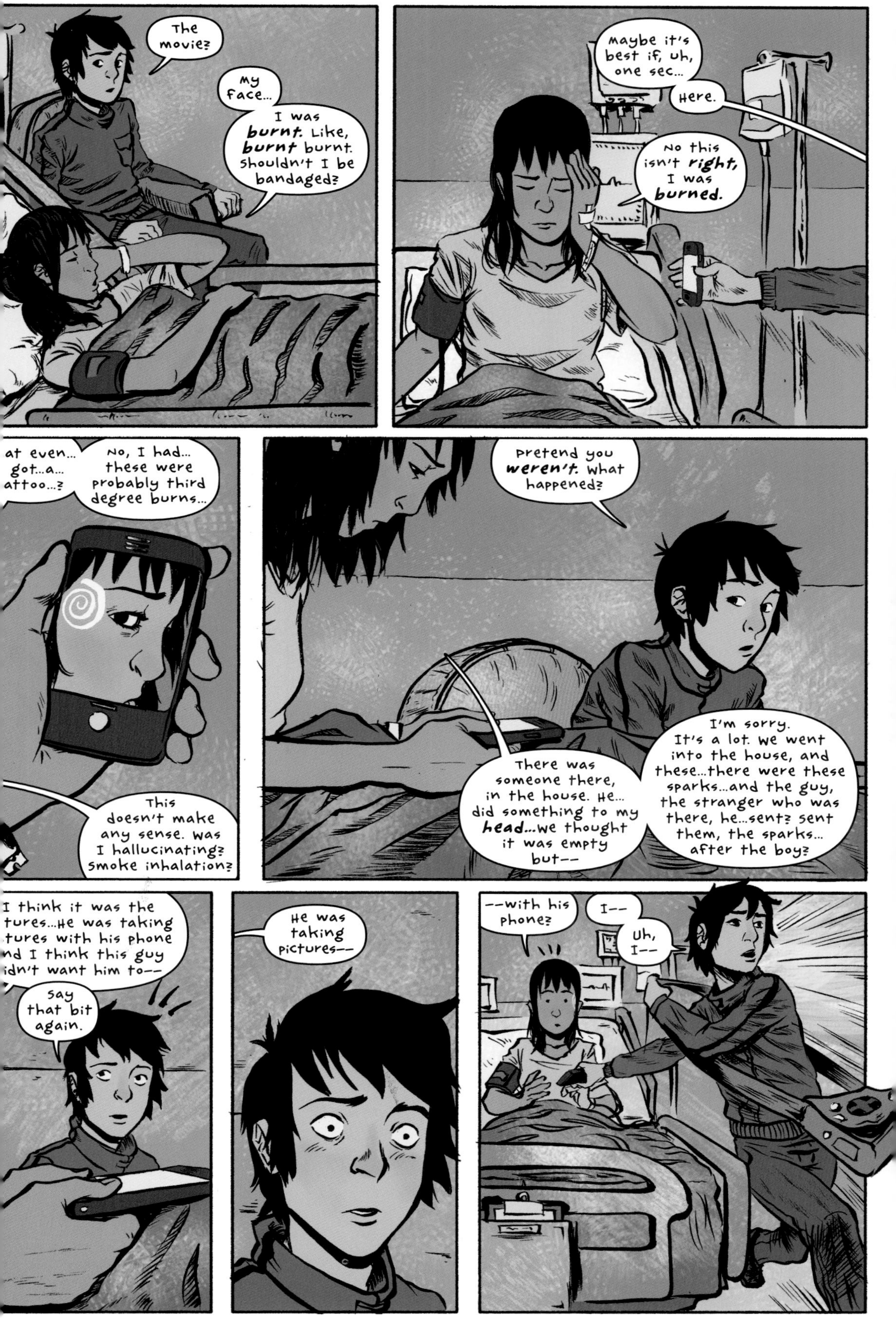
The movie?
My face...
I was burnt. Like, burnt burnt. Shouldn't I be bandaged?
Maybe it's best if, uh, one sec...
Here.
No this isn't right, I was burned.
at even... got...a... attoo...?
No, I had... these were probably third degree burns...
This doesn't make any sense. Was I hallucinating? Smoke inhalation?
Pretend you weren't. What happened?
There was someone there, in the house. He... did something to my head...we thought it was empty but--
I'm sorry. It's a lot. We went into the house, and these...there were these sparks...and the guy, the stranger who was there, he...sent? sent them, the sparks... after the boy?
I think it was the tures...He was taking tures with his phone nd I think this guy idn't want him to--
Say that bit again.
He was taking pictures--
--with his phone?
I--
Uh, I--

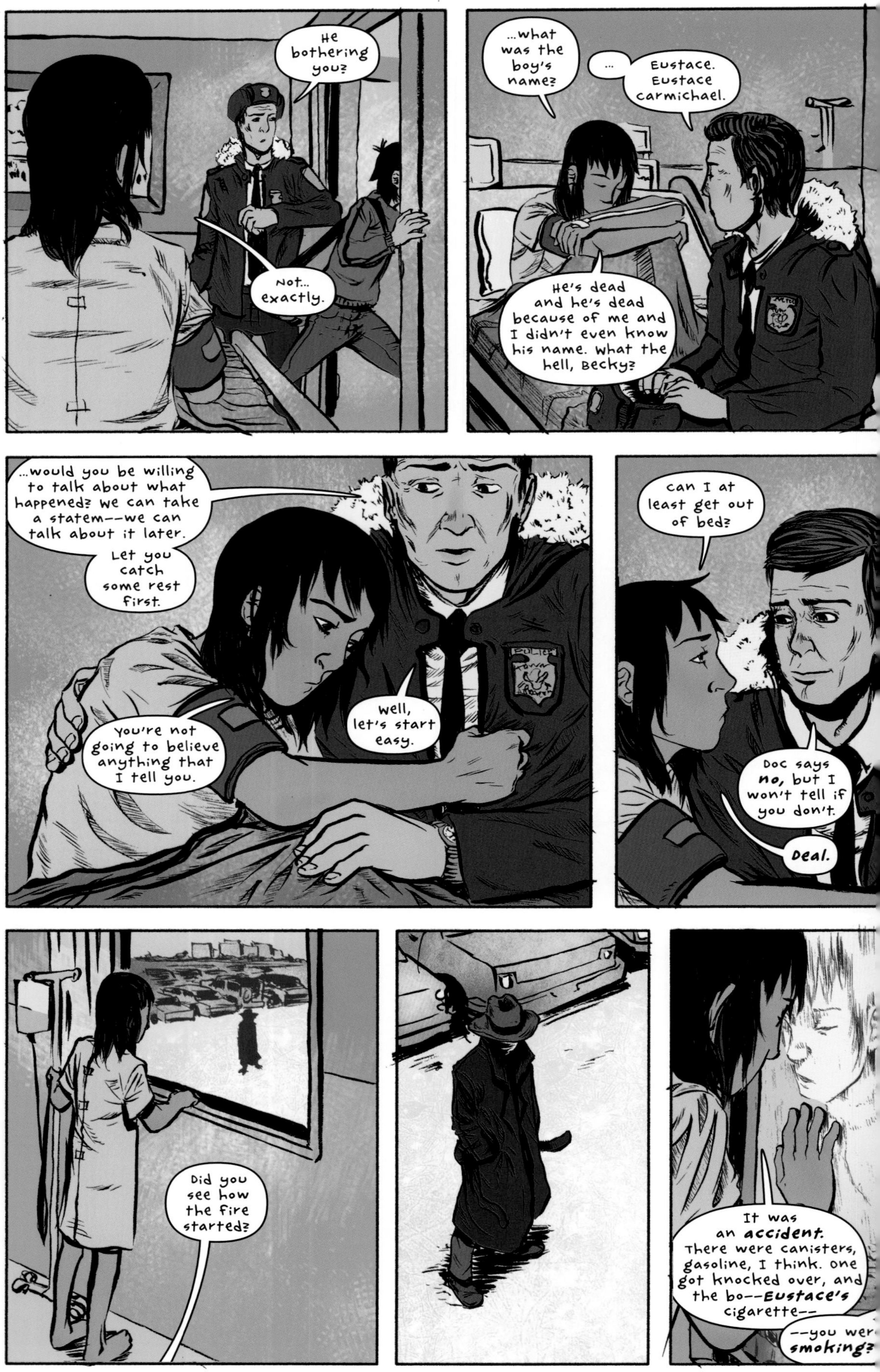
He bothering you?
Not... exactly.
...what was the boy's name?
...
Eustace. Eustace Carmichael.
He's dead and he's dead because of me and I didn't even know his name. What the hell, Becky?
...would you be willing to talk about what happened? We can take a statem--we can talk about it later.
Let you catch some rest first.
You're not going to believe anything that I tell you.
Well, let's start easy.
Can I at least get out of bed?
Doc says **no**, but I won't tell if you don't.
Deal.
Did you see how the fire started?
It was an **accident.** There were canisters, gasoline, I think. One got knocked over, and the bo--**Eustace's** cigarette--
--you wer **smoking?**

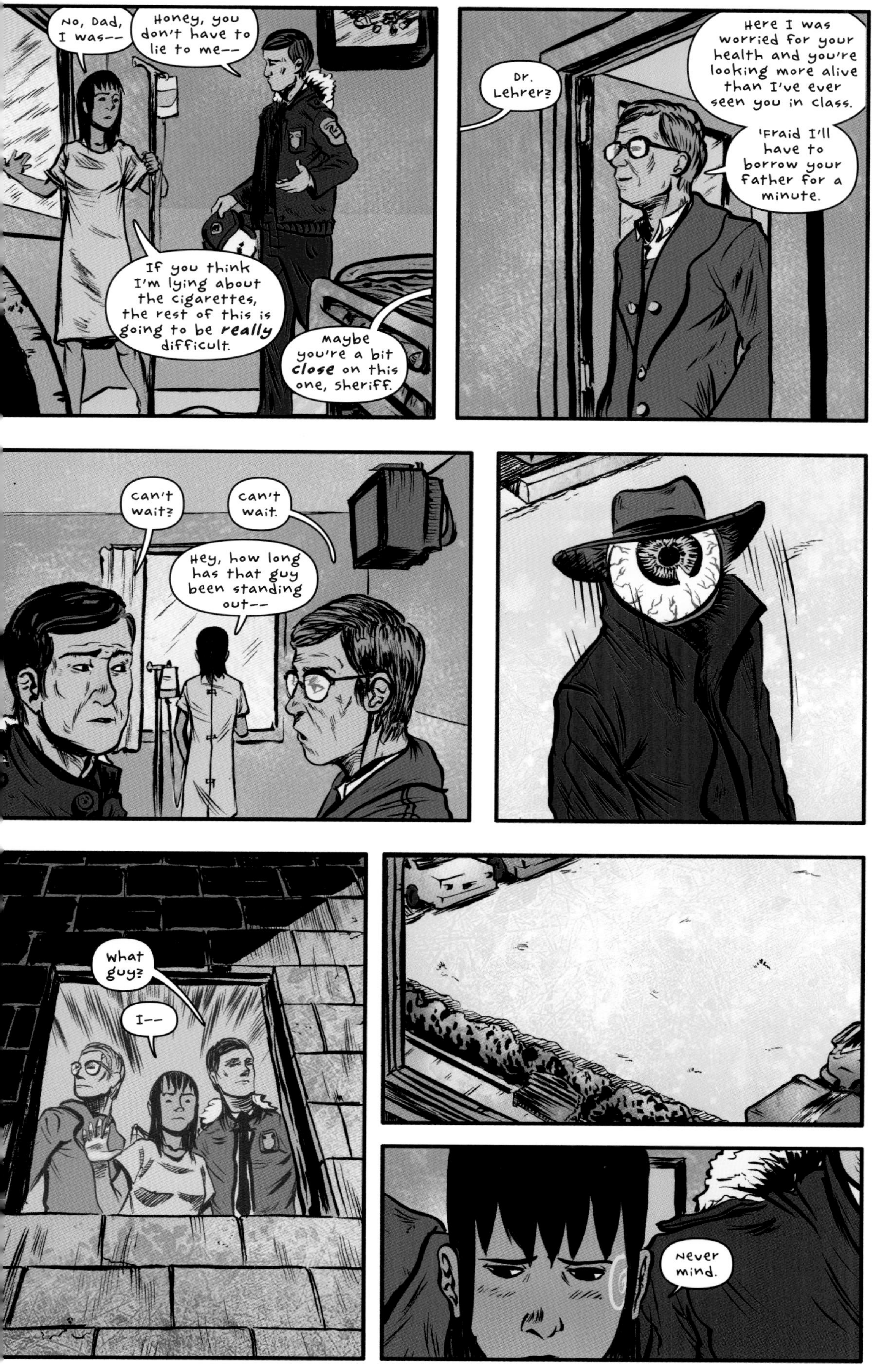
No, Dad, I was--
Honey, you don't have to lie to me--
If you think I'm lying about the cigarettes, the rest of this is going to be ***really*** difficult.
Maybe you're a bit ***close*** on this one, sheriff.
Dr. Lehrer?
Here I was worried for your health and you're looking more alive than I've ever seen you in class.
'Fraid I'll have to borrow your father for a minute.
Can't wait?
Can't wait.
Hey, how long has that guy been standing out--
What guy?
I--
Never mind.

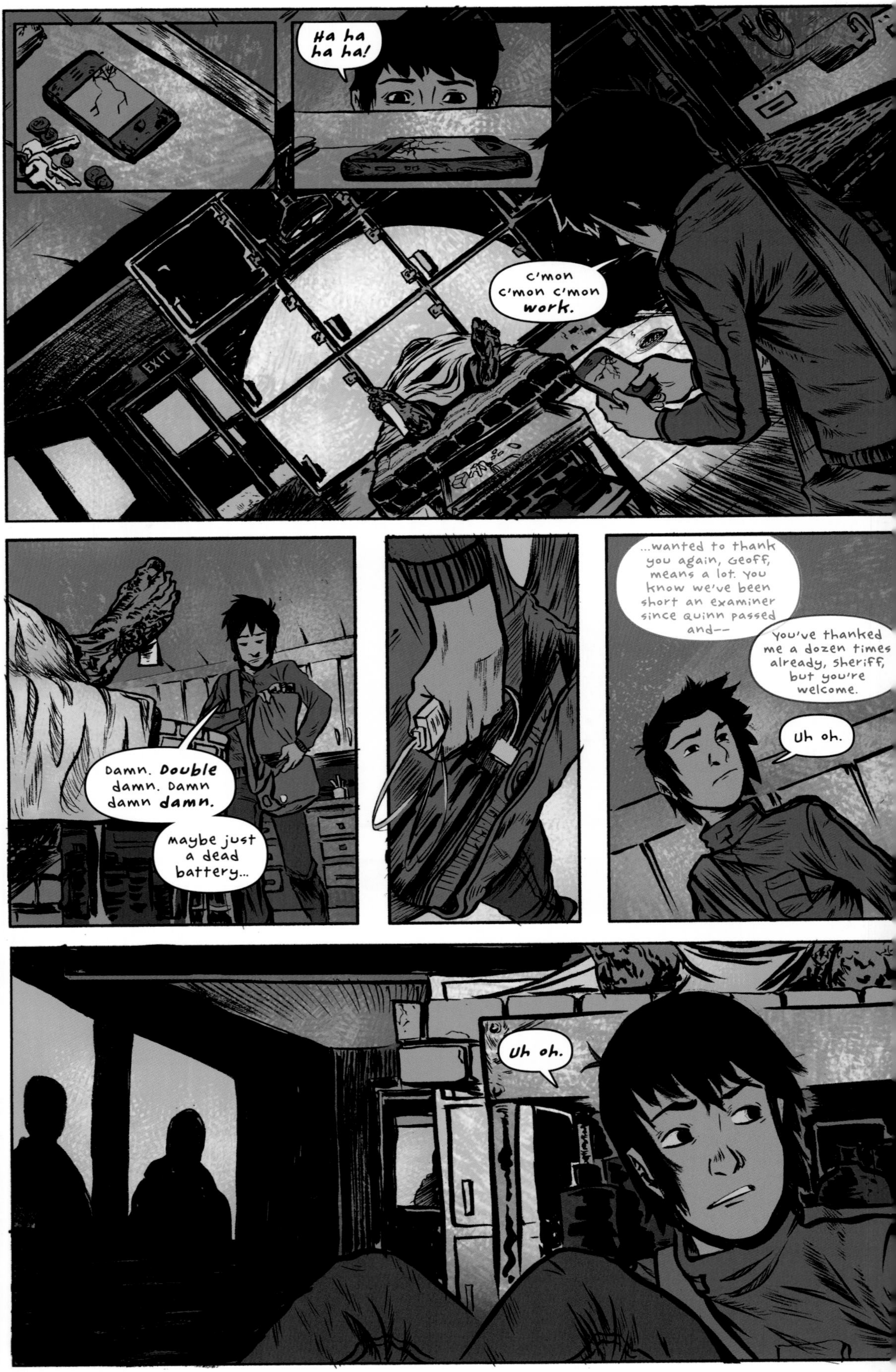
Ha ha ha ha!
c'mon c'mon c'mon work.
Damn. Double damn. Damn damn damn.
maybe just a dead battery...
...wanted to thank you again, Geoff, means a lot. You know we've been short an examiner since Quinn passed and--
You've thanked me a dozen times already, sheriff, but you're welcome.
Uh oh.
Uh oh.

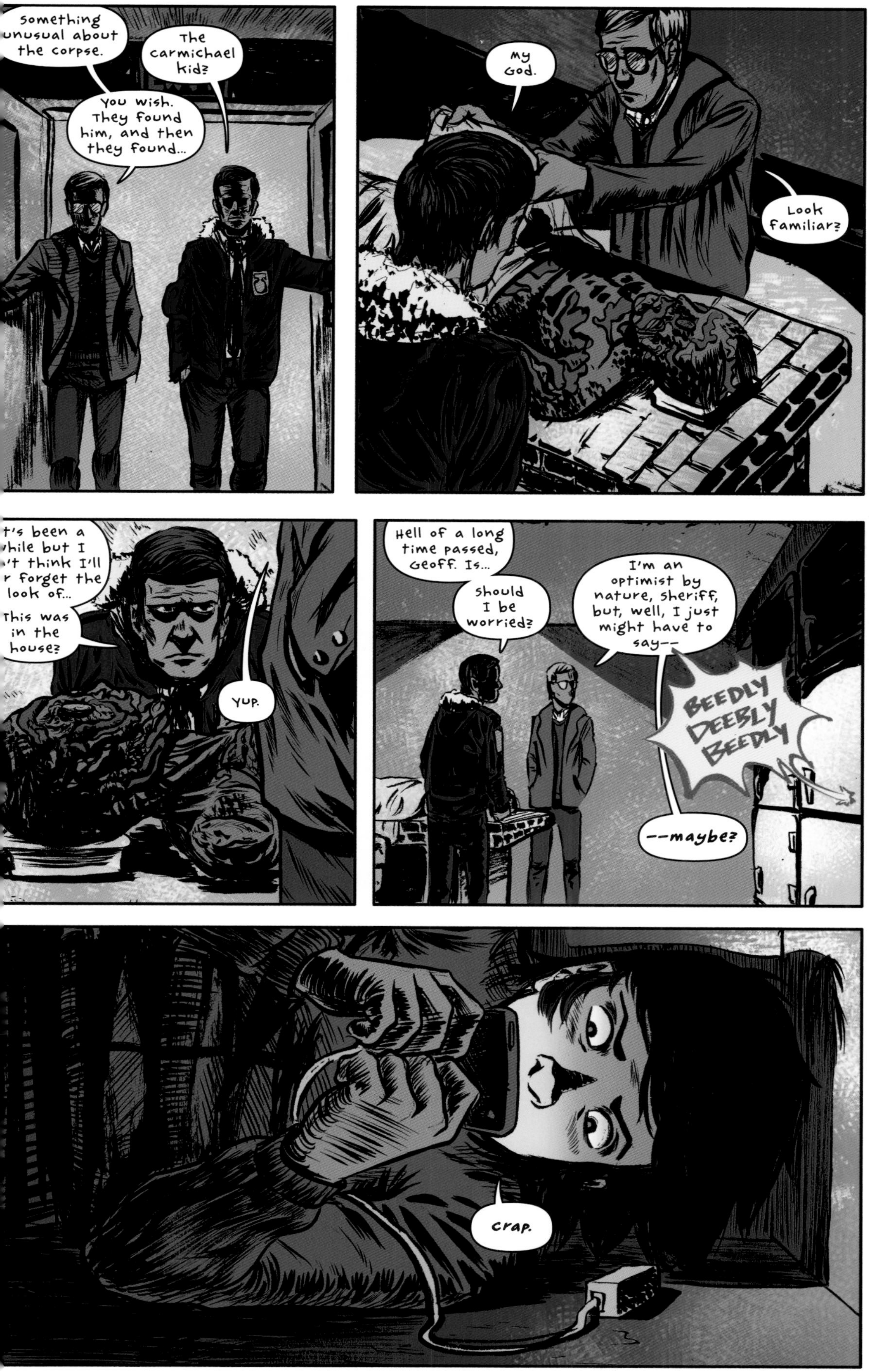
Something unusual about the corpse.
The Carmichael kid?
You wish. They found him, and then they found...
My God.
Look familiar?
t's been a while but I 't think I'll r forget the look of...
This was in the house?
Yup.
Hell of a long time passed, Geoff. Is...
Should I be worried?
I'm an optimist by nature, sheriff, but, well, I just might have to say--
BEEDLY DEEBLY BEEDLY
--maybe?
Crap.

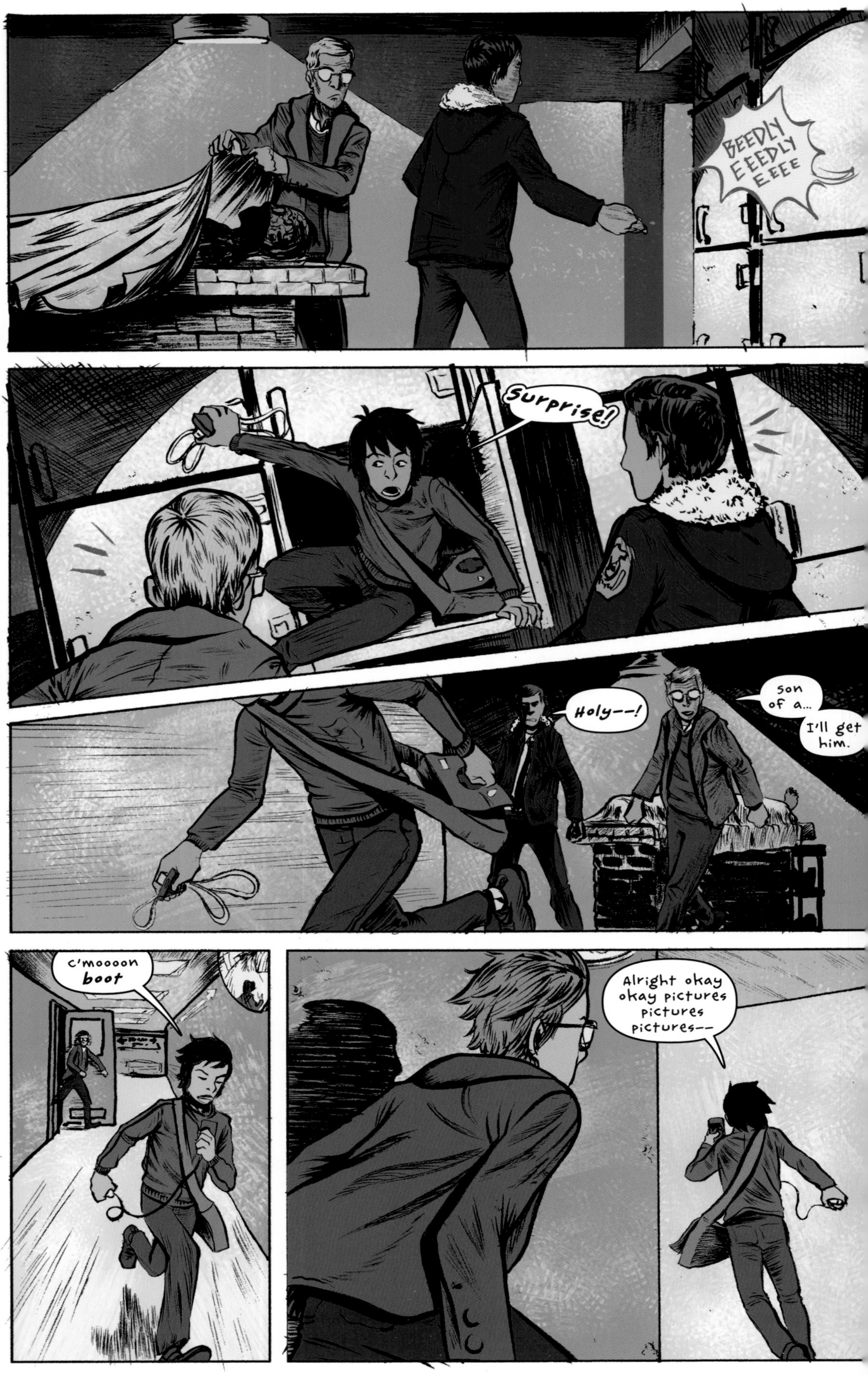
BEEDLY EEEDLY EEEE
Surprise!
Holy--!
son of a...
I'll get him.
c'moooon boot
Alright okay okay pictures pictures pictures--

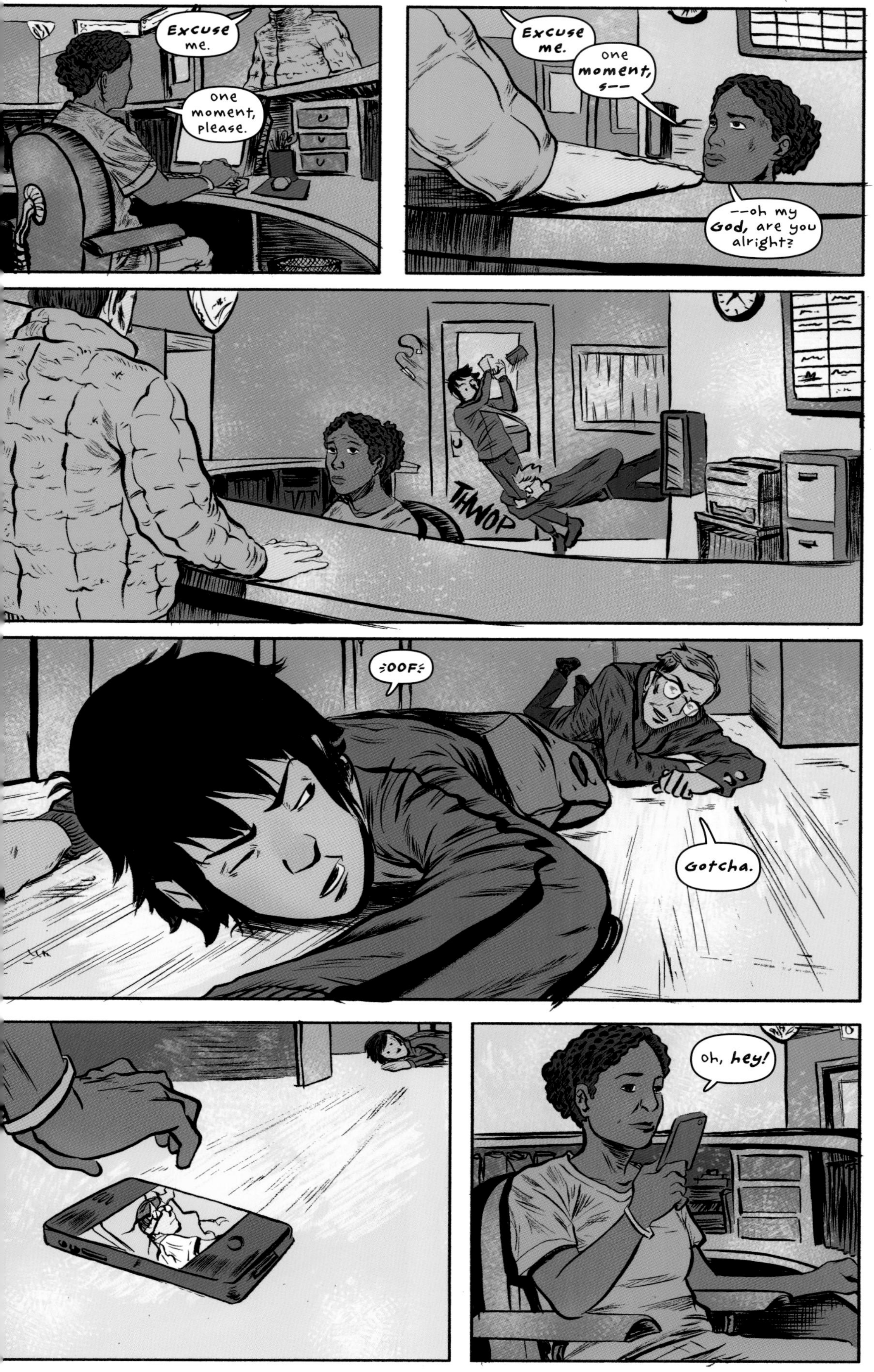

Excuse me.
one moment, please.
Excuse me.
one moment, s--
--oh my God, are you alright?
THWOP
OOF
Gotcha.
oh, hey!

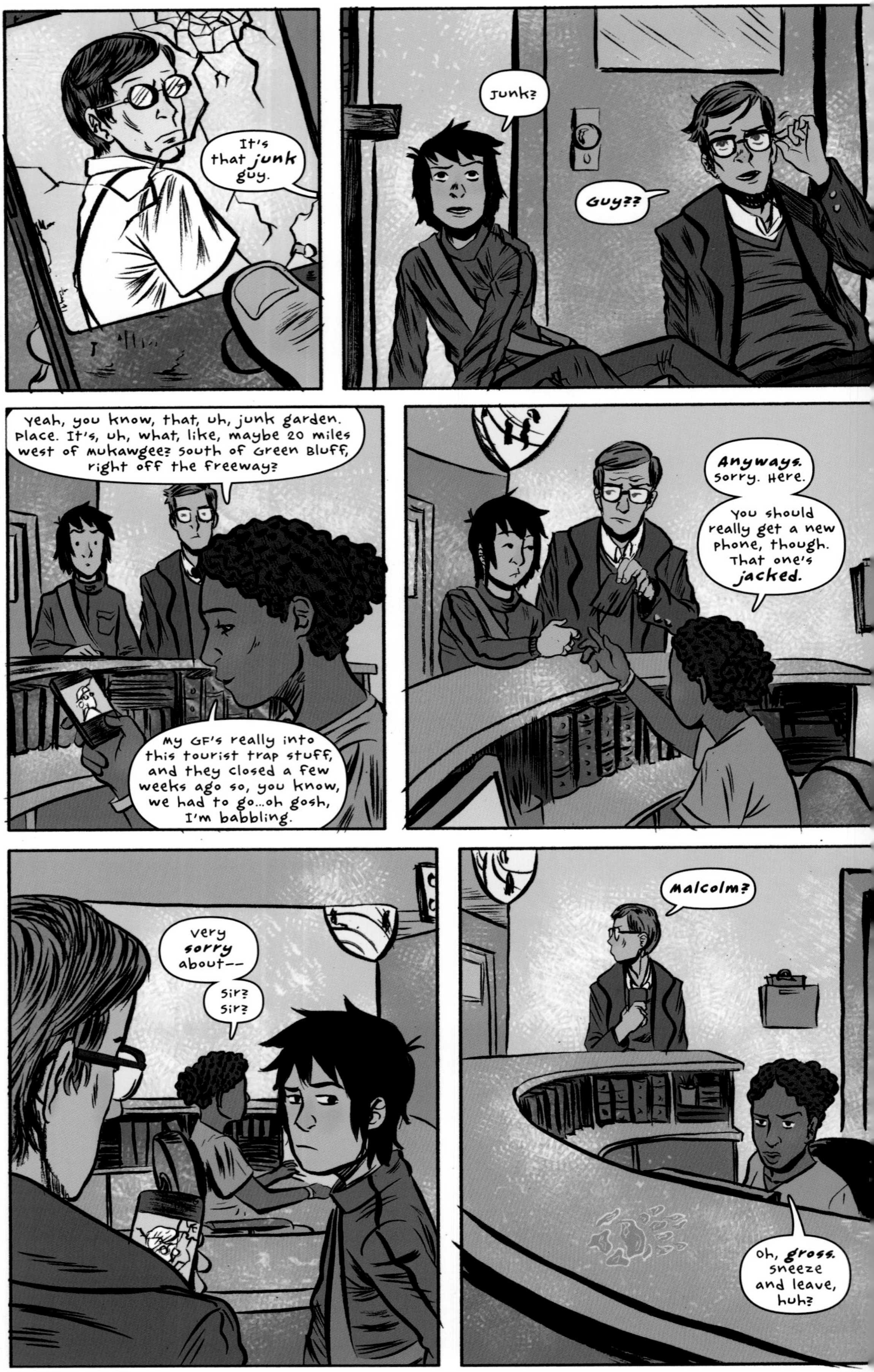
It's that junk guy.
Junk?
Guy??
Yeah, you know, that, uh, junk garden. Place. It's, uh, what, like, maybe 20 miles west of Mukawgee? South of Green Bluff, right off the freeway?
My GF's really into this tourist trap stuff, and they closed a few weeks ago so, you know, we had to go...oh gosh, I'm babbling.
Anyways. Sorry. Here.
You should really get a new phone, though. That one's jacked.
Very sorry about--
Sir? Sir?
Malcolm?
Oh, gross. Sneeze and leave, huh?

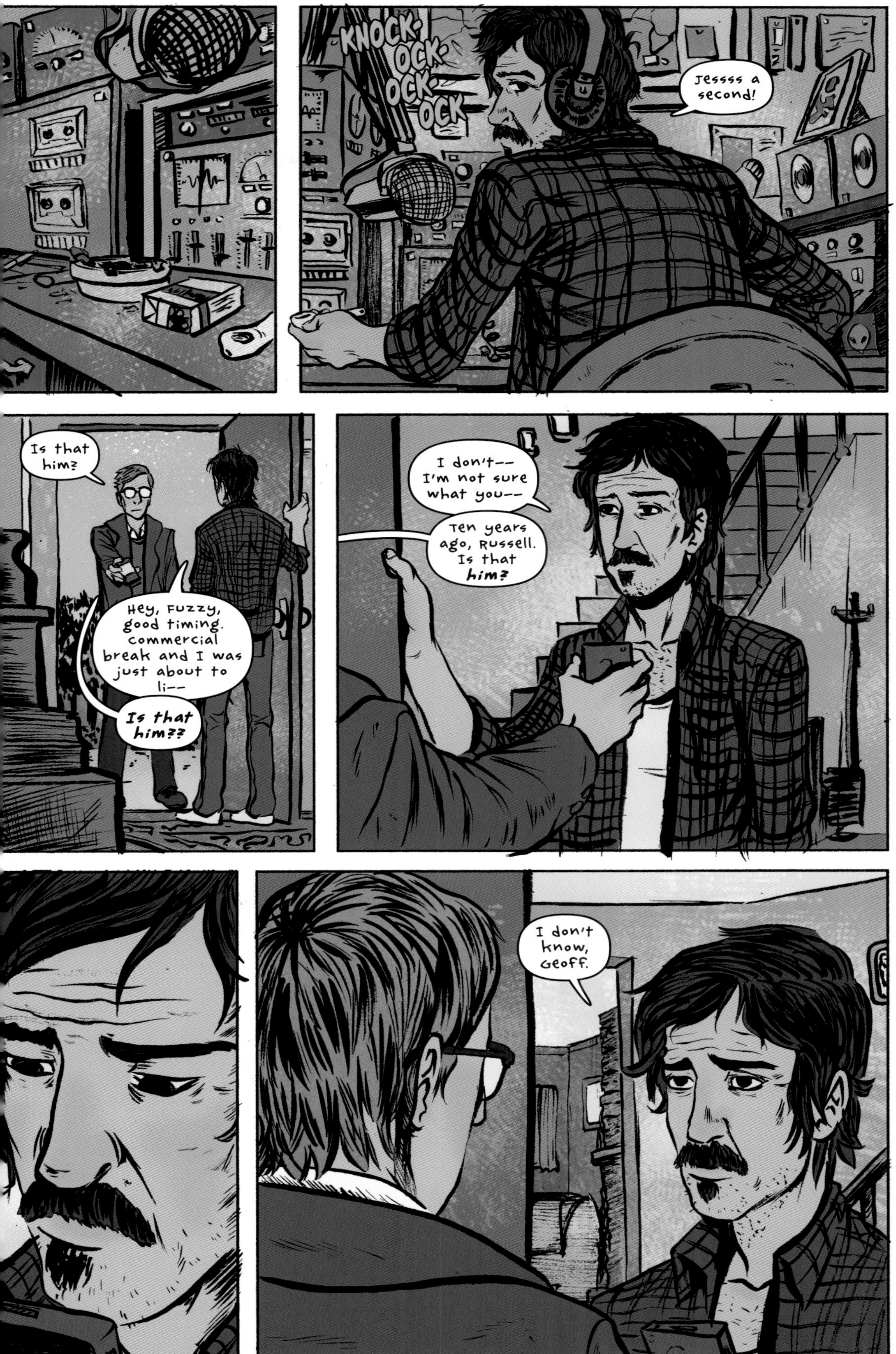

KNOCK-OCK-OCK-OCK
Jessss a second!
Is that him?
Hey, Fuzzy, good timing. commercial break and I was just about to li--
Is that him??
I don't-- I'm not sure what you--
Ten years ago, Russell. Is that him?
I don't know, Geoff.

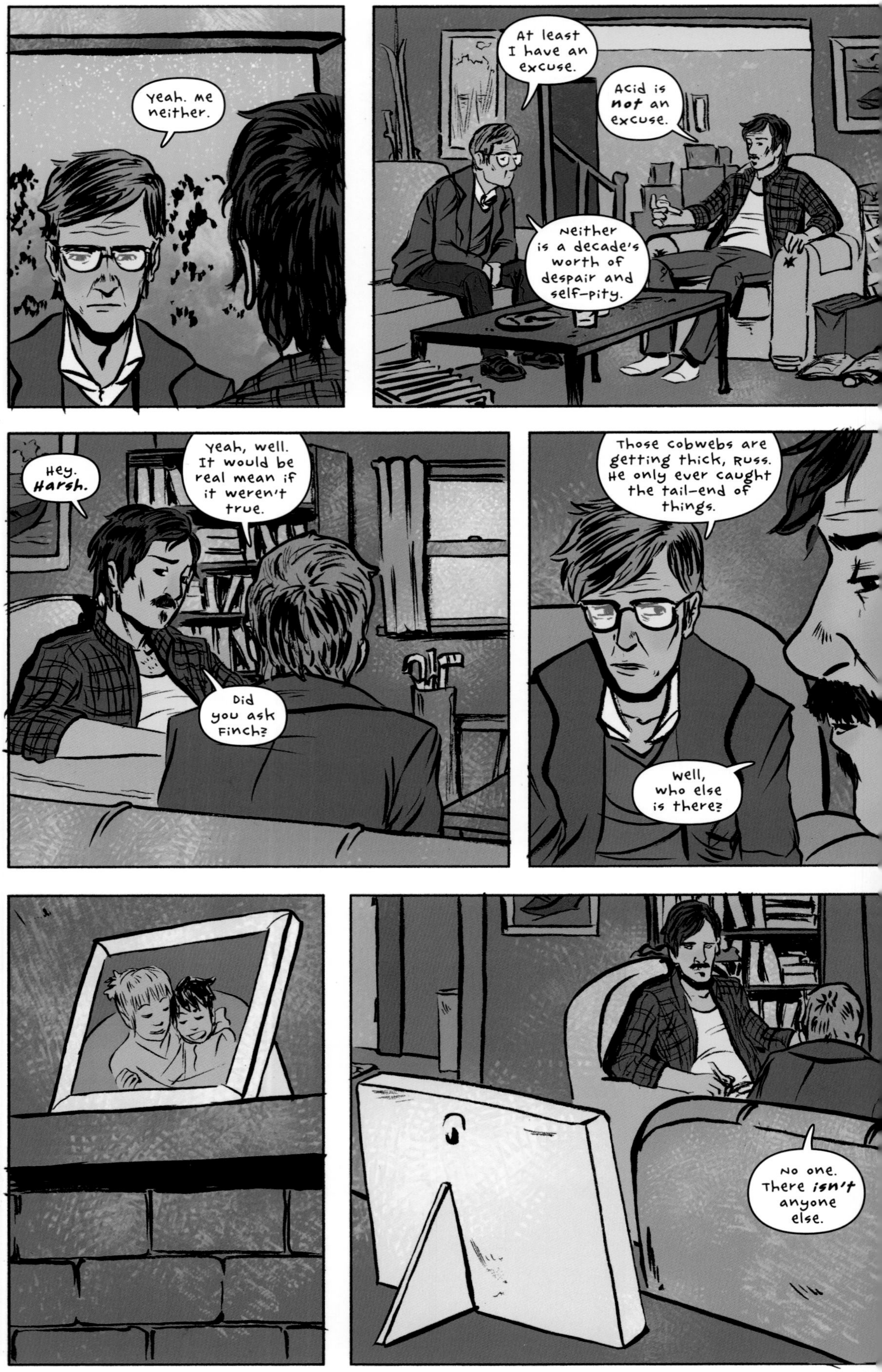
Yeah. Me neither.
At least I have an excuse.
Acid is *not* an excuse.
Neither is a decade's worth of despair and self-pity.
Hey. ***Harsh.***
Yeah, well. It would be real mean if it weren't true.
Did you ask Finch?
Those cobwebs are getting thick, Russ. He only ever caught the tail-end of things.
Well, who else is there?
No one. There ***isn't*** anyone else.

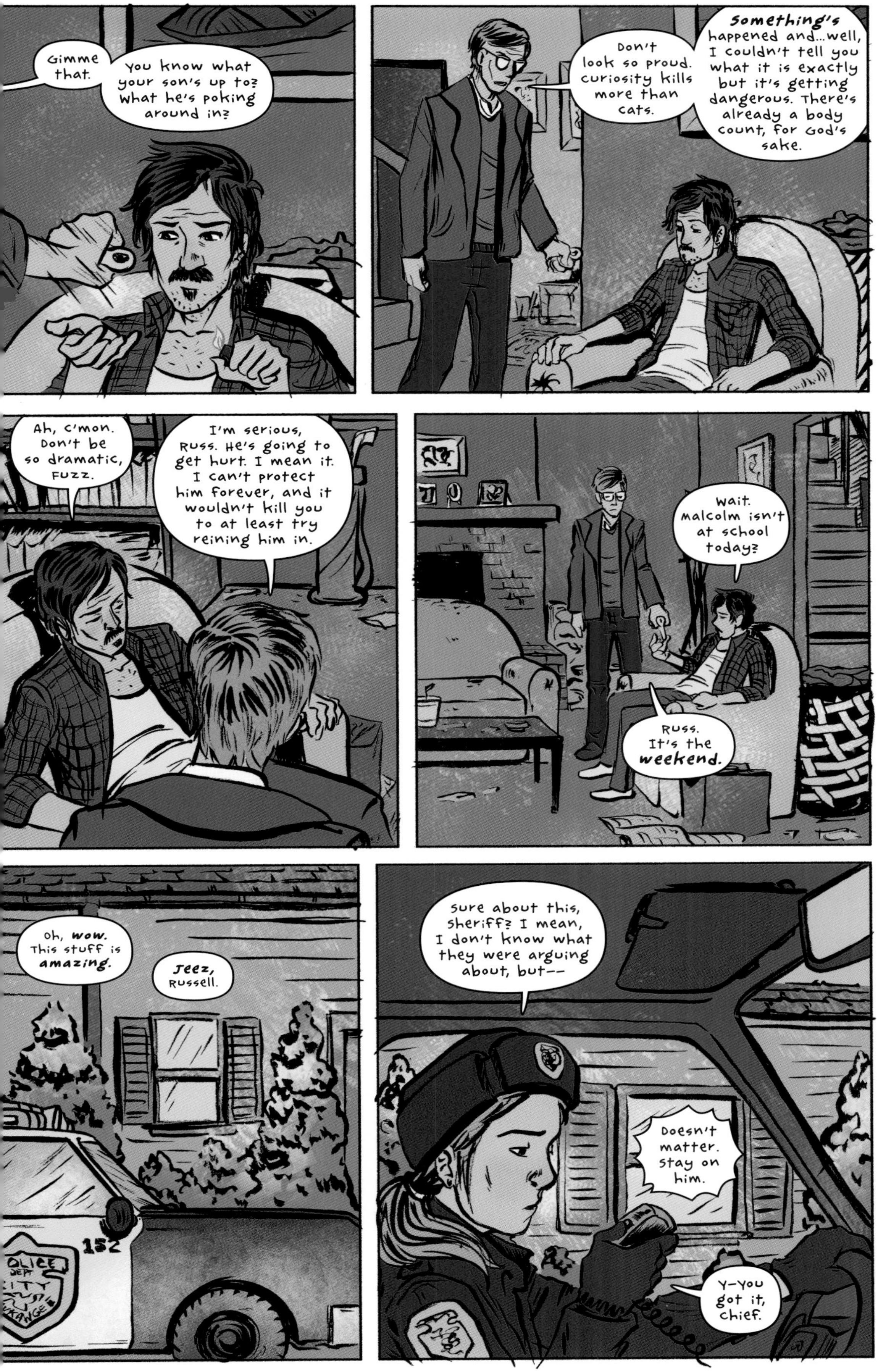
Gimme that.
You know what your son's up to? What he's poking around in?
Don't look so proud. Curiosity kills more than cats.
Something's happened and...well, I couldn't tell you what it is exactly but it's getting dangerous. There's already a body count, for God's sake.
Ah, c'mon. Don't be so dramatic, Fuzz.
I'm serious, Russ. He's going to get hurt. I mean it. I can't protect him forever, and it wouldn't kill you to at least try reining him in.
Wait. Malcolm isn't at school today?
Russ. It's the weekend.
Oh, wow. This stuff is amazing.
Jeez, Russell.
152
Sure about this, sheriff? I mean, I don't know what they were arguing about, but--
Doesn't matter. Stay on him.
Y-You got it, chief.

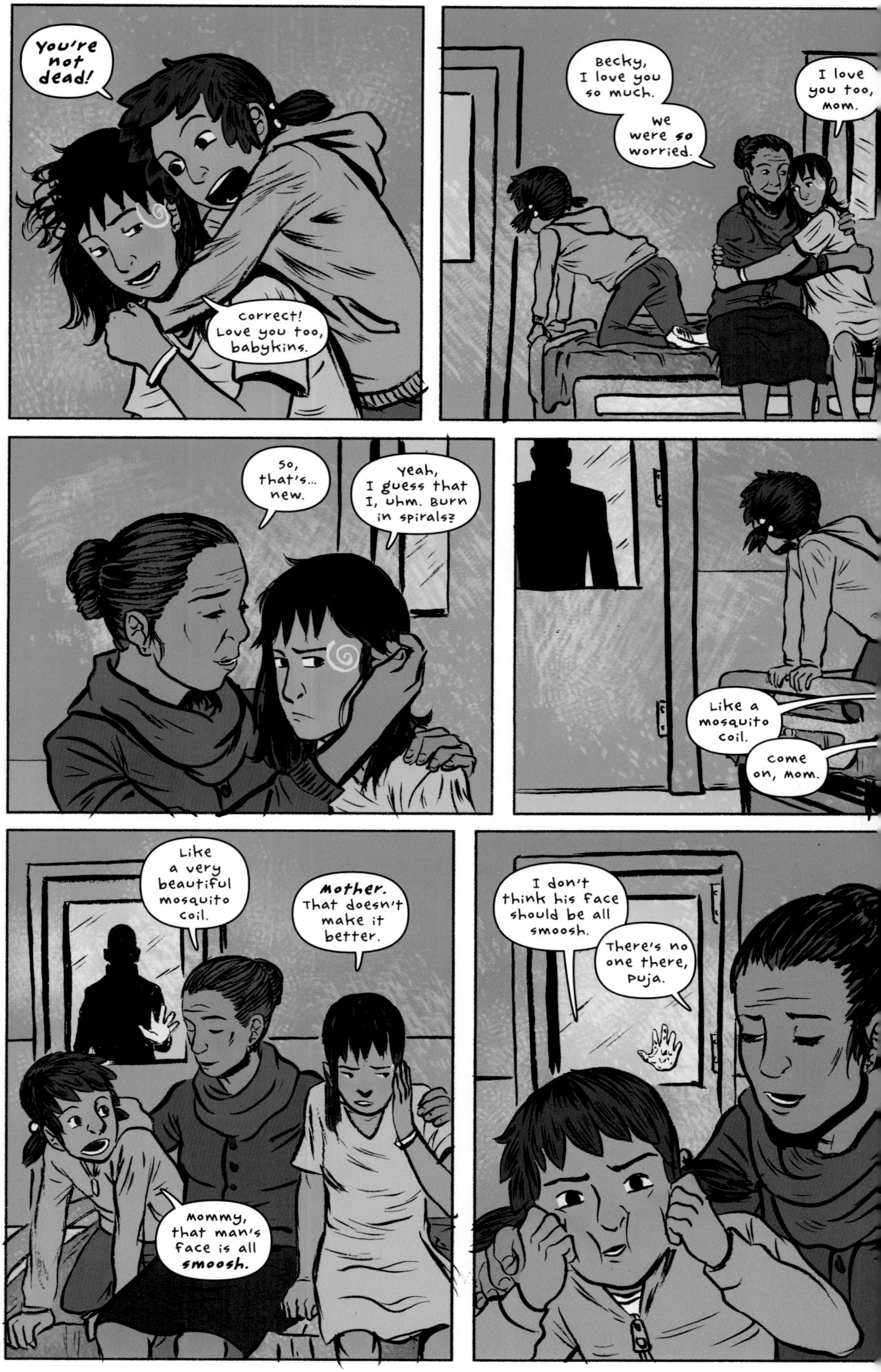
You're not dead!
Correct! Love you too, babykins.
Becky, I love you so much.
We were so worried.
I love you too, mom.
So, that's... new.
Yeah, I guess that I, uhm. Burn in spirals?
Like a mosquito coil.
Come on, mom.
Like a very beautiful mosquito coil.
Mother. That doesn't make it better.
Mommy, that man's face is all smoosh.
I don't think his face should be all smoosh.
There's no one there, Puja.

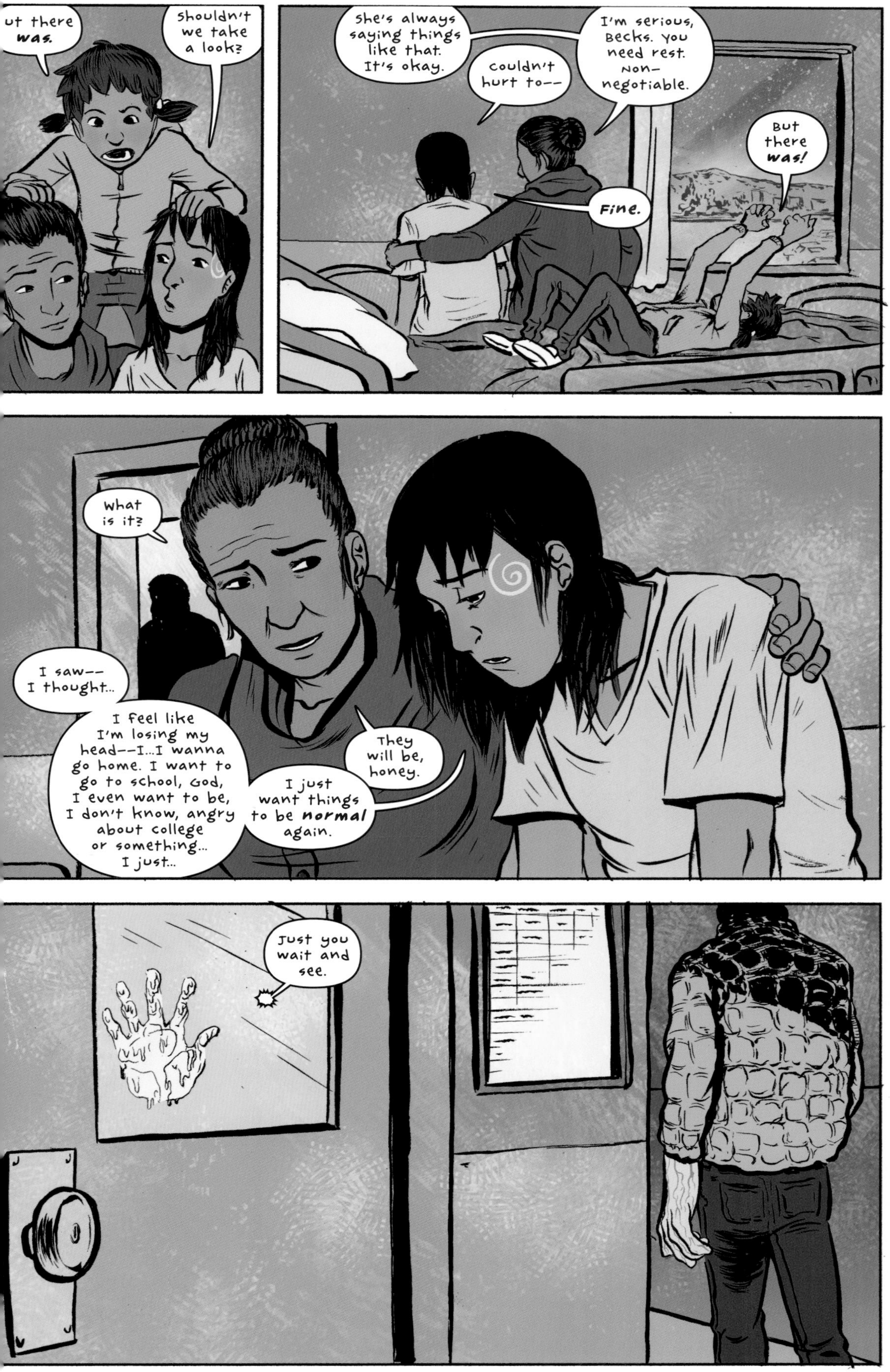
ut there **was.**
Shouldn't we take a look?
She's always saying things like that. It's okay.
Couldn't hurt to--
I'm serious, Becks. You need rest. Non-negotiable.
But there **was!**
Fine.
What is it?
I saw-- I thought...
I feel like I'm losing my head--I...I wanna go home. I want to go to school, God, I even want to be, I don't know, angry about college or something... I just...
I just want things to be **normal** again.
They will be, honey.
Just you wait and see.

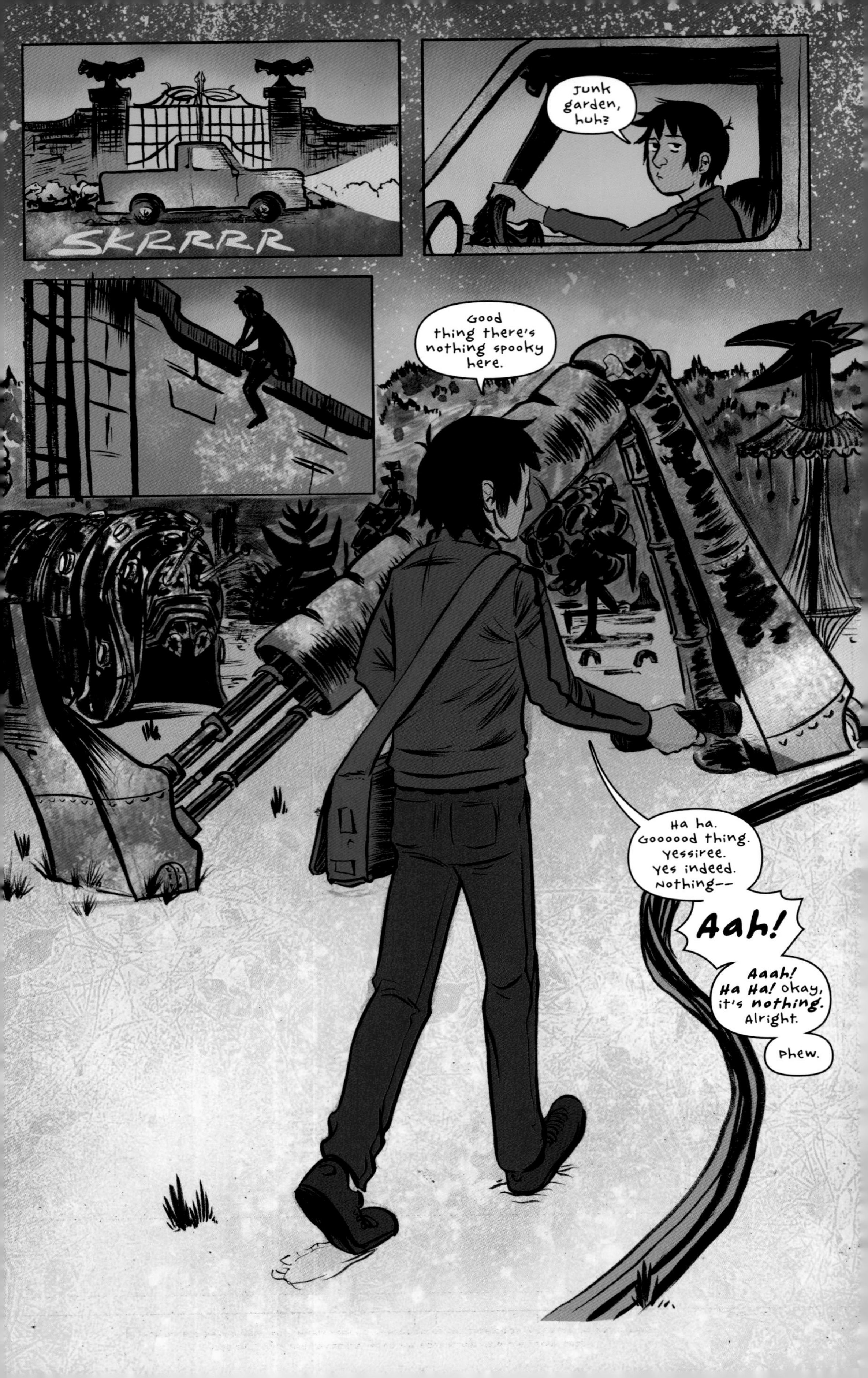
SKRRRR
Junk garden, huh?
Good thing there's nothing spooky here.
Ha ha. Goooood thing. Yessiree. Yes indeed. Nothing--
Aah!
Aaah! Ha Ha! Okay, it's nothing. Alright.
Phew.

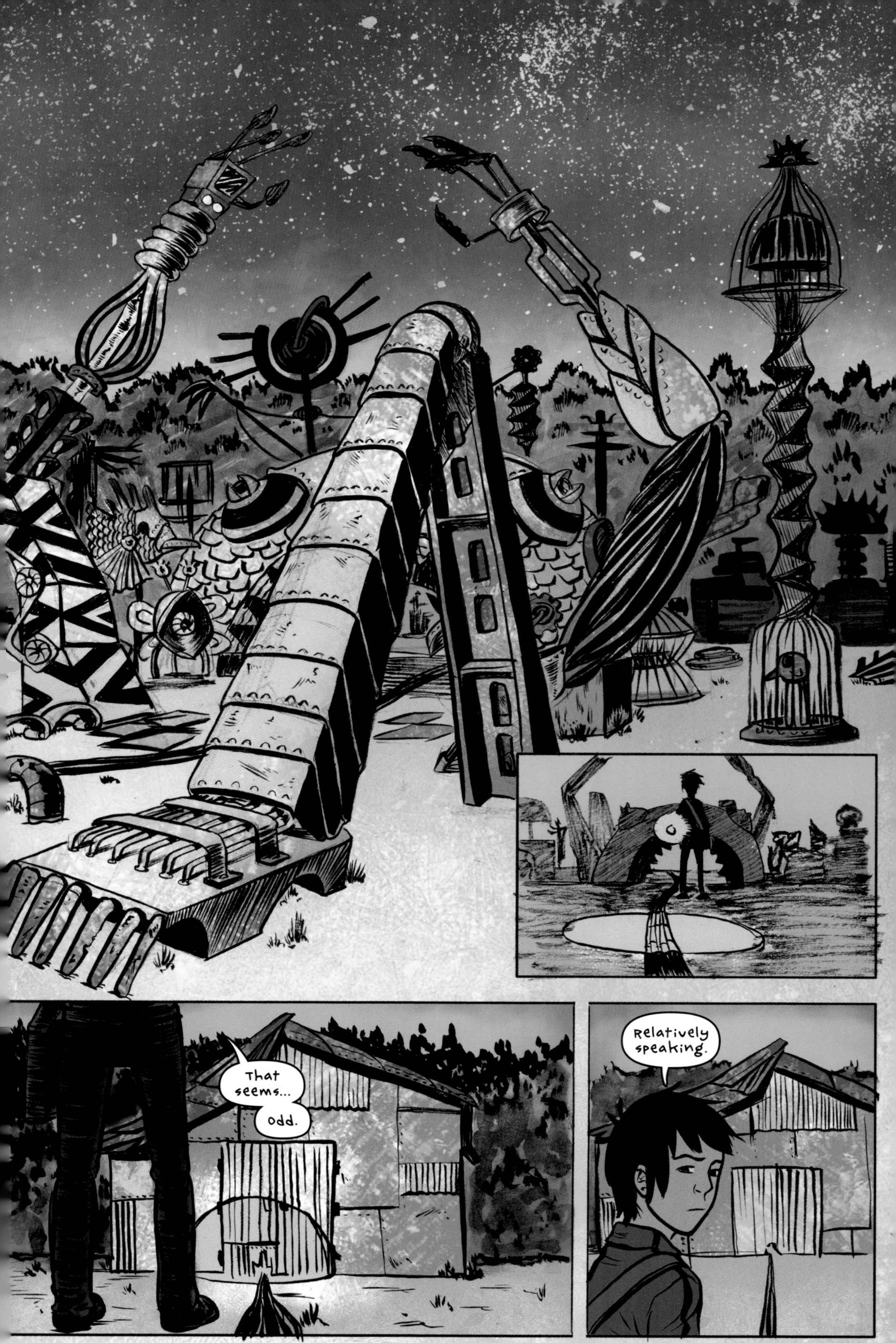
That seems...
odd.
Relatively speaking.

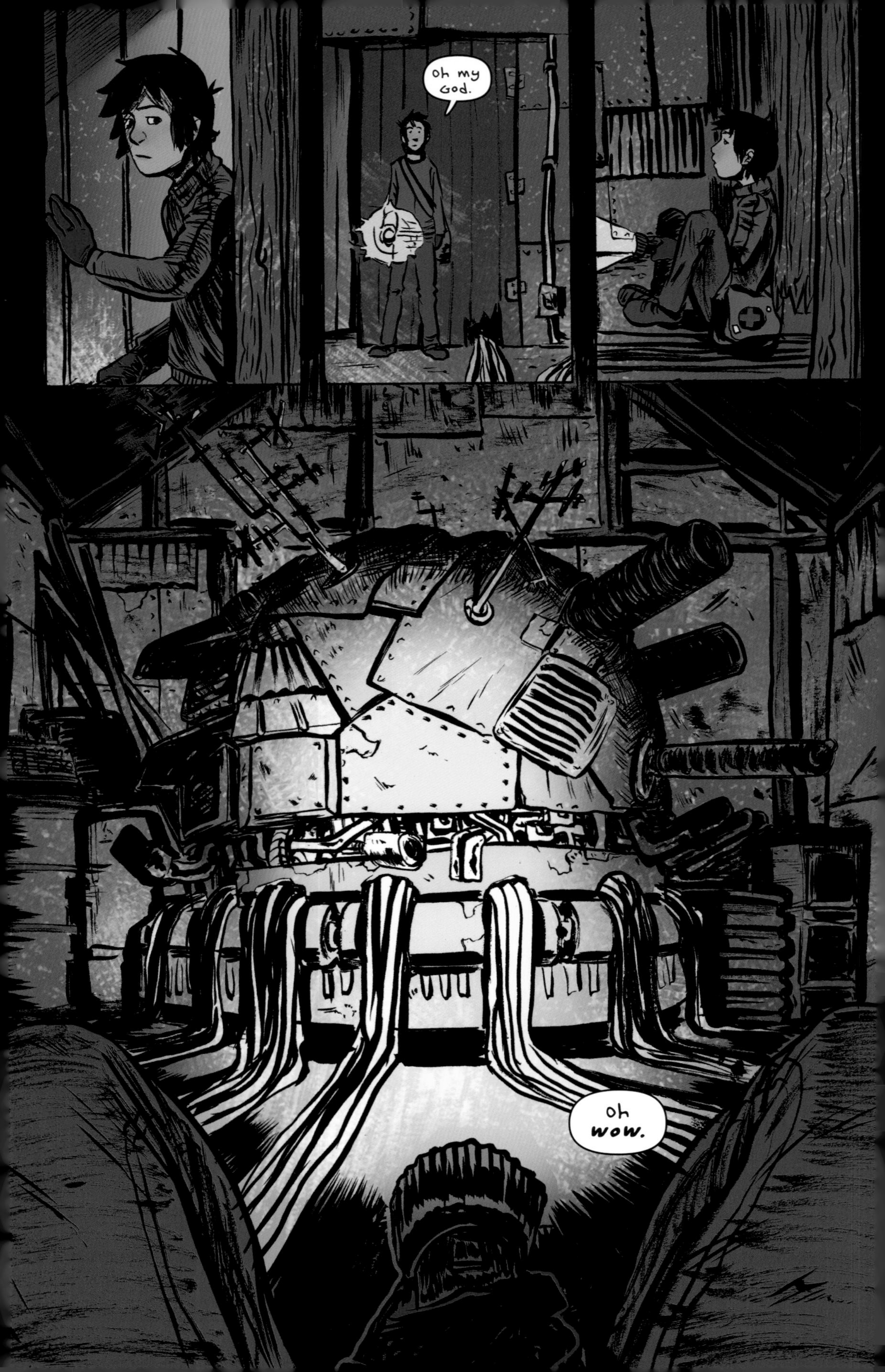
Oh my God.
Oh wow.

t·h·r·e·e

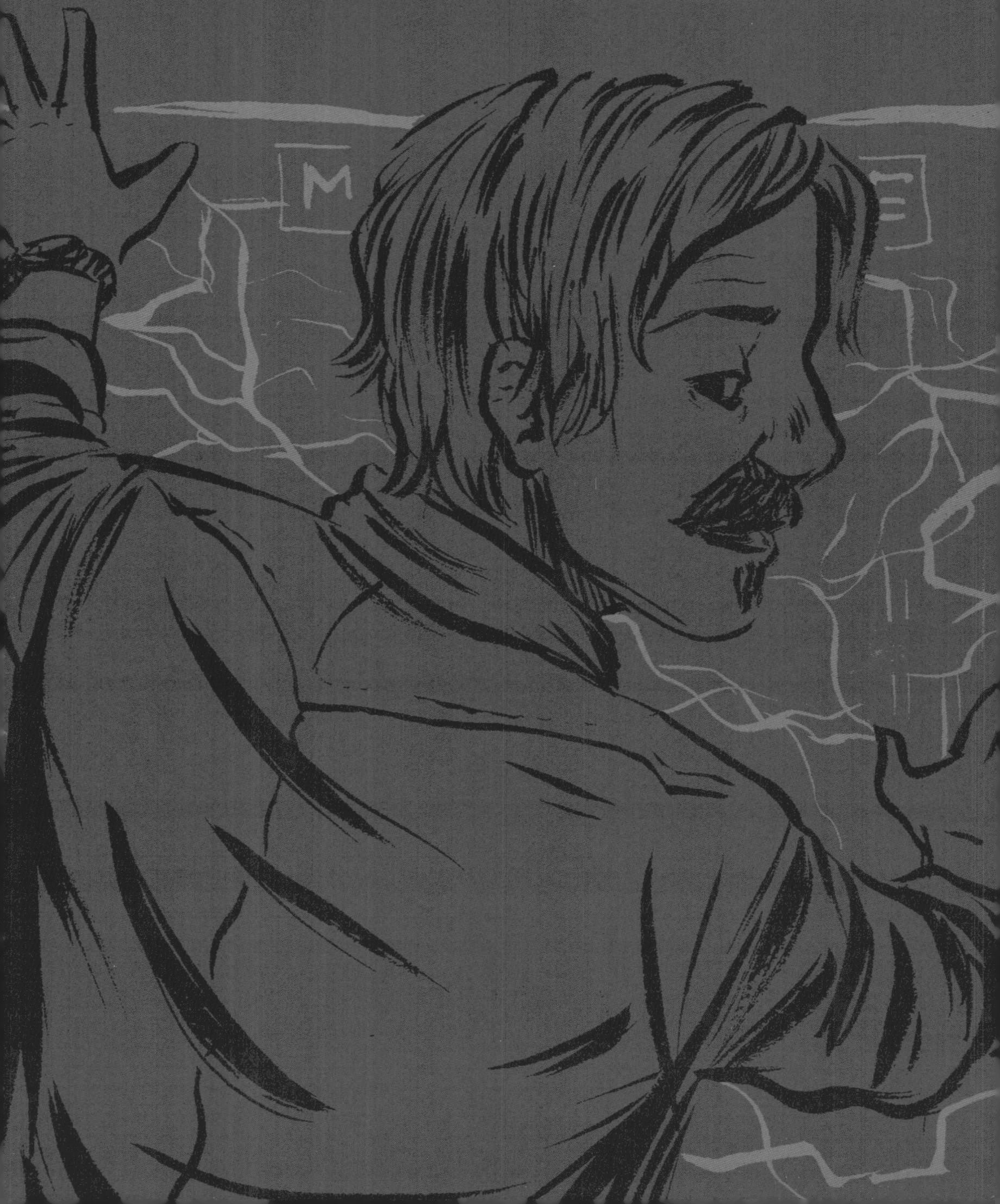
M

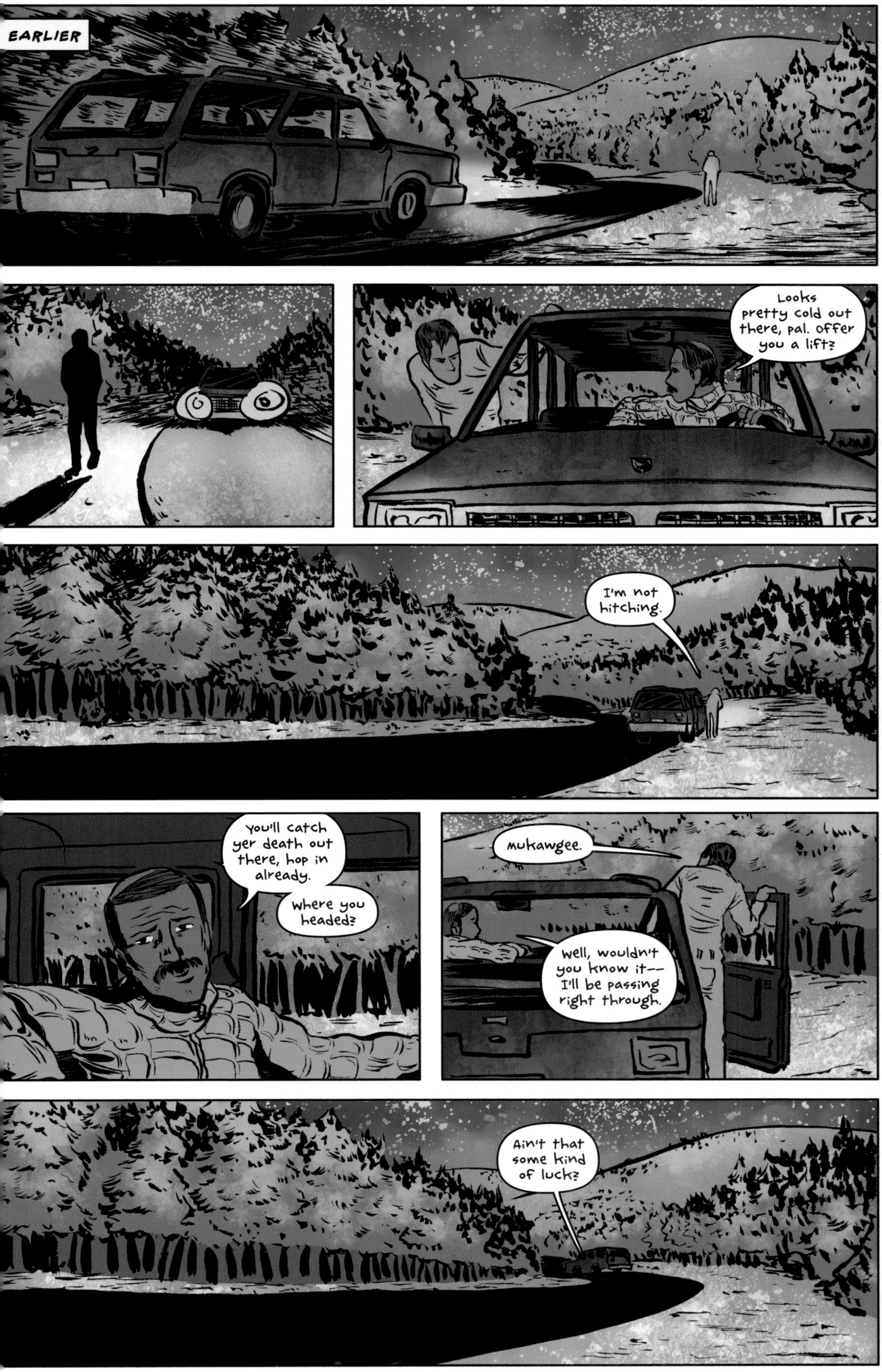
EARLIER
Looks pretty cold out there, pal. Offer you a lift?
I'm not hitching.
You'll catch yer death out there, hop in already.
Where you headed?
Mukawgee.
Well, wouldn't you know it-- I'll be passing right through.
Ain't that some kind of luck?

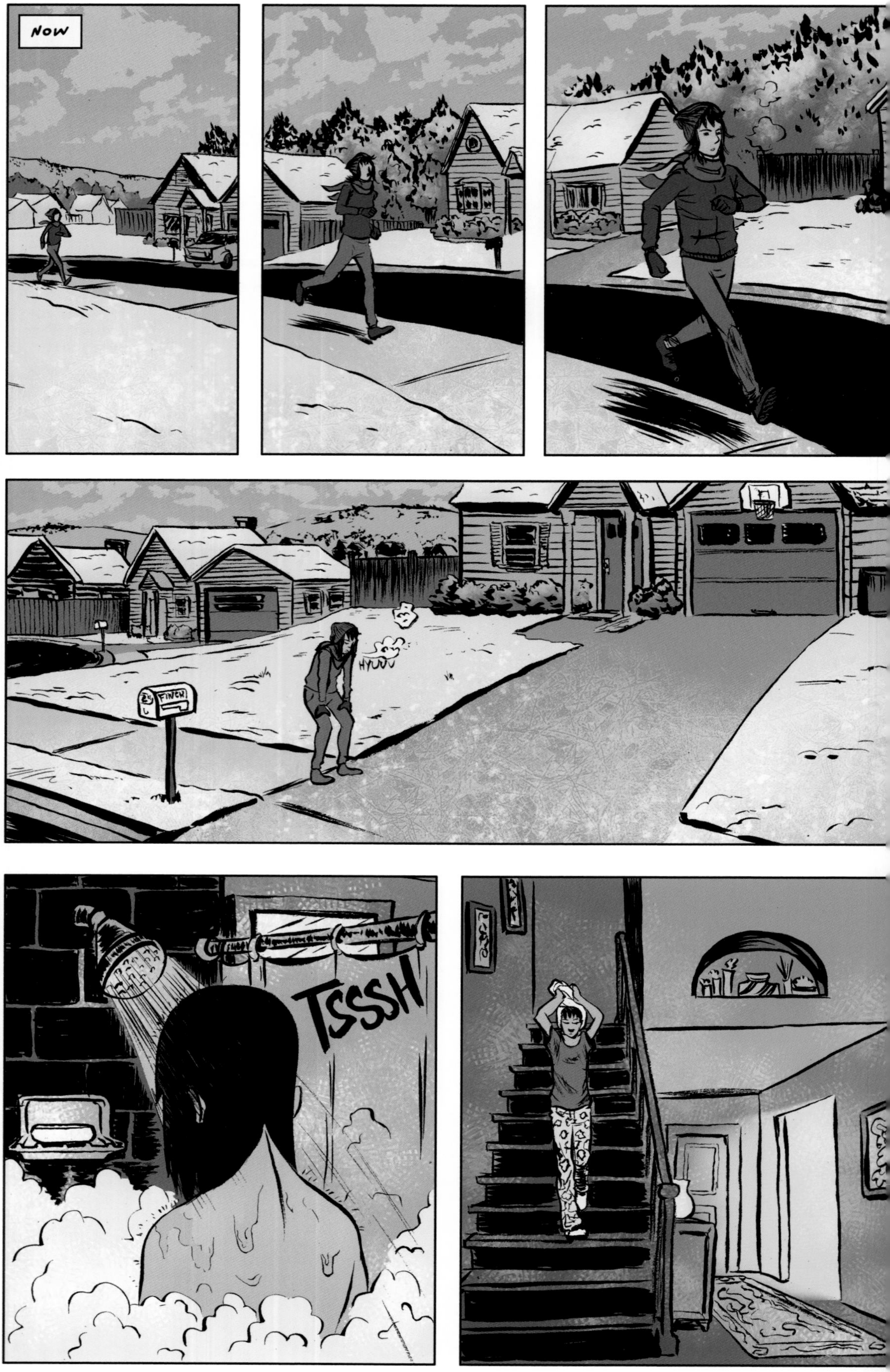
NOW
FINCH
HYUUU
TSSSH

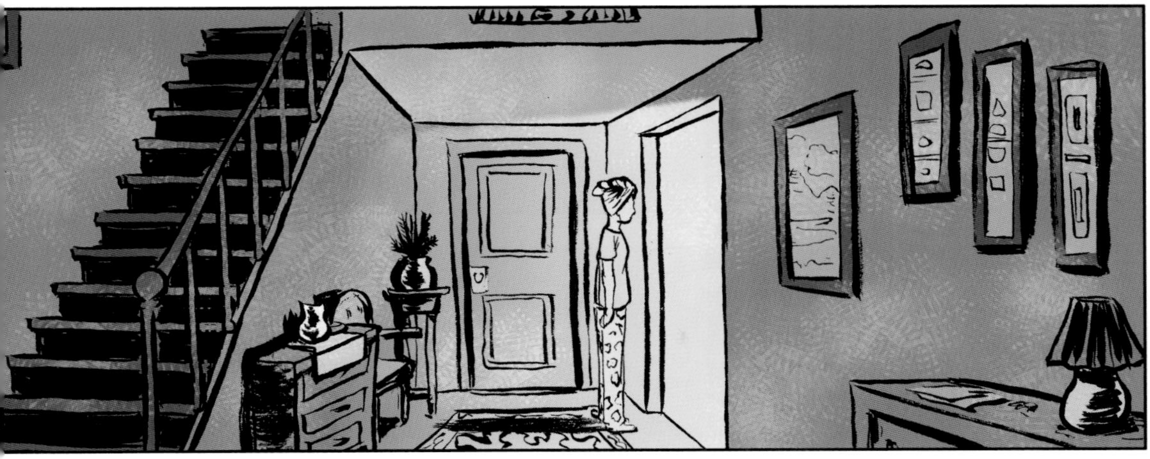

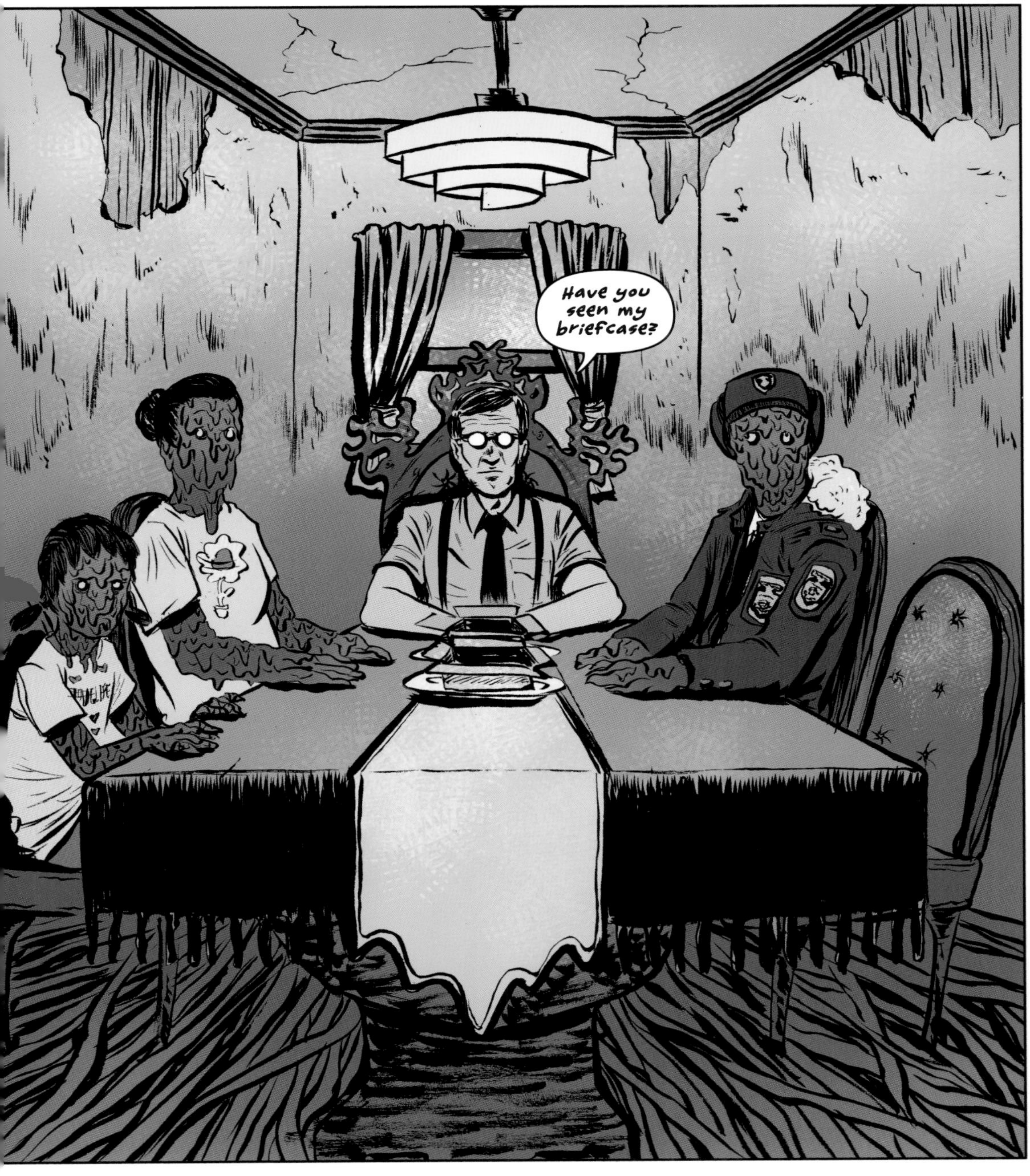
Have you seen my briefcase?

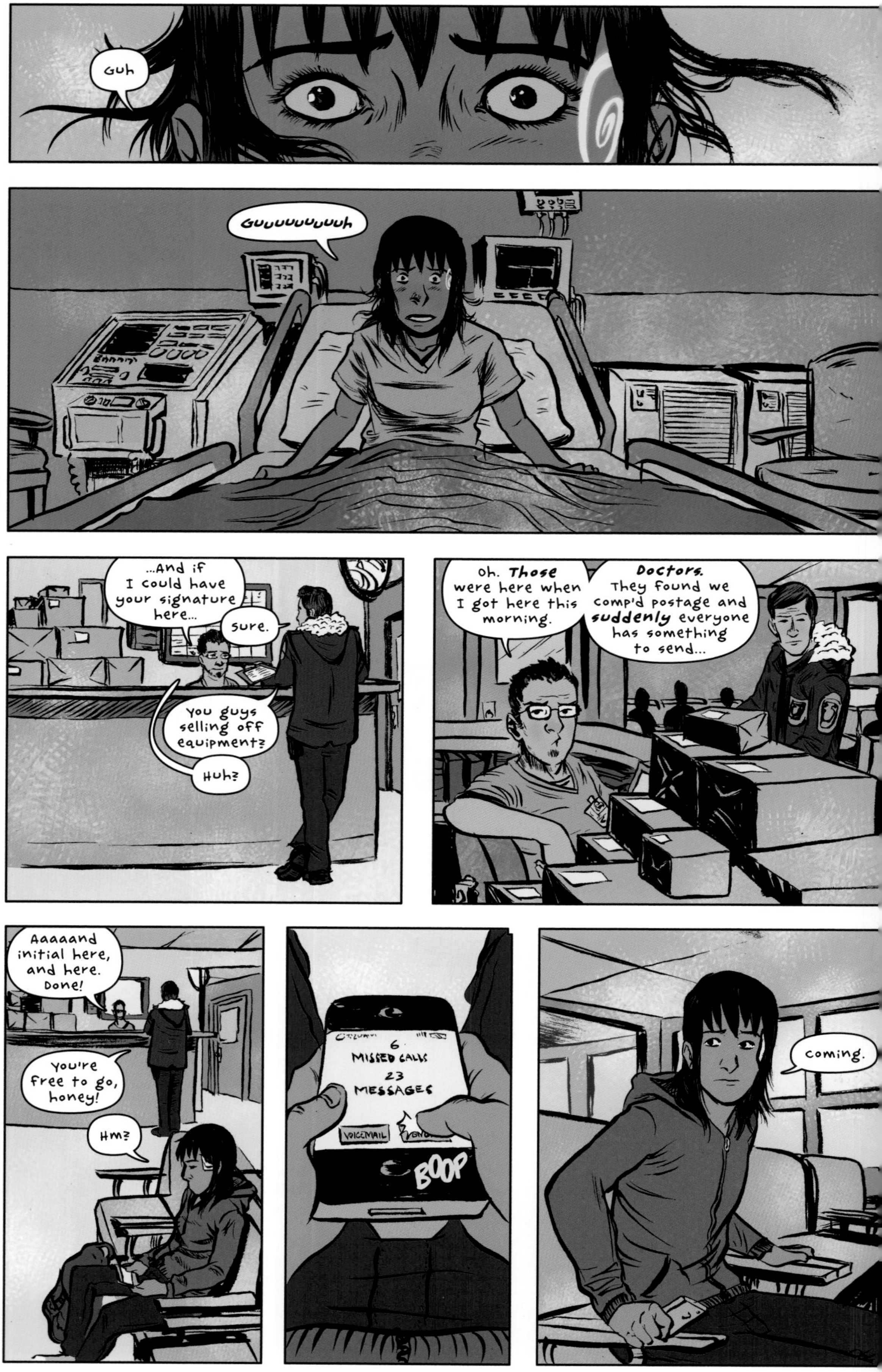
Guh
GUUUUUUUUUh
...And if I could have your signature here...
Sure.
You guys selling off equipment?
Huh?
Oh. Those were here when I got here this morning.
Doctors. They found we comp'd postage and suddenly everyone has something to send...
Aaaaand initial here, and here. Done!
You're free to go, honey!
Hm?
6 MISSED CALLS
23 MESSAGES
VOICEMAIL
BOOP
Coming.

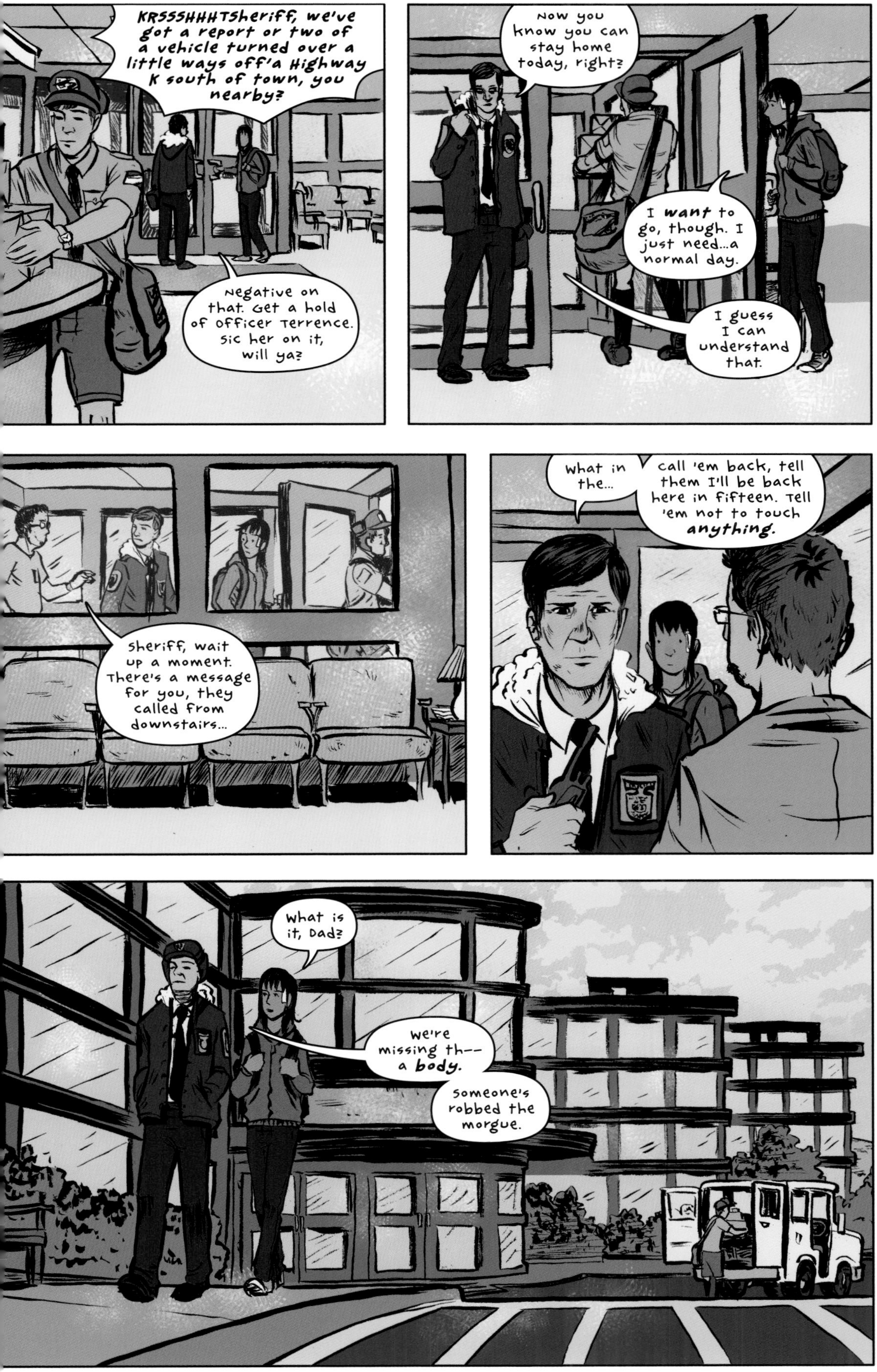
KRSSSHHHTSheriff, we've got a report or two of a vehicle turned over a little ways off'a Highway K south of town, you nearby?
Negative on that. Get a hold of Officer Terrence. Sic her on it, will ya?
Now you know you can stay home today, right?
I want to go, though. I just need...a normal day.
I guess I can understand that.
Sheriff, wait up a moment. There's a message for you, they called from downstairs...
What in the...
Call 'em back, tell them I'll be back here in fifteen. Tell 'em not to touch anything.
What is it, Dad?
We're missing th-- a body.
Someone's robbed the morgue.

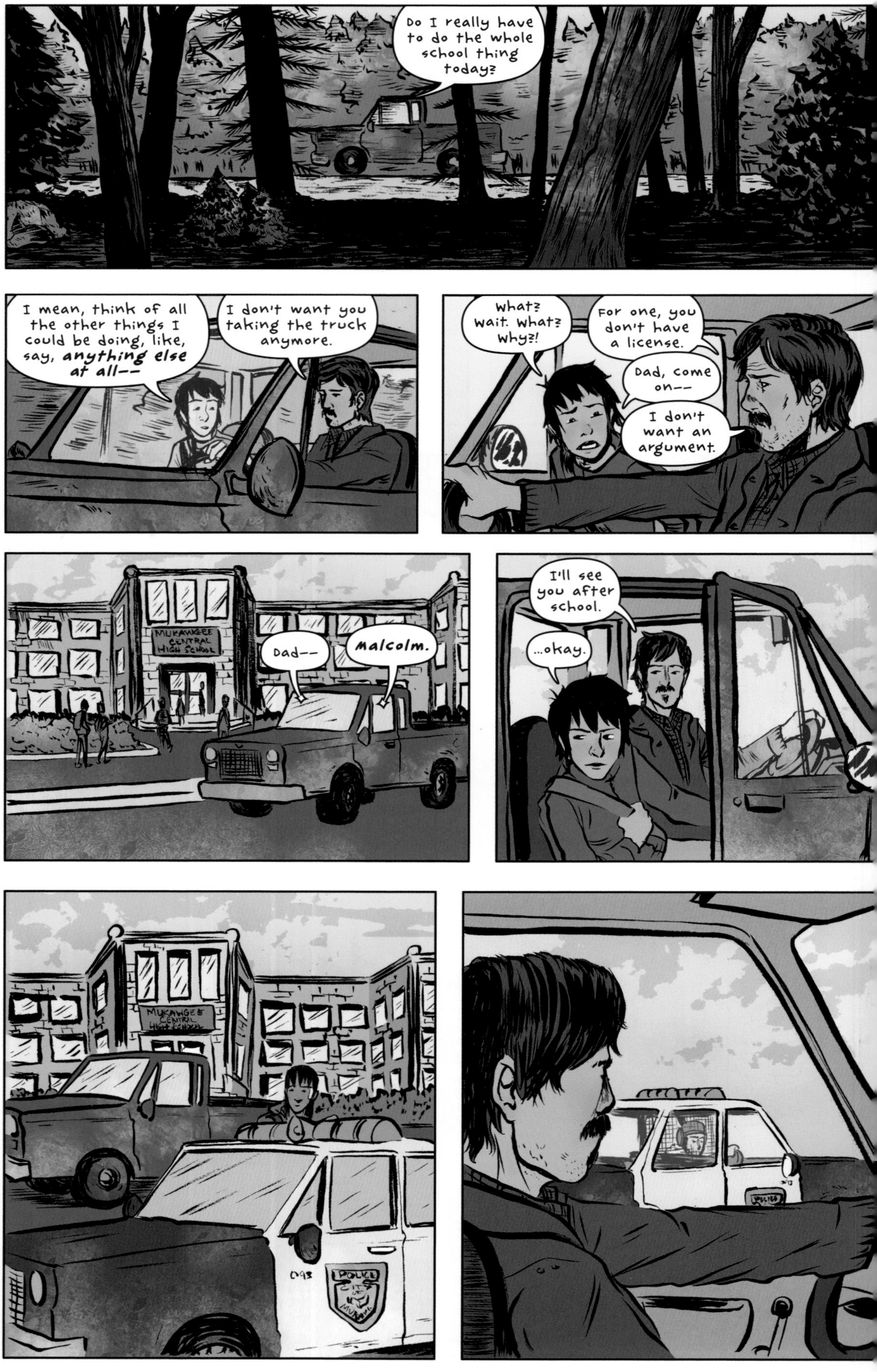
Do I really have to do the whole school thing today?
I mean, think of all the other things I could be doing, like, say, **anything else at all--**
I don't want you taking the truck anymore.
What? Wait. What? Why?!
For one, you don't have a license.
Dad, come on--
I don't want an argument.
MUKAWGEE CENTRAL HIGH SCHOOL
Dad--
Malcolm.
I'll see you after school.
...okay.
MUKAWGEE CENTRAL HIGH SCHOOL
POLICE

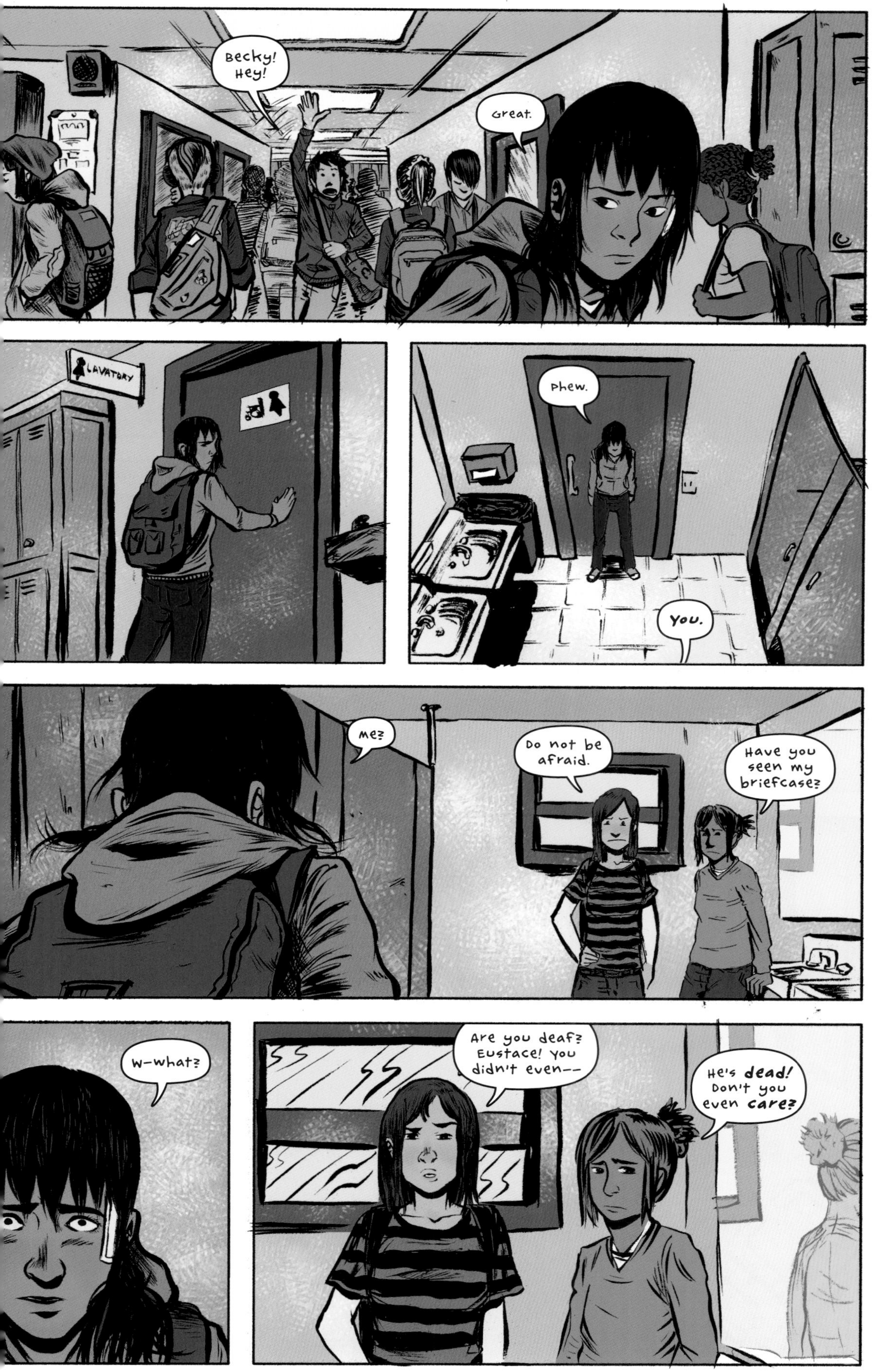
Becky! Hey!
Great.
LAVATORY
Phew.
You.
Me?
Do not be afraid.
Have you seen my briefcase?
W-what?
Are you deaf? Eustace! You didn't even--
He's **dead!** Don't you even **care?**

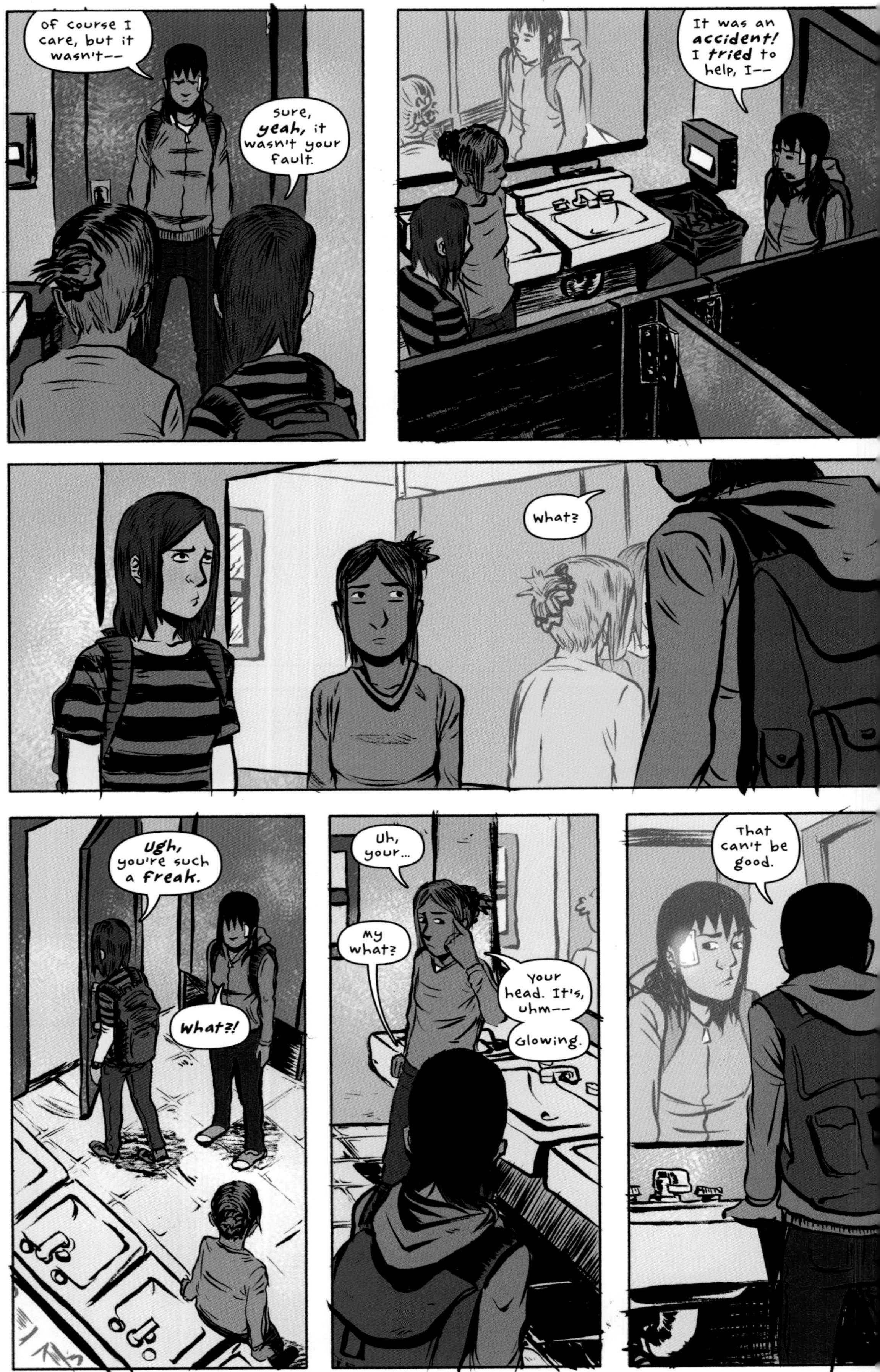
Of course I care, but it wasn't--
Sure, yeah, it wasn't your fault.
It was an accident! I tried to help, I--
What?
Ugh, you're such a freak.
What?!
Uh, your...
My what?
Your head. It's, uhm--
Glowing.
That can't be good.

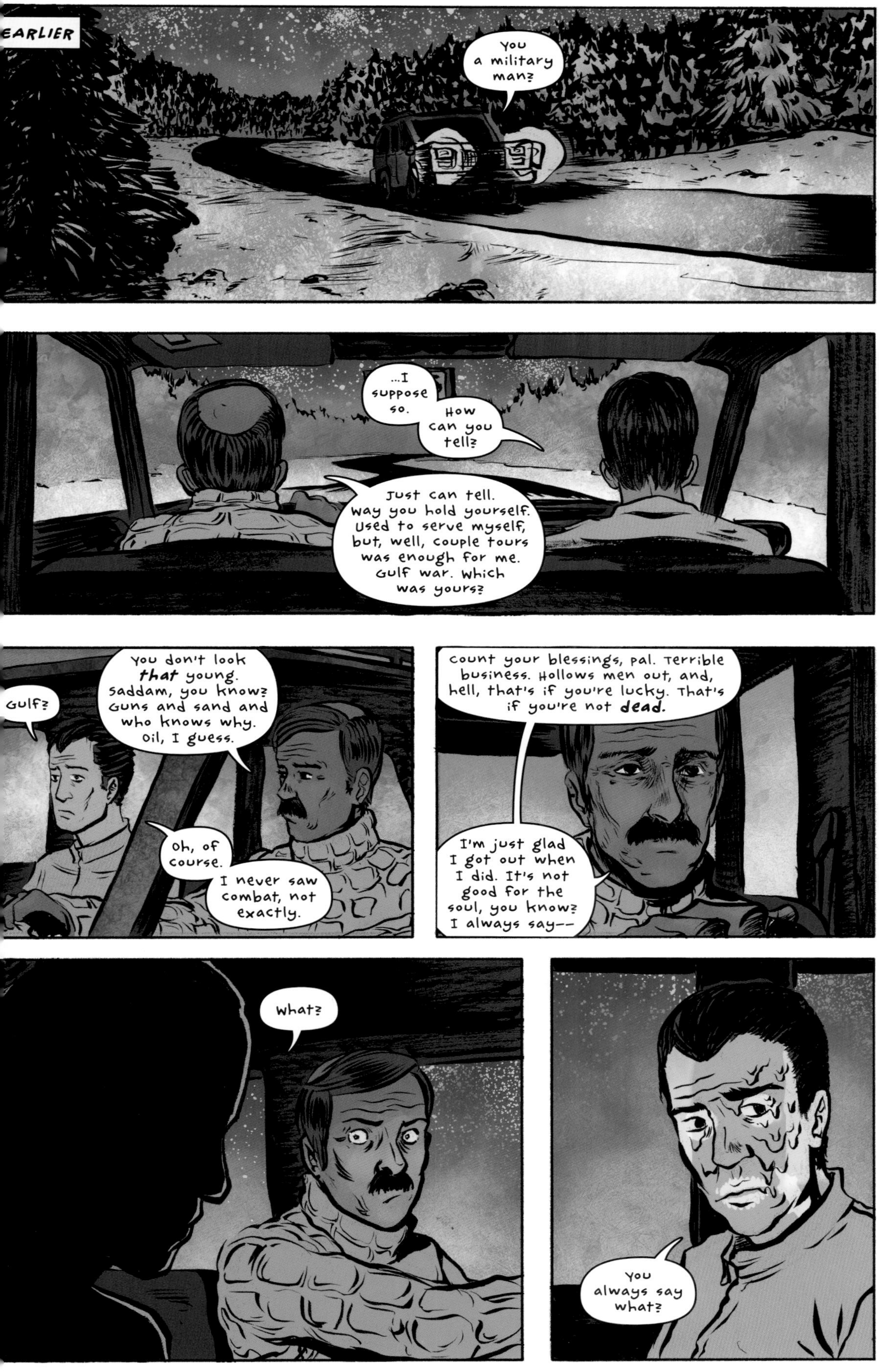
EARLIER
You a military man?
...I suppose so.
How can you tell?
Just can tell. Way you hold yourself. Used to serve myself, but, well, couple tours was enough for me. Gulf war. Which was yours?
Gulf?
You don't look *that* young. Saddam, you know? Guns and sand and who knows why. Oil, I guess.
Oh, of course.
I never saw combat, not exactly.
Count your blessings, pal. Terrible business. Hollows men out, and, hell, that's if you're lucky. That's if you're not **dead.**
I'm just glad I got out when I did. It's not good for the soul, you know? I always say--
What?
You always say what?

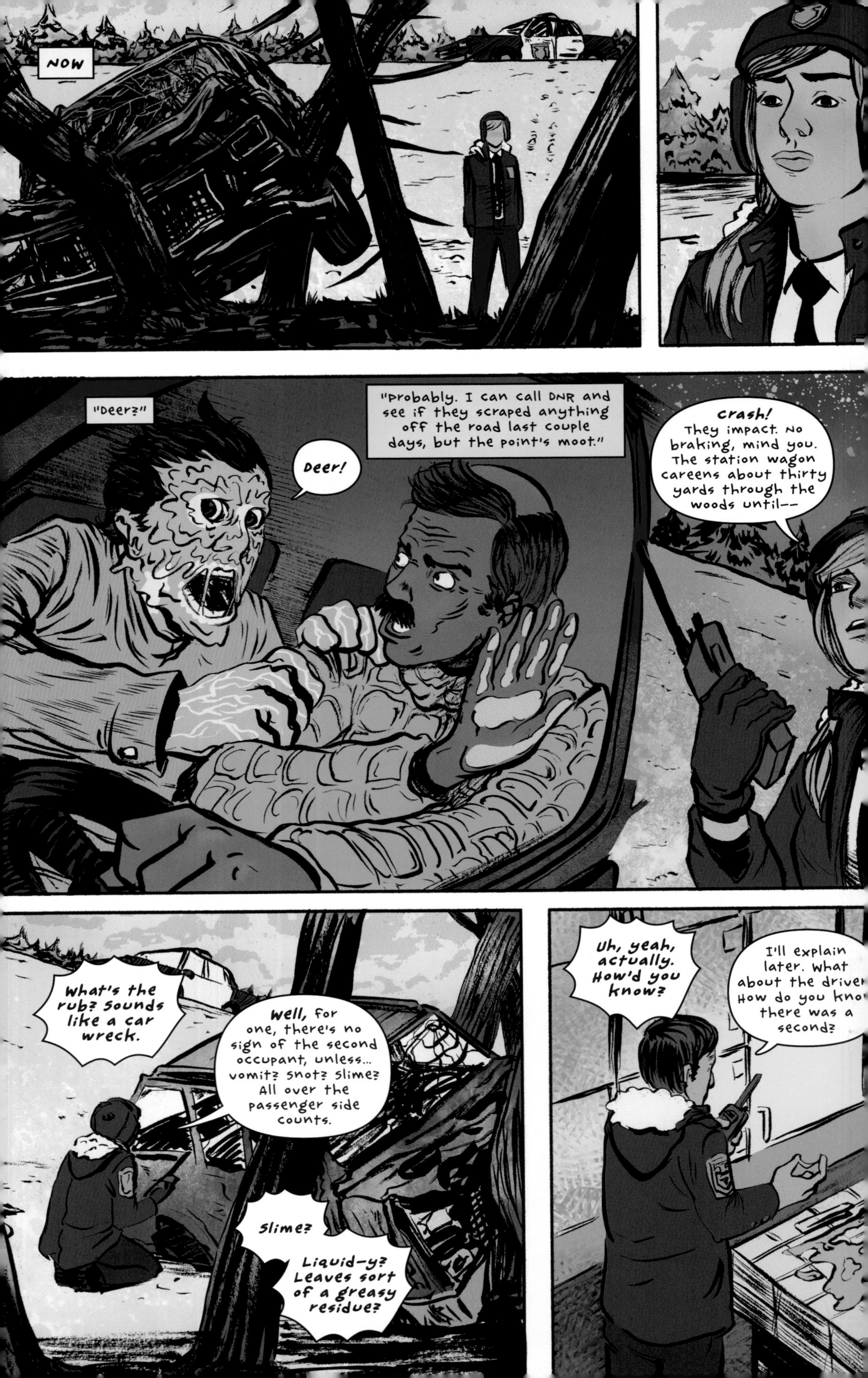
NOW
"Deer?"
Deer!
"Probably. I can call DNR and see if they scraped anything off the road last couple days, but the point's moot."
Crash! They impact. No braking, mind you. The station wagon careens about thirty yards through the woods until--
What's the rub? Sounds like a car wreck.
Well, for one, there's no sign of the second occupant, unless... vomit? Snot? Slime? All over the passenger side counts.
Slime?
Liquid-y? Leaves sort of a greasy residue?
Uh, yeah, actually. How'd you know?
I'll explain later. What about the driver? How do you know there was a second?

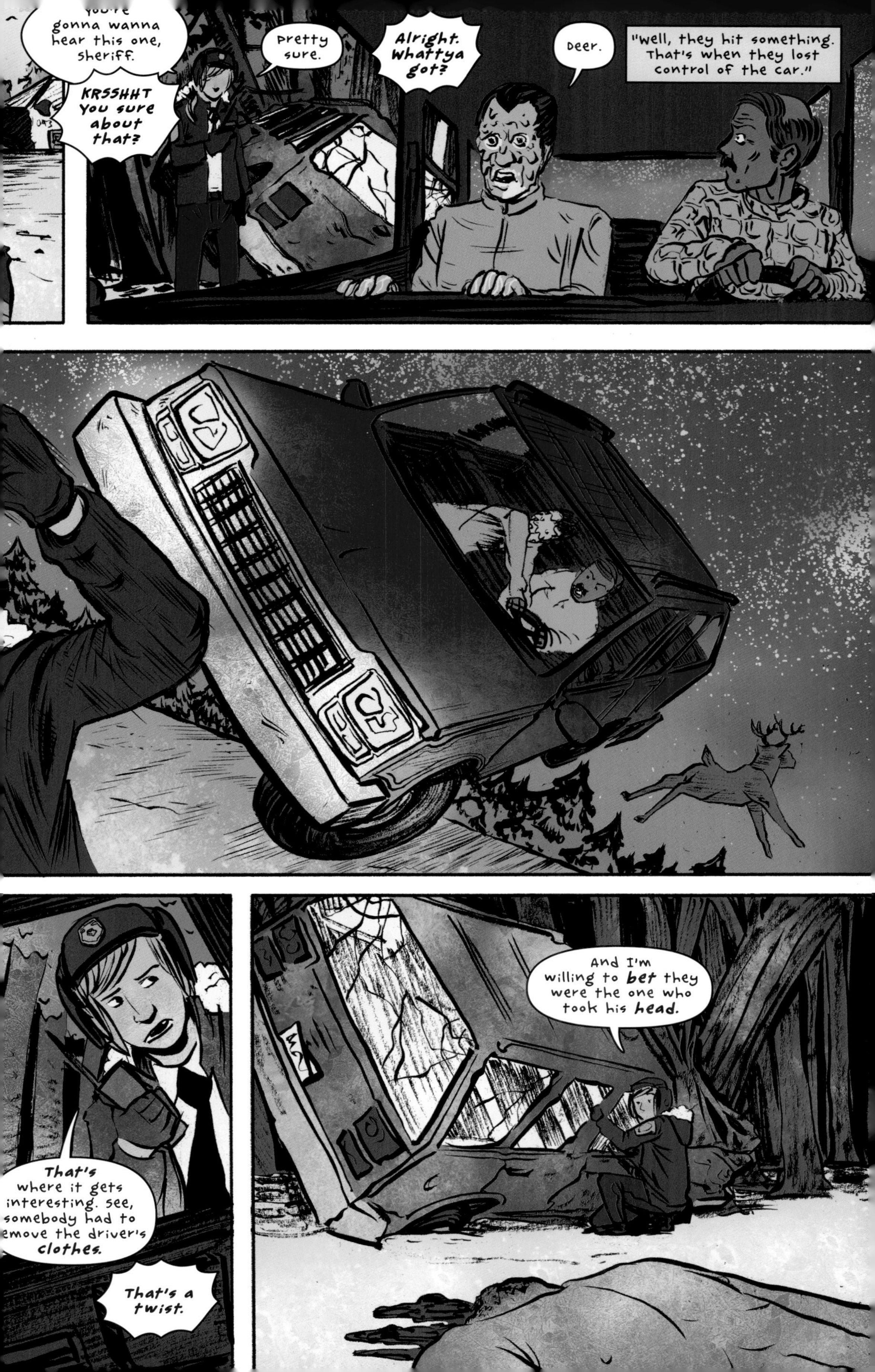
You're gonna wanna hear this one, sheriff.
KRSSHHT You sure about that?
Pretty sure.
Alright. Whattya got?
Deer.
"Well, they hit something. That's when they lost control of the car."
That's where it gets interesting. See, somebody had to remove the driver's clothes.
That's a twist.
And I'm willing to bet they were the one who took his head.

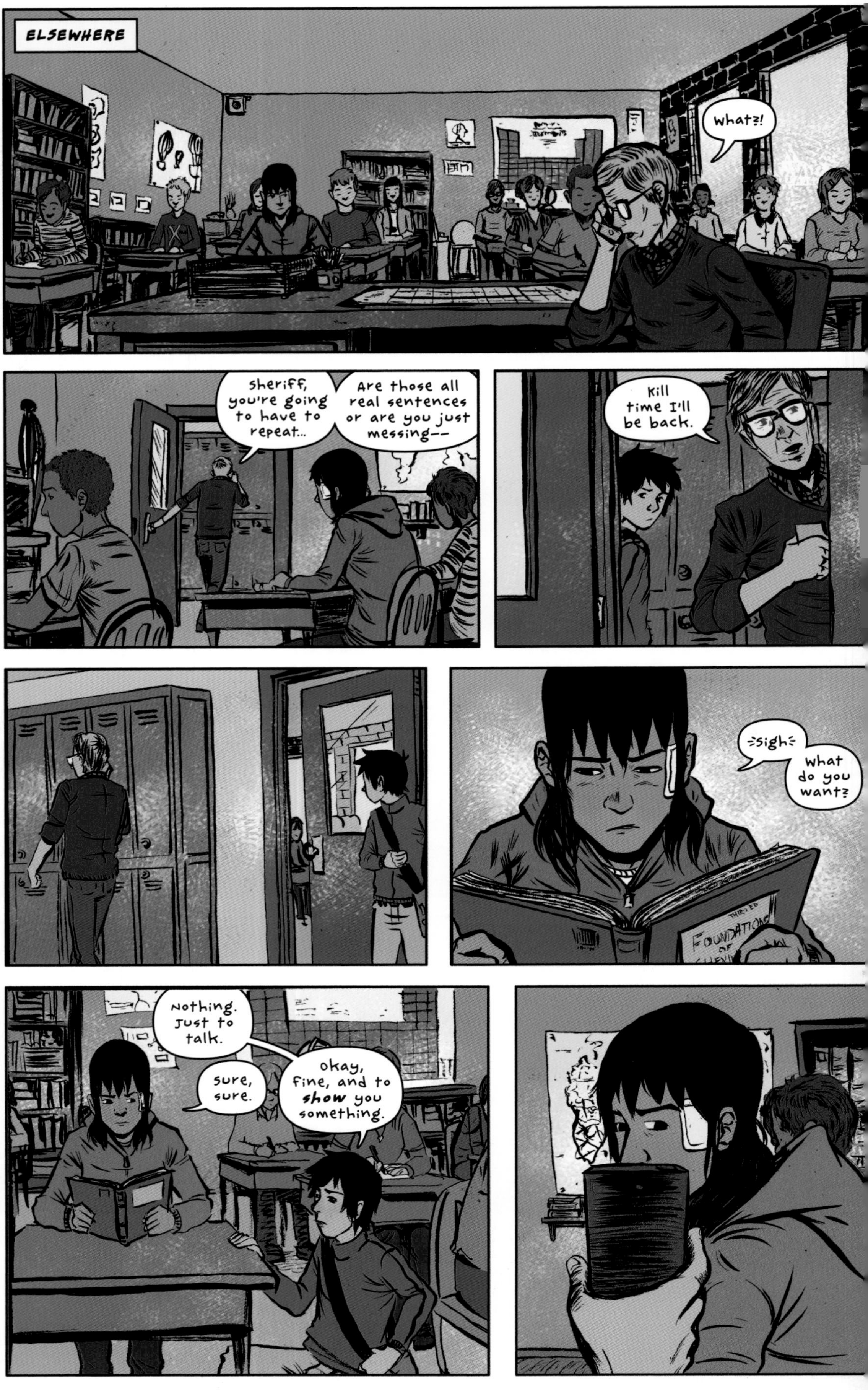
ELSEWHERE
What?!
Sheriff, you're going to have to repeat...
Are those all real sentences or are you just messing--
Kill time I'll be back.
:sigh:
What do you want?
Nothing. Just to talk.
Sure, sure.
Okay, fine, and to *show* you something.

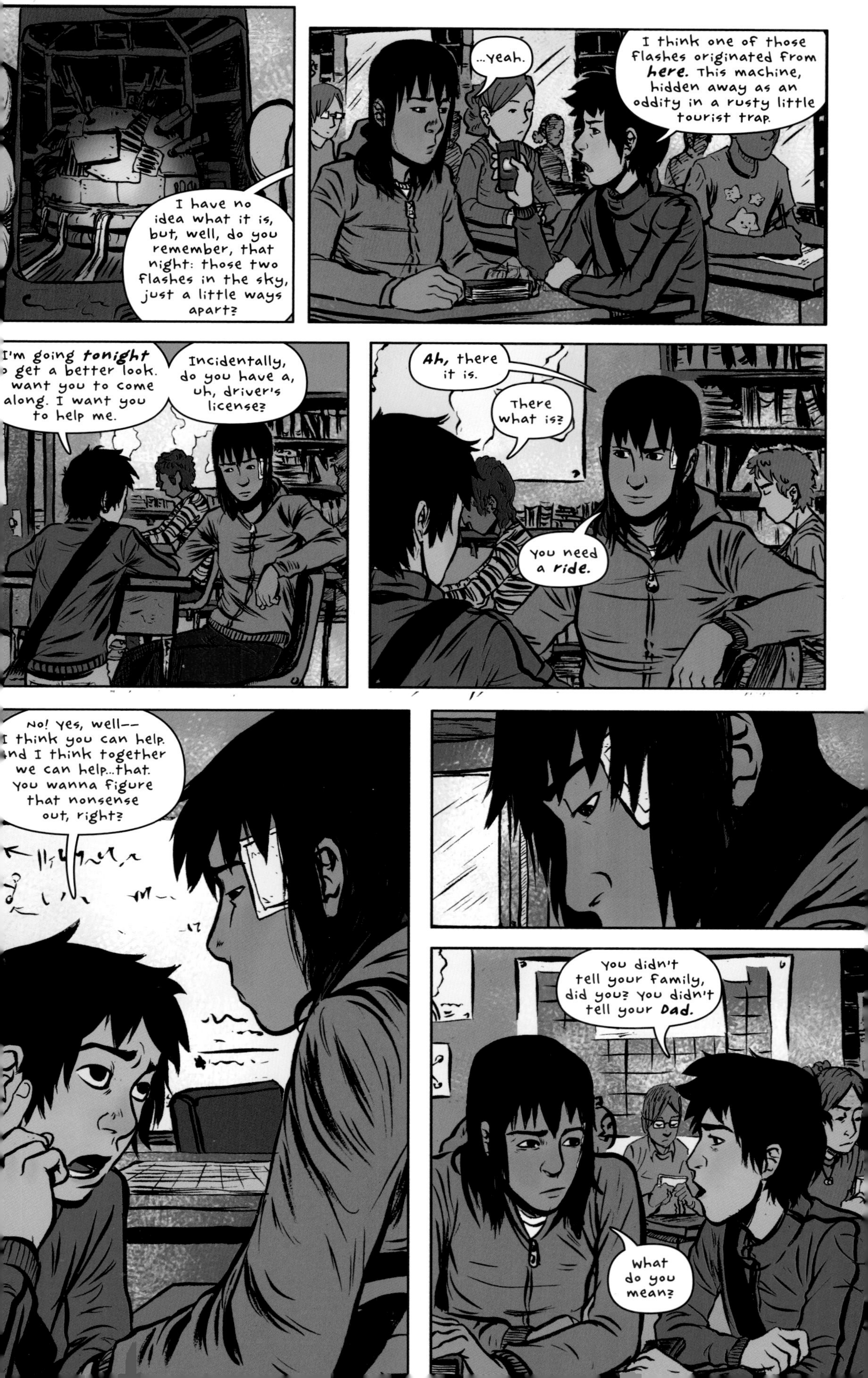
I have no idea what it is, but, well, do you remember, that night: those two flashes in the sky, just a little ways apart?
...yeah.
I think one of those flashes originated from **here**. This machine, hidden away as an oddity in a rusty little tourist trap.
I'm going **tonight** o get a better look. want you to come along. I want you to help me.
Incidentally, do you have a, uh, driver's license?
Ah, there it is.
There what is?
You need a **ride.**
No! Yes, well-- I think you can help. nd I think together we can help...that. You wanna figure that nonsense out, right?
You didn't tell your family, did you? You didn't tell your **Dad.**
What do you mean?

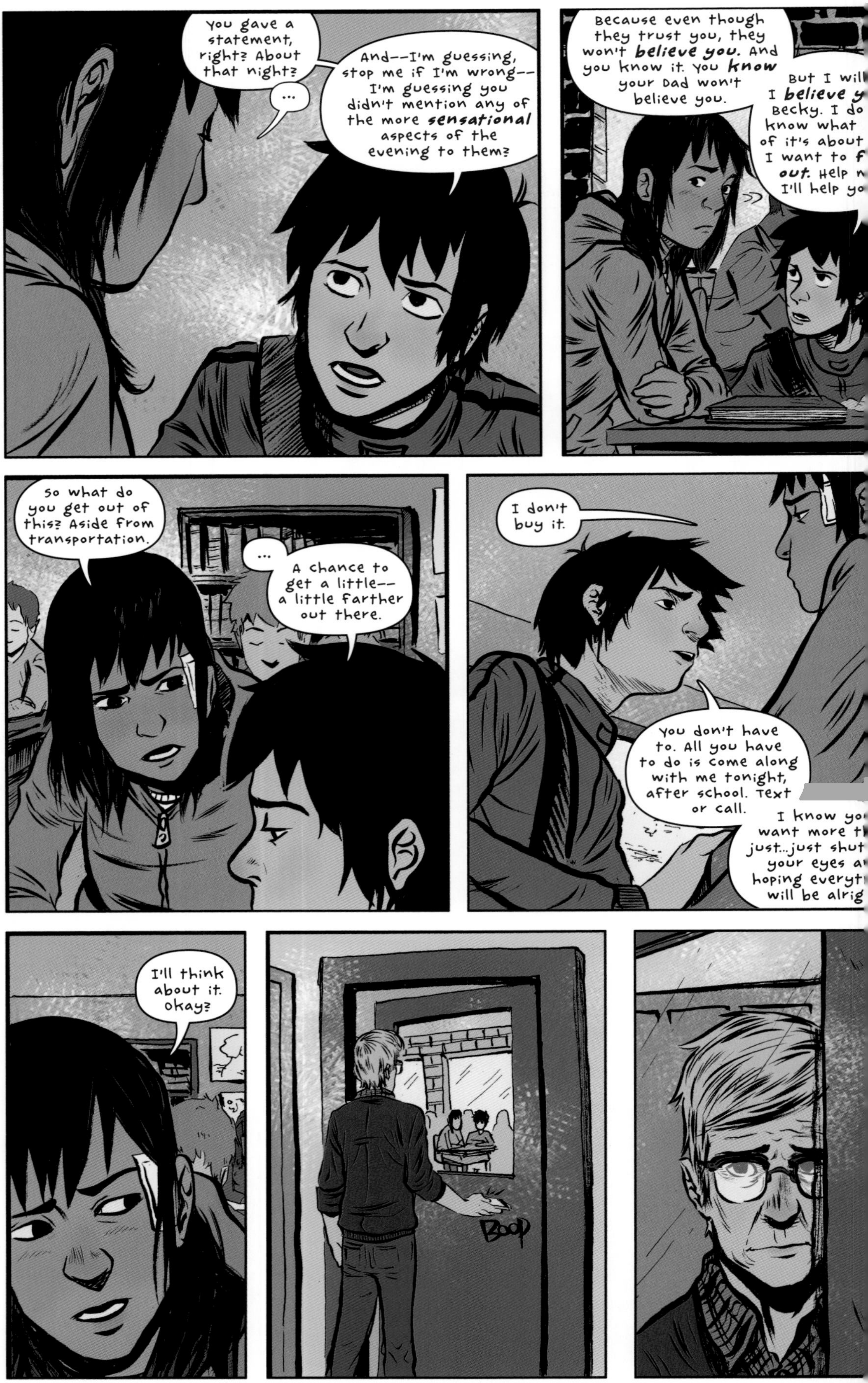
You gave a statement, right? About that night?
...
And--I'm guessing, stop me if I'm wrong--I'm guessing you didn't mention any of the more **sensational** aspects of the evening to them?
Because even though they trust you, they won't **believe you.** And you know it. You **know** your Dad won't believe you.
But I wil I **believe y** Becky. I do know what of it's about I want to f **out.** Help m I'll help yo
So what do you get out of this? Aside from transportation.
...
A chance to get a little--a little farther out there.
I don't buy it.
You don't have to. All you have to do is come along with me tonight, after school. Text or call.
I know yo want more t just...just shut your eyes a hoping everyt will be alrig
I'll think about it. Okay?
BOOP

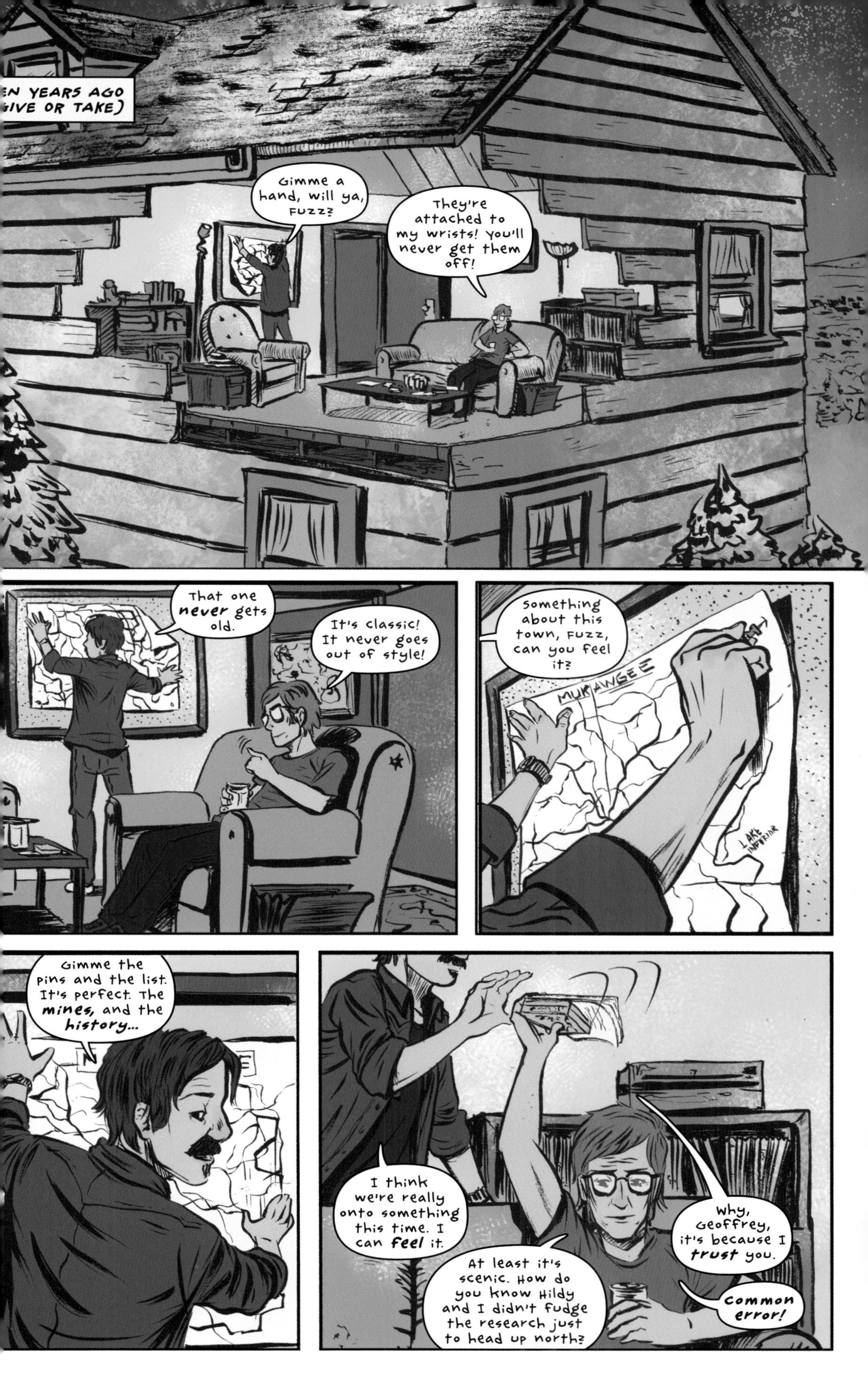

EN YEARS AGO
GIVE OR TAKE)
Gimme a hand, will ya, Fuzz?
They're attached to my wrists! You'll never get them off!
That one **never** gets old.
It's classic! It never goes out of style!
Something about this town, Fuzz, can you feel it?
MUKAWGEE
LAKE INFERIOR
Gimme the pins and the list. It's perfect. The ***mines,*** and the ***history...***
I think we're really onto something this time. I can ***feel*** it.
At least it's scenic. How do you know Hildy and I didn't fudge the research just to head up north?
Why, Geoffrey, it's because I ***trust*** you.
Common error!

It is done! The prince of fuss is put to bed.

oh shucks, lemme say goodnight—

He's already under. You put the covers up and bam! Gone. out like a light.

He must have gotten all of your successful sleep genes.

He must have gotten all of *your*—

Okay! Have you no chill? Some of us are trying to keep our lunches down.

Want one?

I'm good.

I'll take one.

Well, alri Russell, s us a song iron.

Yes! Iron! So the research of the last few months, right? We tracked the most legitimate sightings, contemporary and relatively ancient, for the region.

most every sighting, al *all* of them, are cluste around serious minin activity. mine establish sightings, from *mult* diarists of the perio

when the mine went from open- to underground early 1900s? Anot big spike in activ see where I'm goi with this?

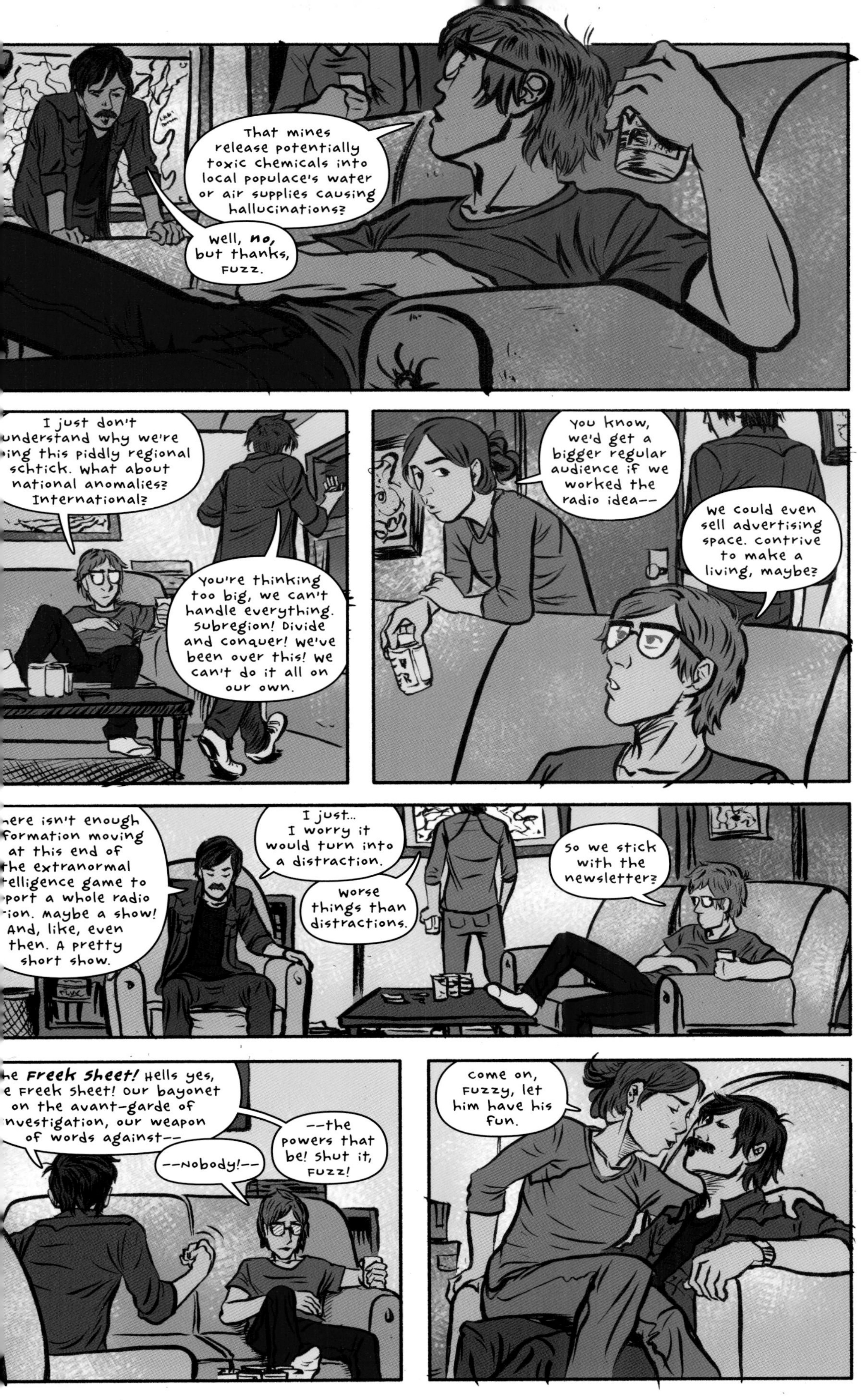
That mines release potentially toxic chemicals into local populace's water or air supplies causing hallucinations?
Well, no, but thanks, Fuzz.
I just don't understand why we're ing this piddly regional schtick. What about national anomalies? International?
You're thinking too big, we can't handle everything. Subregion! Divide and conquer! We've been over this! We can't do it all on our own.
You know, we'd get a bigger regular audience if we worked the radio idea--
We could even sell advertising space. Contrive to make a living, maybe?
here isn't enough formation moving at this end of the extranormal telligence game to port a whole radio ion. Maybe a show! And, like, even then. A pretty short show.
I just... I worry it would turn into a distraction.
Worse things than distractions.
So we stick with the newsletter?
he Freek Sheet! Hells yes, e Freek Sheet! Our bayonet on the avant-garde of nvestigation, our weapon of words against--
--Nobody!--
--the powers that be! Shut it, Fuzz!
Come on, Fuzzy, let him have his fun.

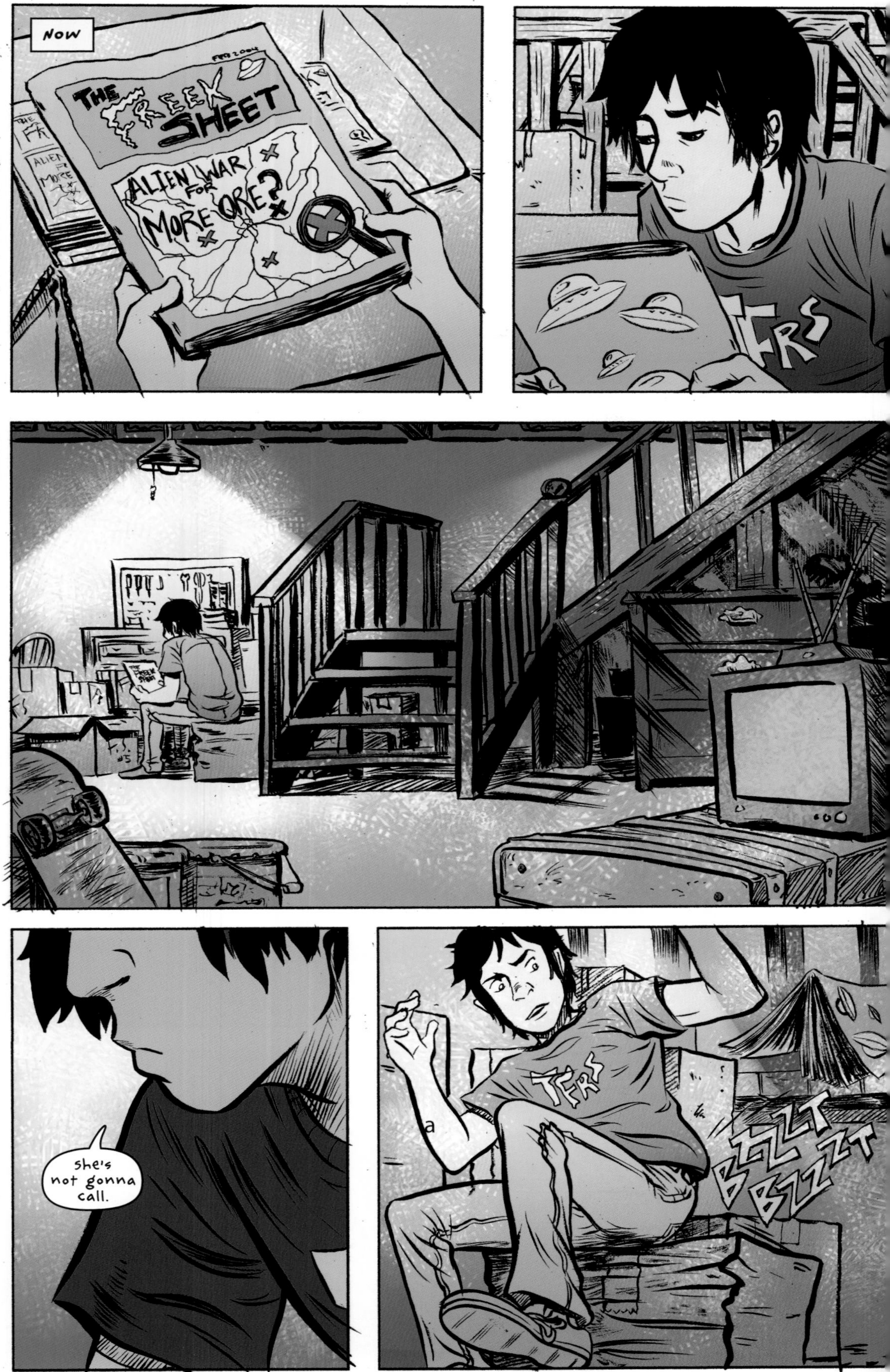
NOW
THE FREEK SHEET
ALIEN WAR FOR MORE ORE?
she's not gonna call.
BZZZT BZZZZT

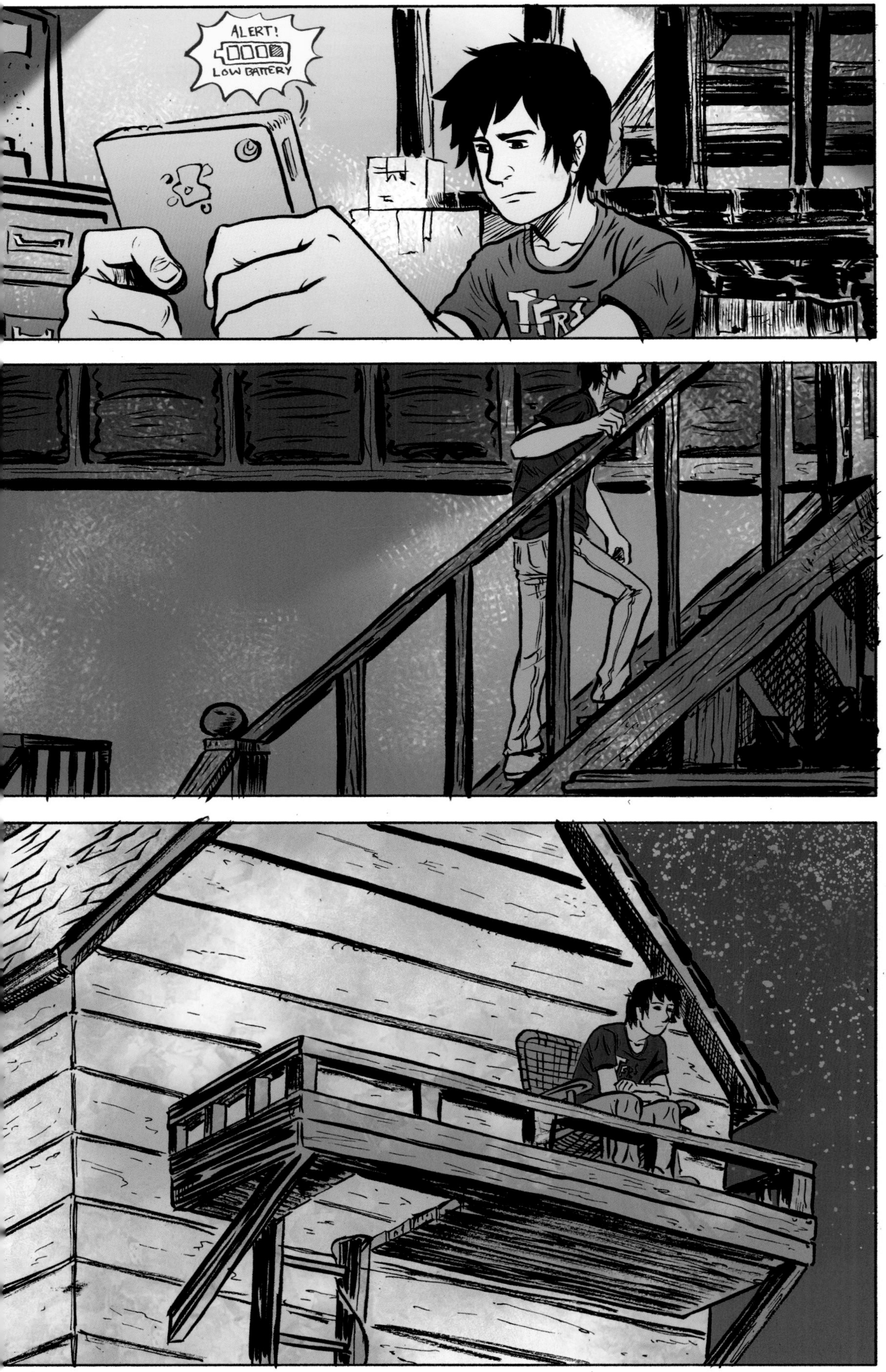
ALERT!
LOW BATTERY
TFRS

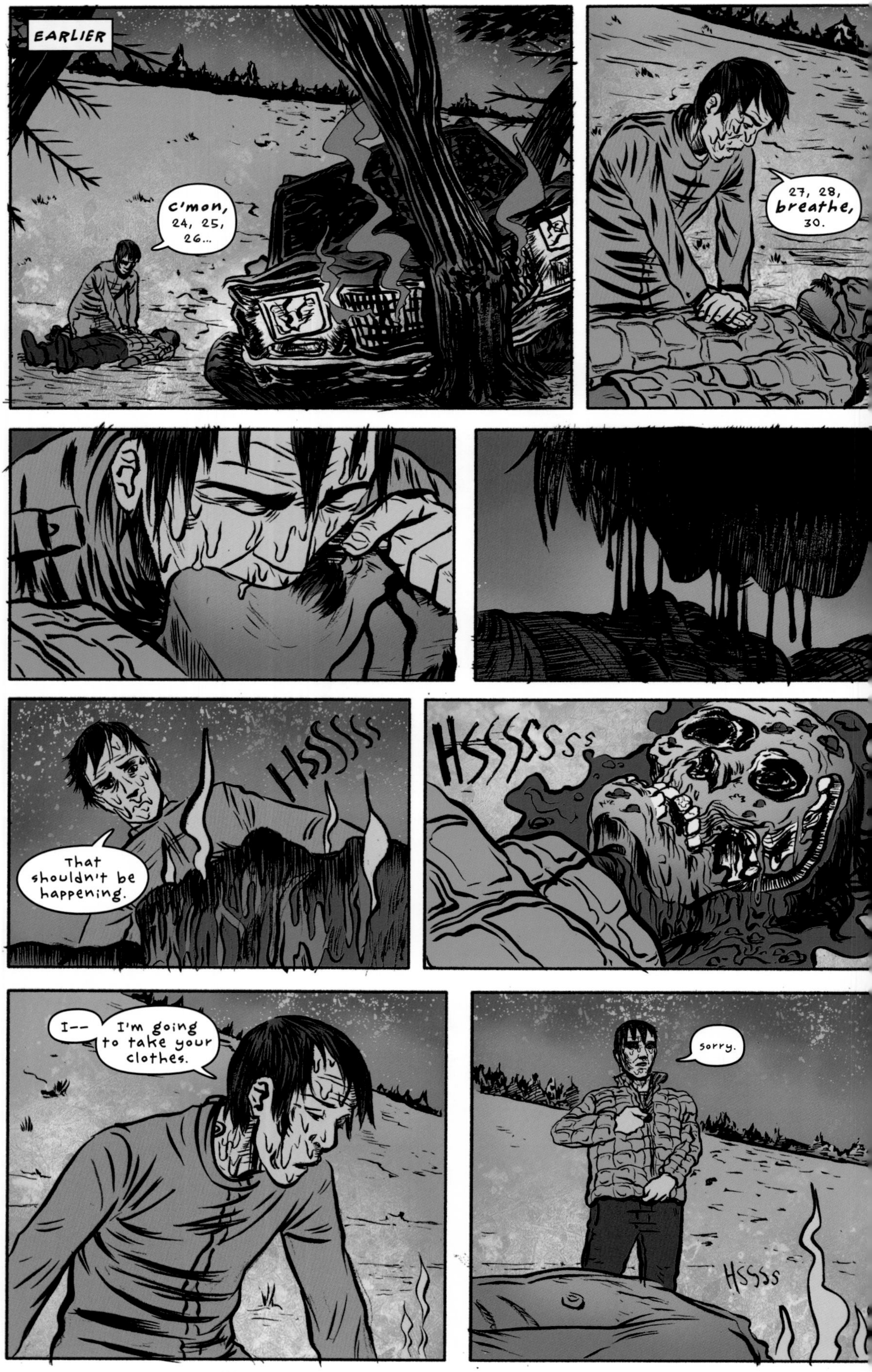
EARLIER
c'mon, 24, 25, 26...
27, 28, breathe, 30.
HSSSSS
That shouldn't be happening.
HSSSSSSS
I--
I'm going to take your clothes.
Sorry.
HSSSS

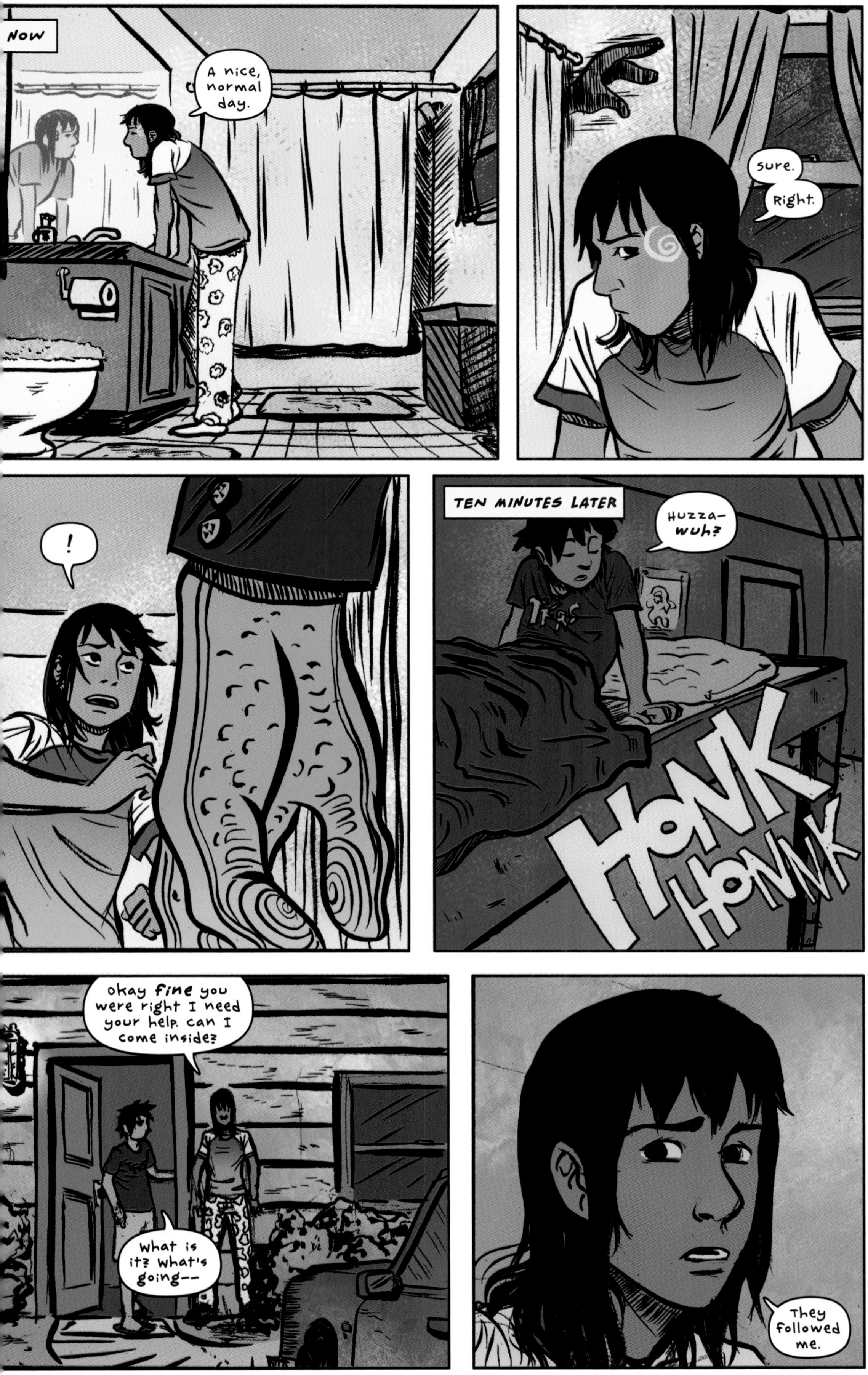
NOW
A nice, normal day.
Sure.
Right.
!
TEN MINUTES LATER
Huzza-wuh?
HONK HONK
okay fine you were right I need your help. can I come inside?
what is it? what's going--
They followed me.

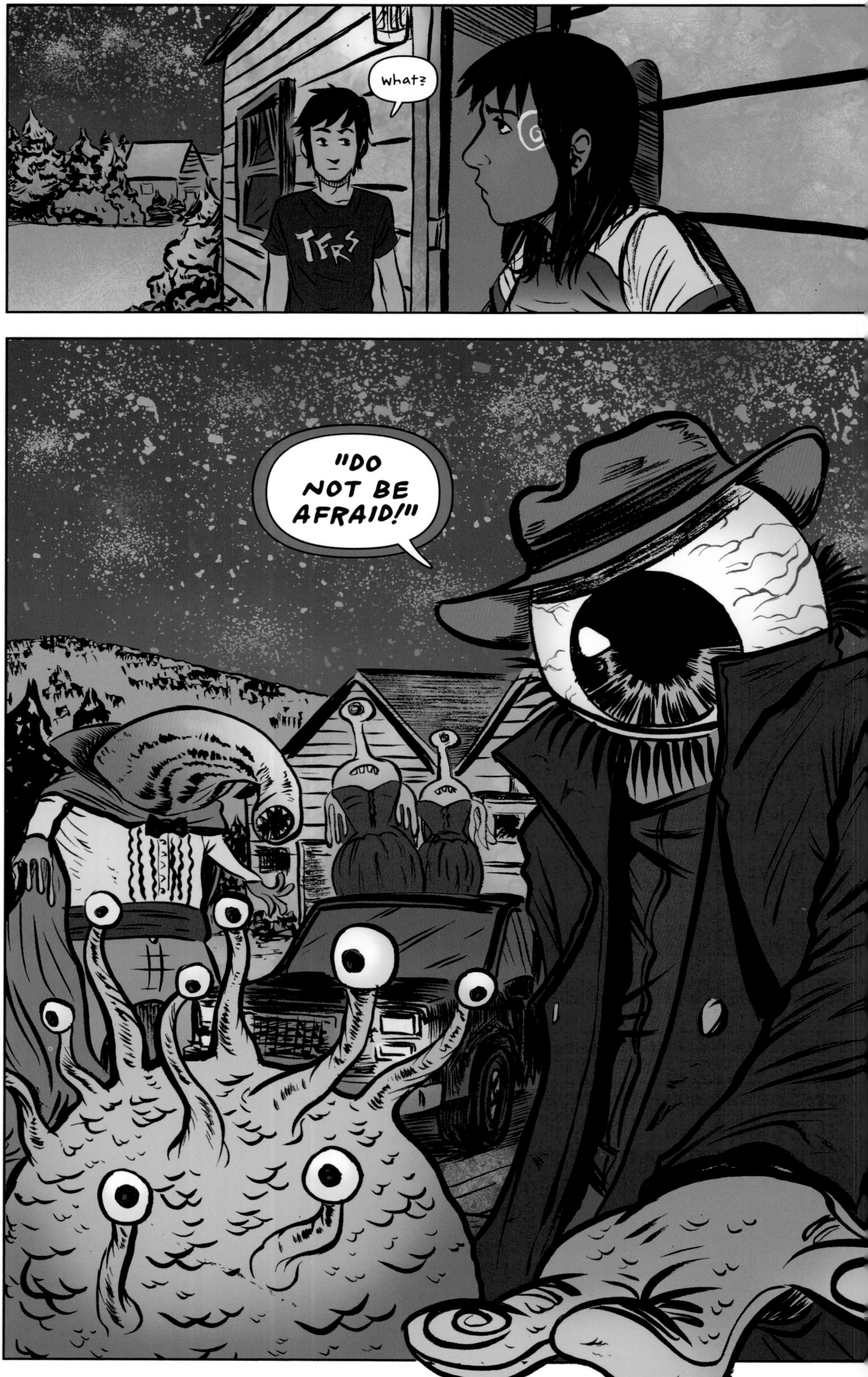
what?
"DO NOT BE AFRAID!"

f·o·u·r

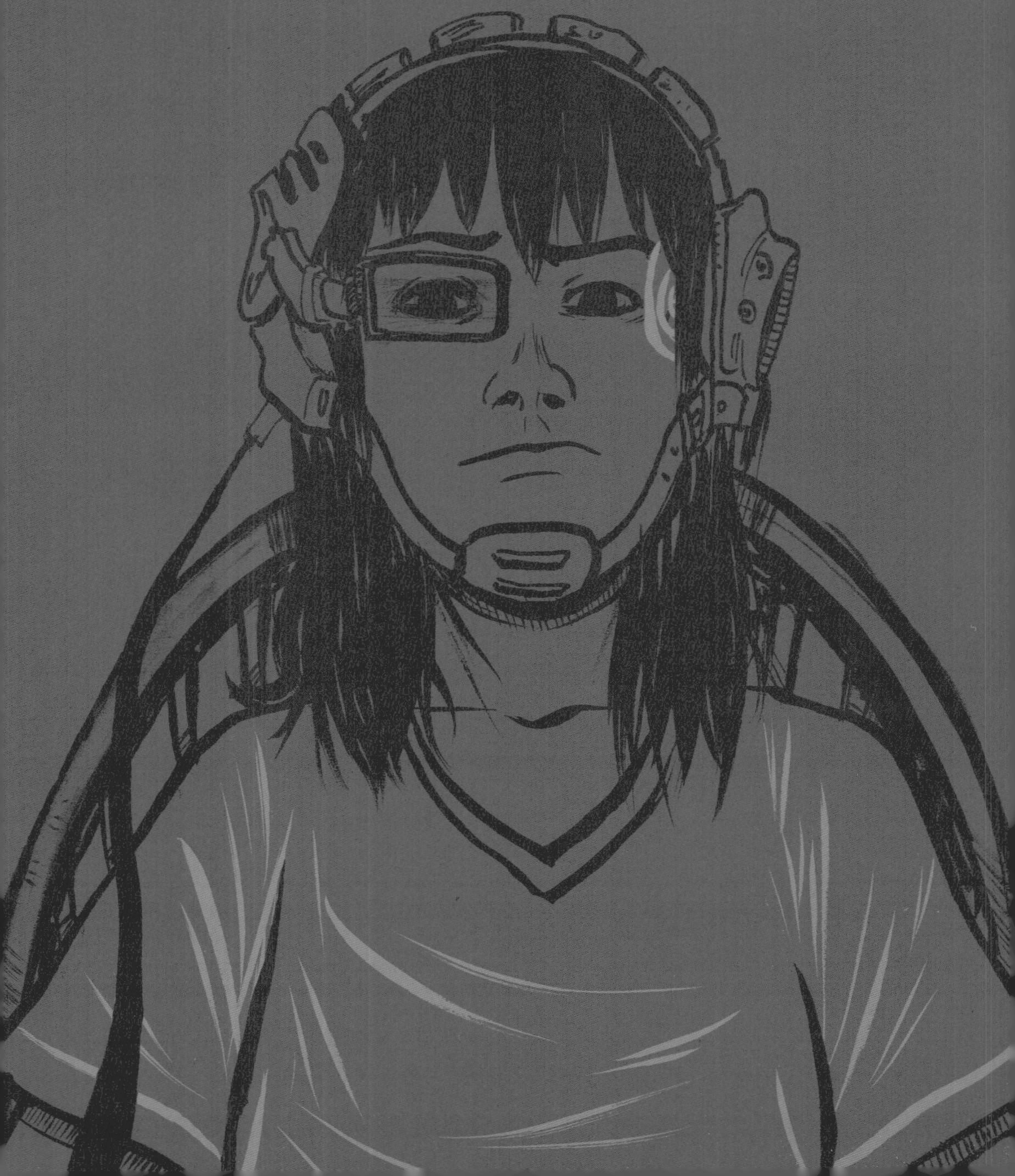

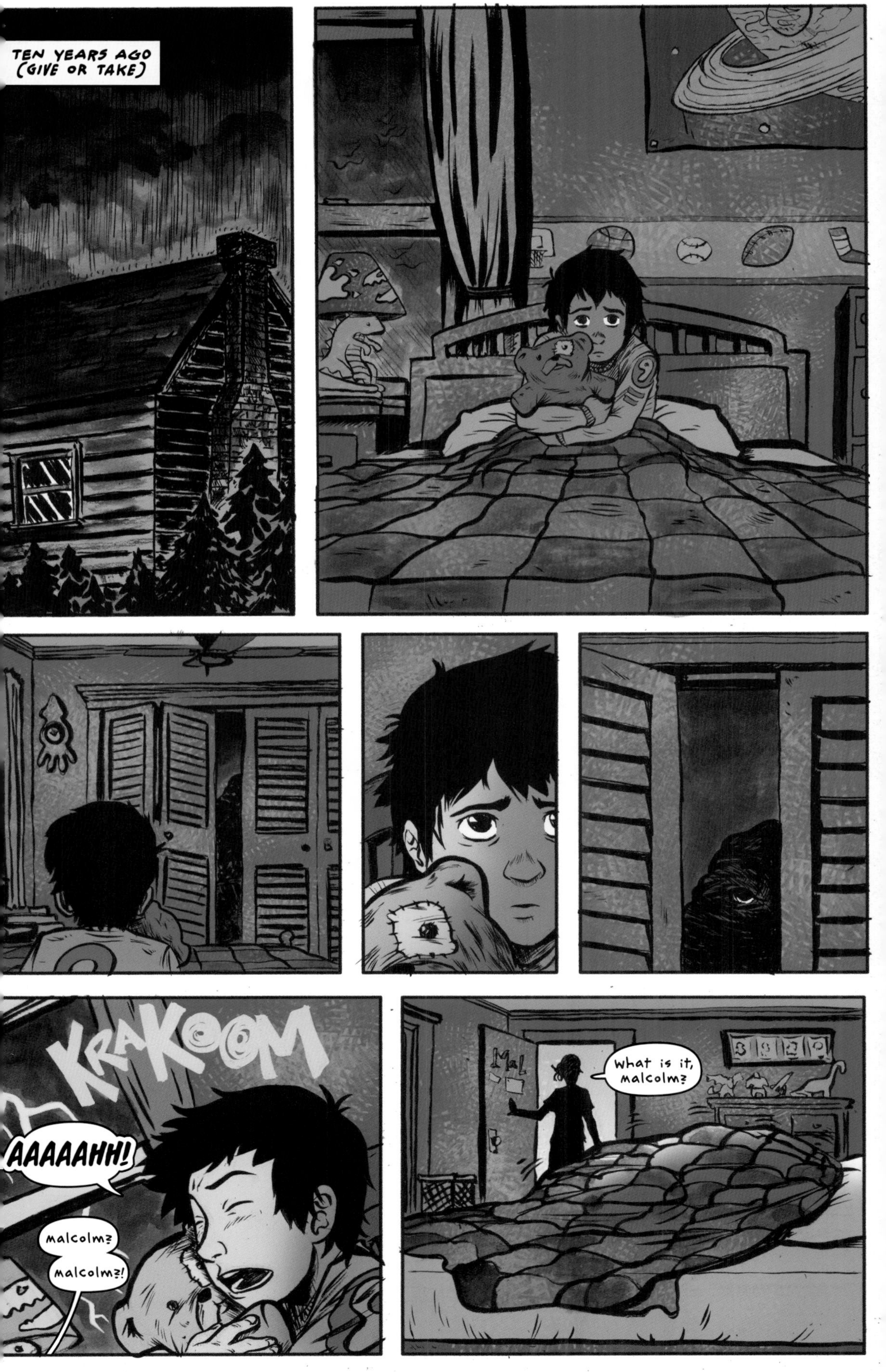
TEN YEARS AGO (GIVE OR TAKE)
KRAKOOM
AAAAAHH!
malcolm?
malcolm?!
MaL
what is it, malcolm?

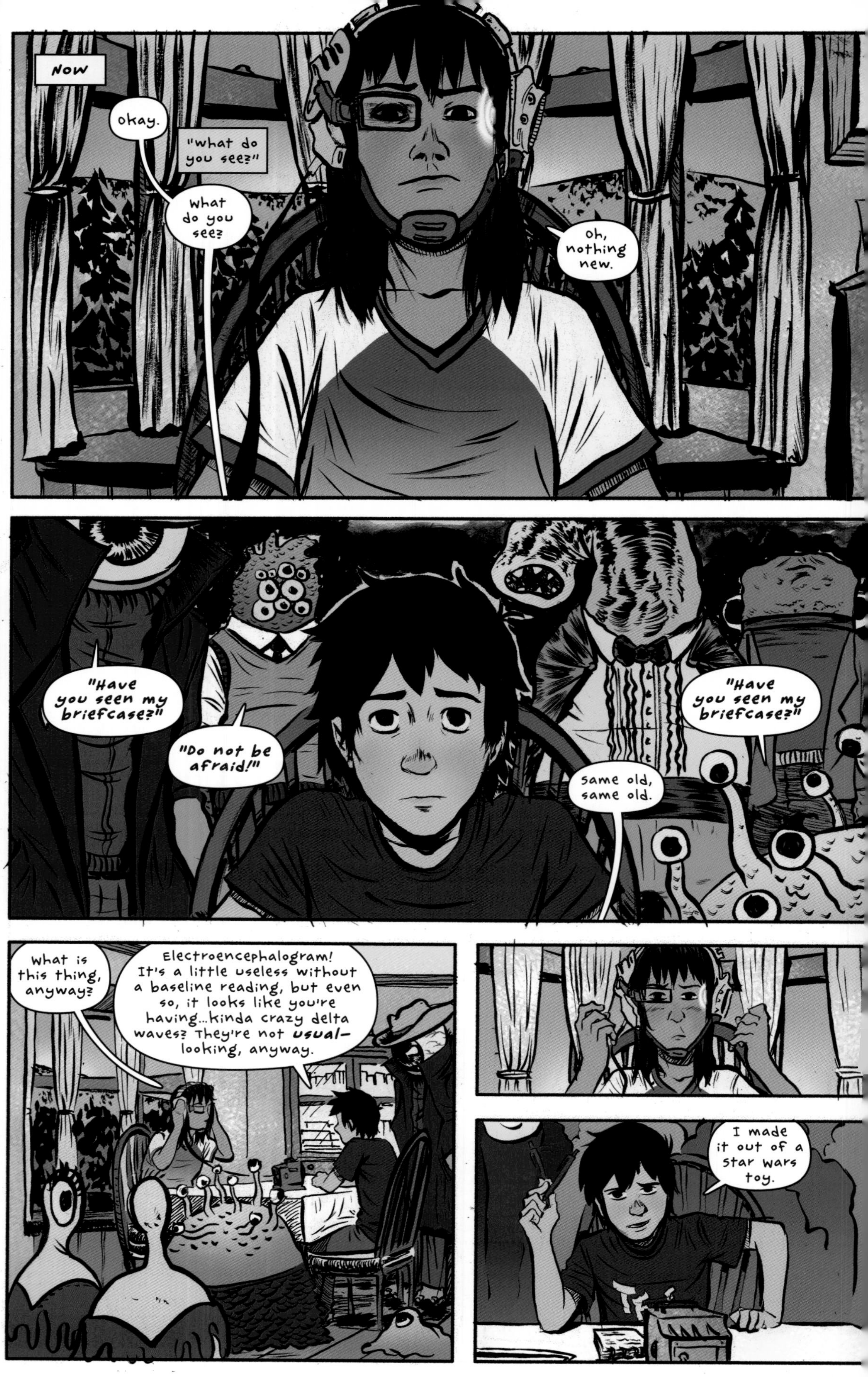
NOW
okay.
"what do you see?"
what do you see?
oh, nothing new.
"Have you seen my briefcase?"
"Do not be afraid!"
"Have you seen my briefcase?"
same old, same old.
what is this thing, anyway?
Electroencephalogram! It's a little useless without a baseline reading, but even so, it looks like you're having...kinda crazy delta waves? They're not usual-looking, anyway.
I made it out of a star wars toy.

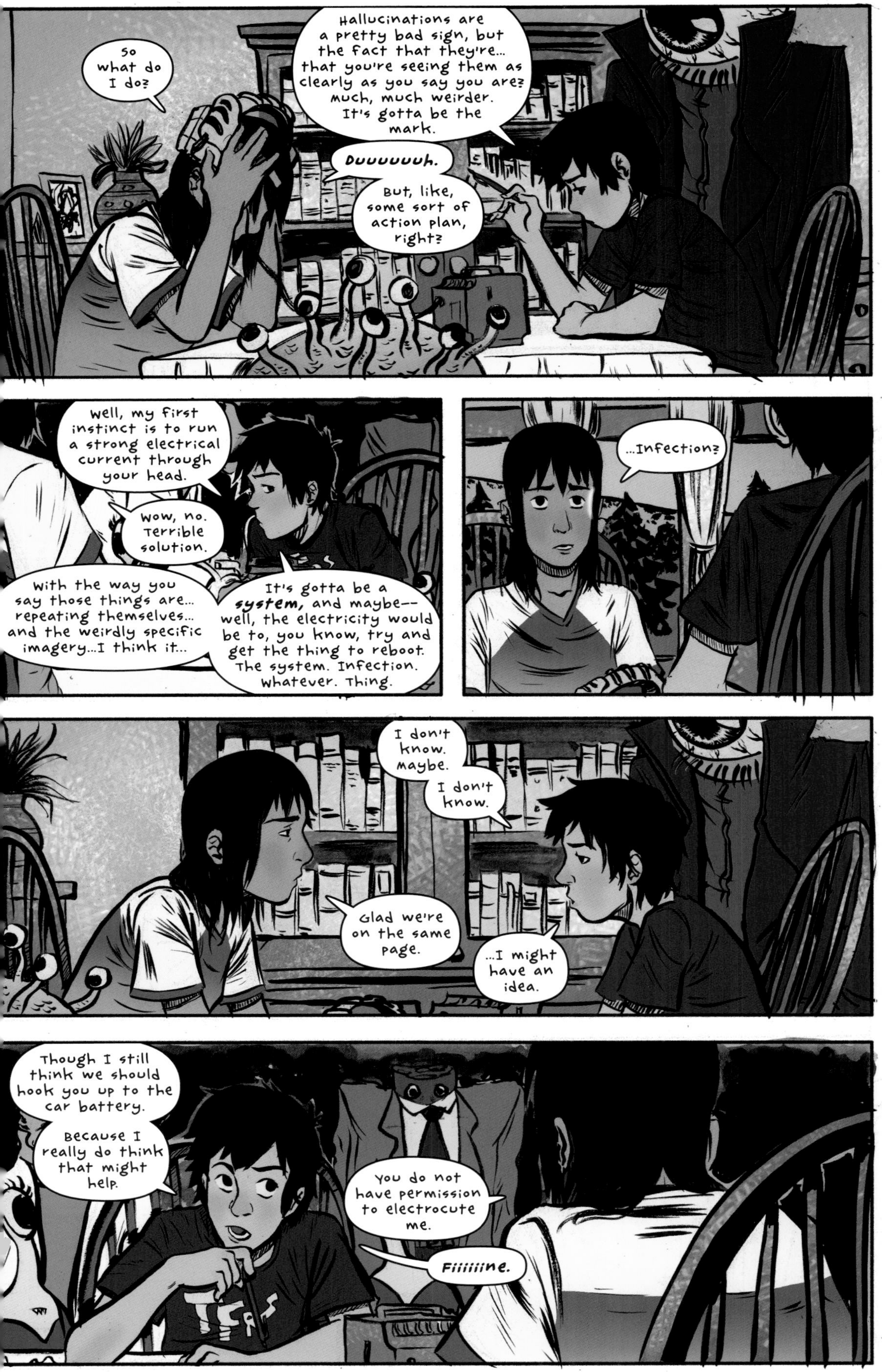
So what do I do?
Hallucinations are a pretty bad sign, but the fact that they're... that you're seeing them as clearly as you say you are? much, much weirder. It's gotta be the mark.
Duuuuuuh.
But, like, some sort of action plan, right?
Well, my first instinct is to run a strong electrical current through your head.
Wow, no. Terrible solution.
With the way you say those things are... repeating themselves... and the weirdly specific imagery...I think it...
It's gotta be a system, and maybe-- well, the electricity would be to, you know, try and get the thing to reboot. The system. Infection. Whatever. Thing.
...Infection?
I don't know. Maybe.
I don't know.
Glad we're on the same page.
...I might have an idea.
Though I still think we should hook you up to the car battery.
Because I really do think that might help.
You do not have permission to electrocute me.
Fiiiiiine.

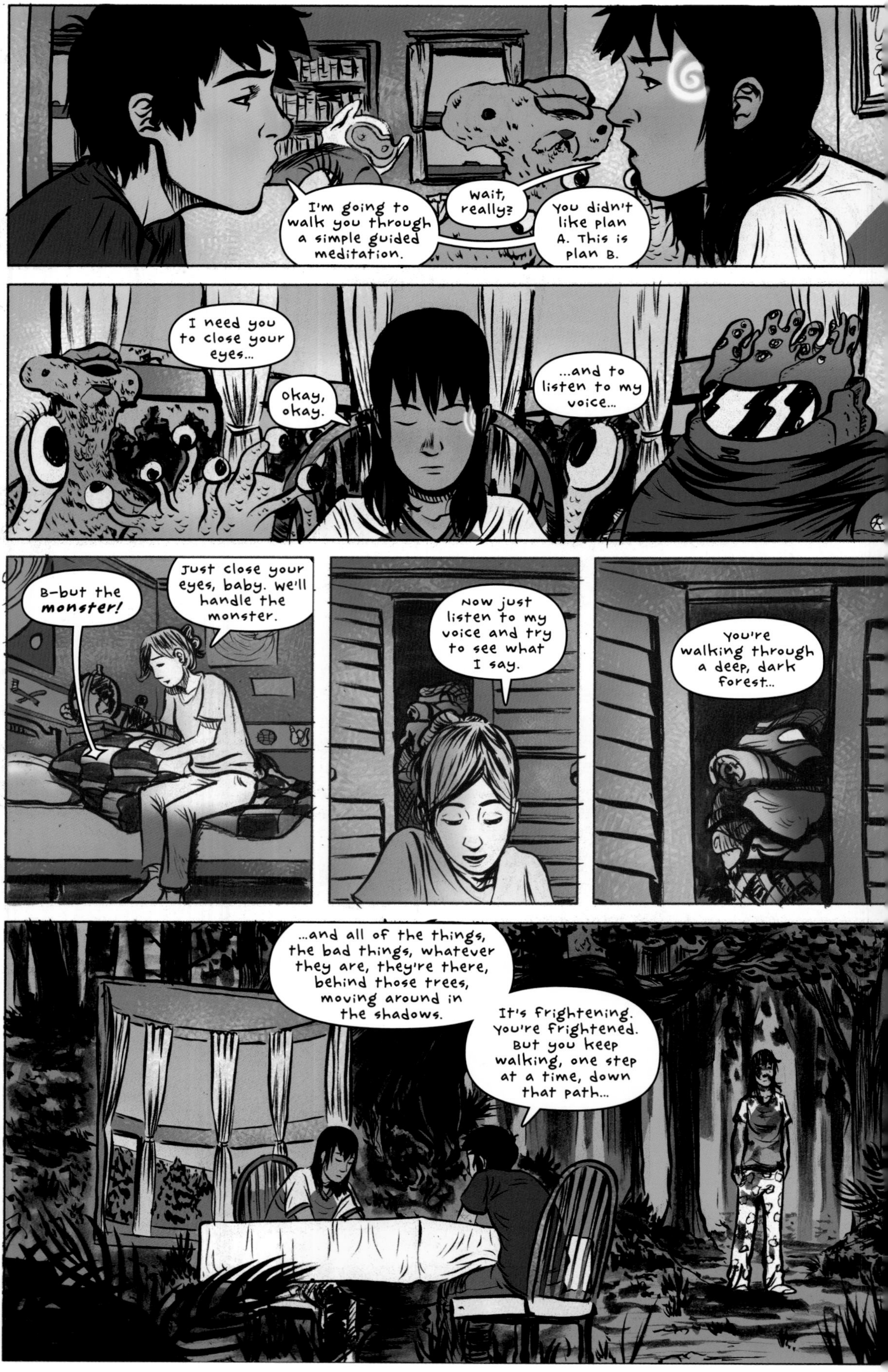
I'm going to walk you through a simple guided meditation.
Wait, really?
You didn't like plan A. This is plan B.
I need you to close your eyes...
Okay, okay.
...and to listen to my voice...
B-but the **monster!**
Just close your eyes, baby. We'll handle the monster.
Now just listen to my voice and try to see what I say.
You're walking through a deep, dark forest...
...and all of the things, the bad things, whatever they are, they're there, behind those trees, moving around in the shadows.
It's frightening. You're frightened. But you keep walking, one step at a time, down that path...

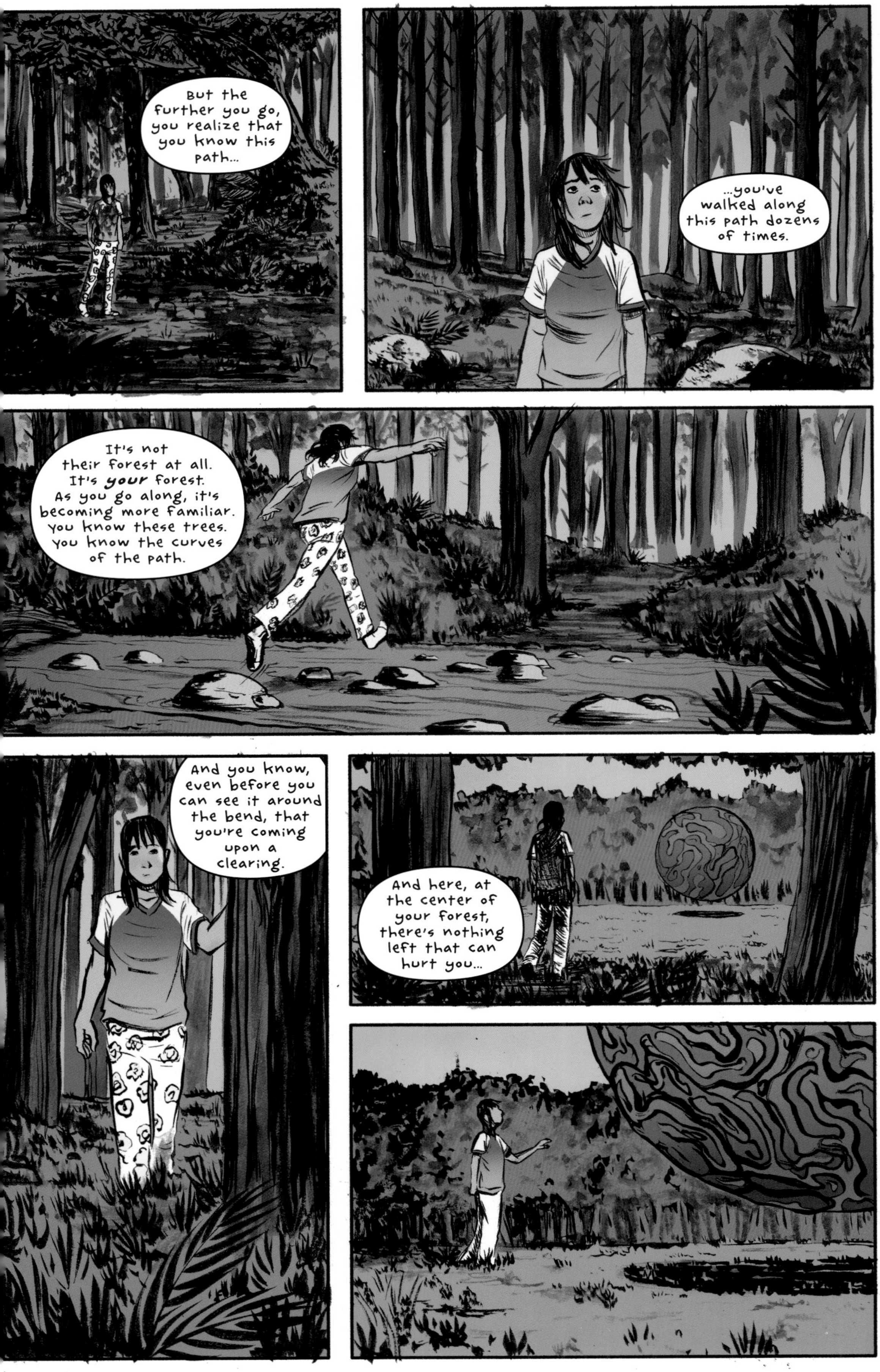
But the further you go, you realize that you know this path...
...you've walked along this path dozens of times.
It's not their forest at all. It's *your* forest. As you go along, it's becoming more familiar. You know these trees. You know the curves of the path.
And you know, even before you can see it around the bend, that you're coming upon a clearing.
And here, at the center of your forest, there's nothing left that can hurt you...

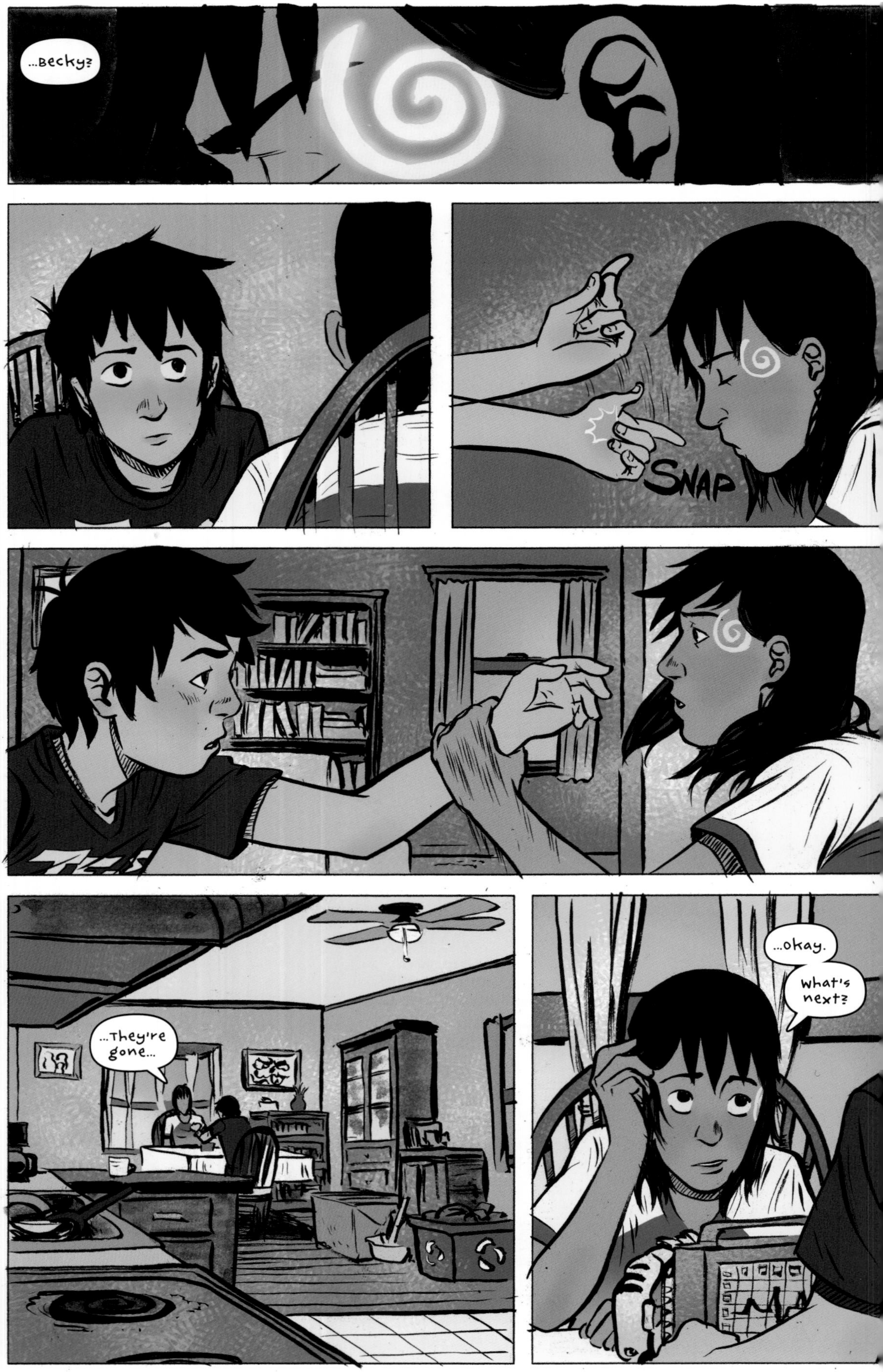
...Becky?
SNAP
...They're gone...
...okay.
What's next?

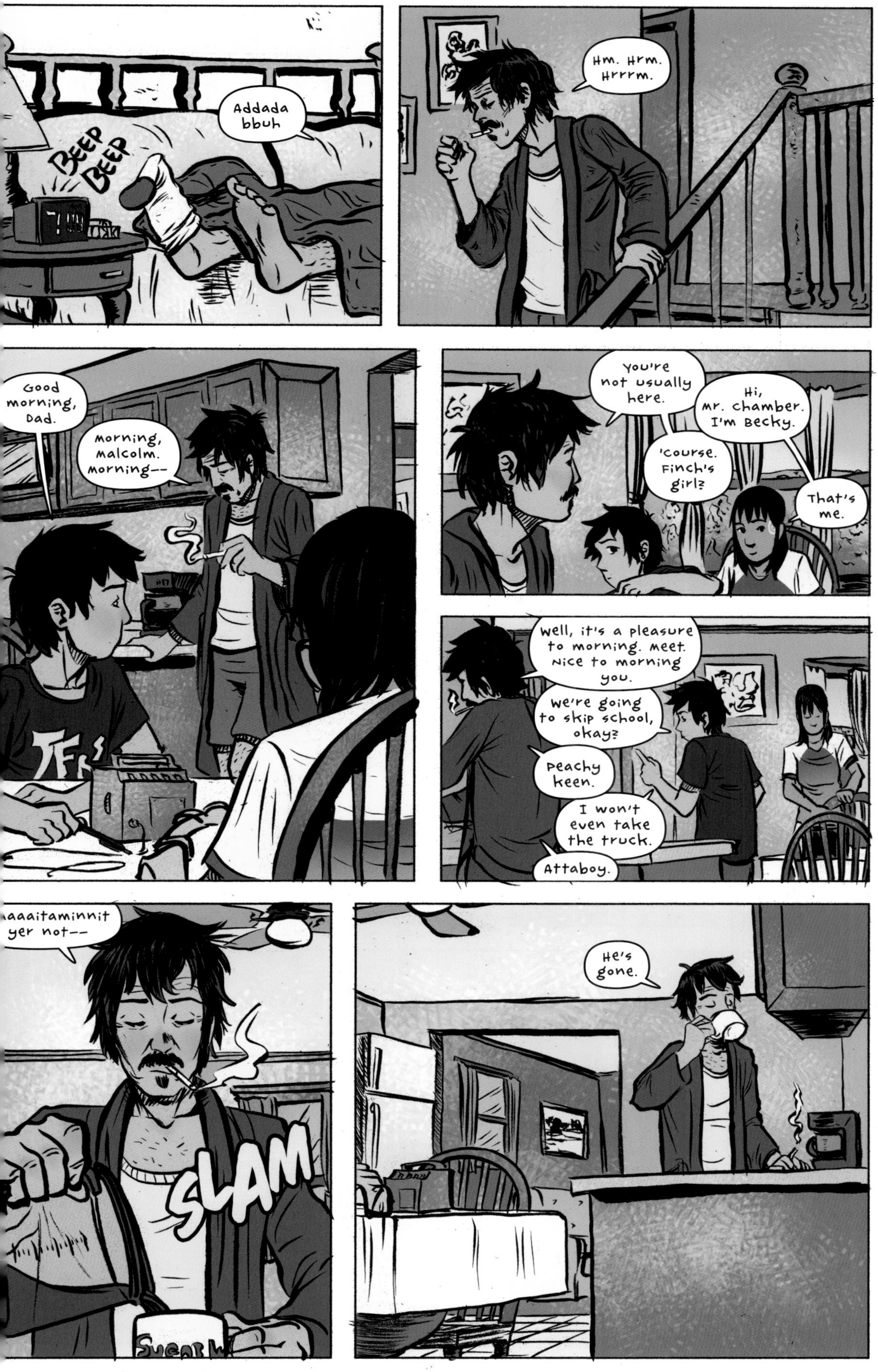
BEEP BEEP
Addada bbuh
Hm. Hrm. Hrrrm.
Good morning, Dad.
Morning, Malcolm. Morning--
You're not usually here.
Hi, Mr. Chamber. I'm Becky.
'Course. Finch's girl?
That's me.
Well, it's a pleasure to morning. Meet. Nice to morning you.
We're going to skip school, okay?
Peachy keen.
I won't even take the truck.
Attaboy.
aaaitaminnit yer not--
SLAM
He's gone.

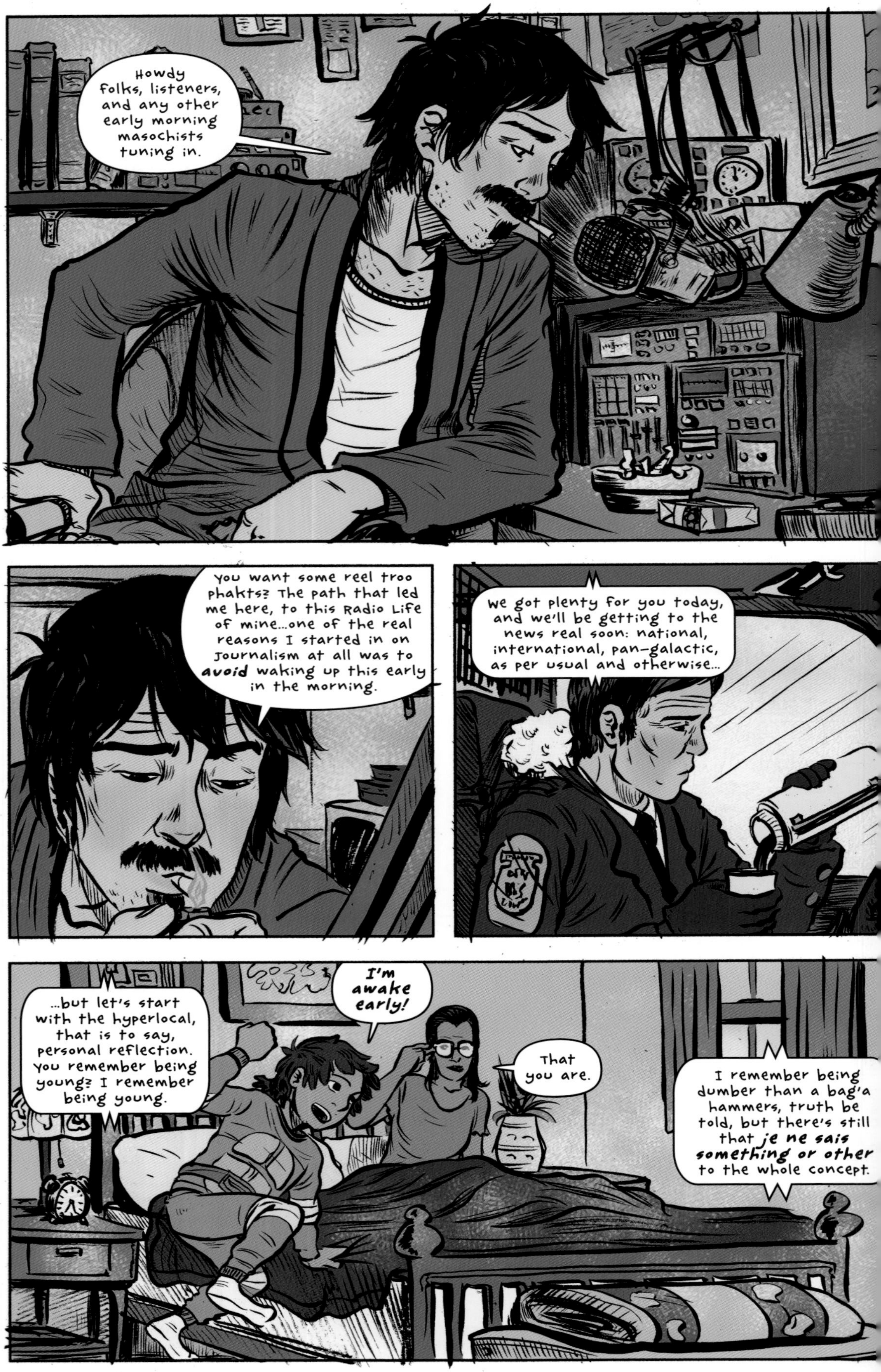
Howdy folks, listeners, and any other early morning masochists tuning in.
You want some reel troo phakts? The path that led me here, to this Radio Life of mine...one of the real reasons I started in on Journalism at all was to *avoid* waking up this early in the morning.
We got plenty for you today, and we'll be getting to the news real soon: national, international, pan-galactic, as per usual and otherwise...
...but let's start with the hyperlocal, that is to say, personal reflection. You remember being young? I remember being young.
I'm awake early!
That you are.
I remember being dumber than a bag'a hammers, truth be told, but there's still that ***je ne sais something or other*** to the whole concept.

But I know that there's nothing more I'd have hated than someone putting me back on the path, whatever the hell that is.

Becky, do you--

children ostensibly being the future and all, I suppose they deserve their chances to make a mess of the mess we've all made of things. So! Allow me to offer a toast--

--and anyone grasping a champagne flute or a cuppa coffee can feel free to join--

PEEBLE-EEP
PEEBLE-EEP
PEEBLE-EEP
PEEBL--

Hey, honey bundles.

veda, my lovely, why?

ou love it. I'm calling --have you een Becky today?

What? No. Is everything--

Well, the car's gone, her running shoes are here, and her phone is on the dresser.

Becky?

Should I be worried?

...

--a toast to that next generation running off on their own adventures. May they avoid all our failings and never find their own. God bless their strivings.

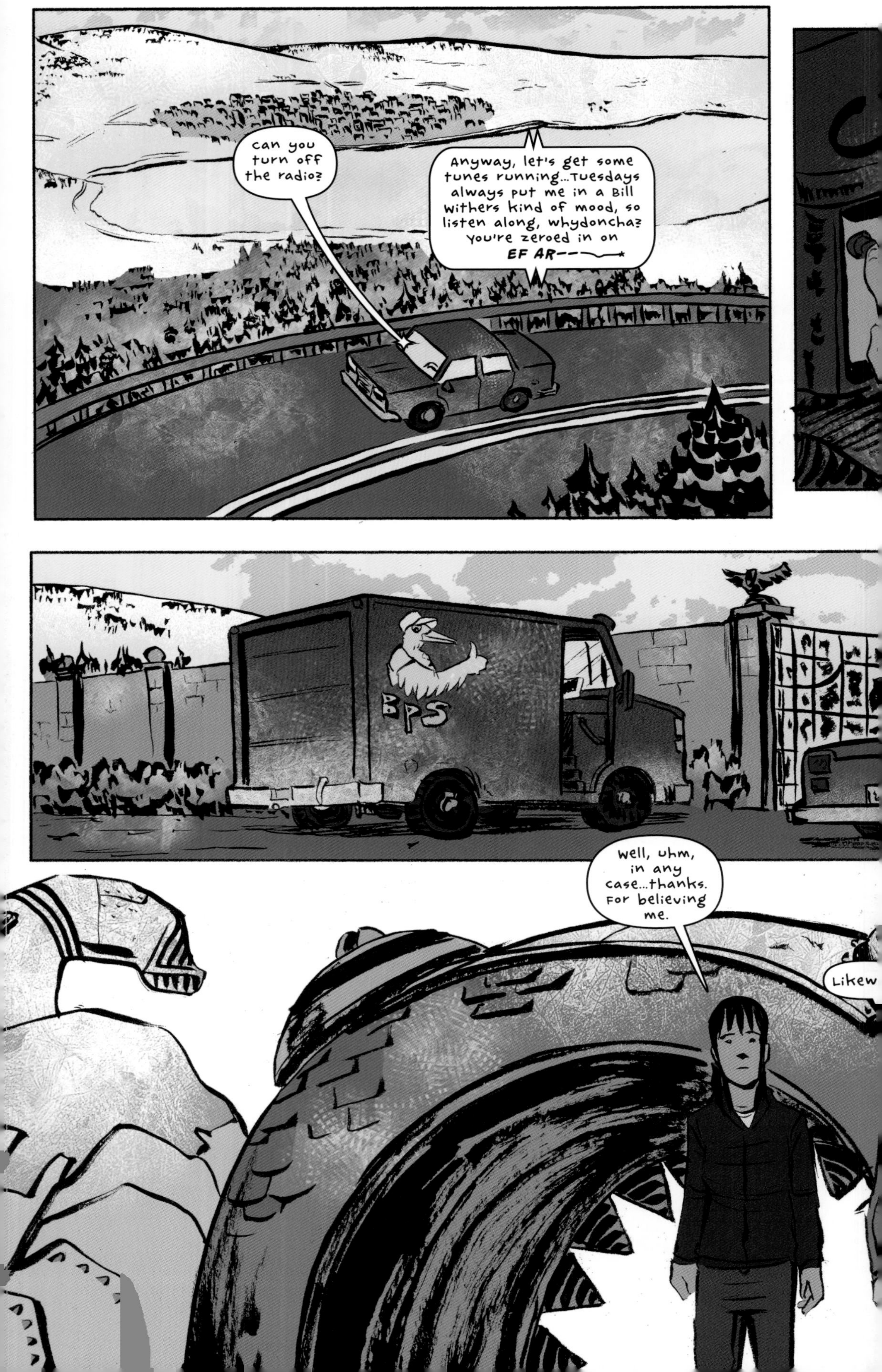
can you turn off the radio?
Anyway, let's get some tunes running...Tuesdays always put me in a Bill Withers kind of mood, so listen along, whydoncha? You're zeroed in on EF AR---
BPS
Well, uhm, in any case...thanks. For believing me.
Likew

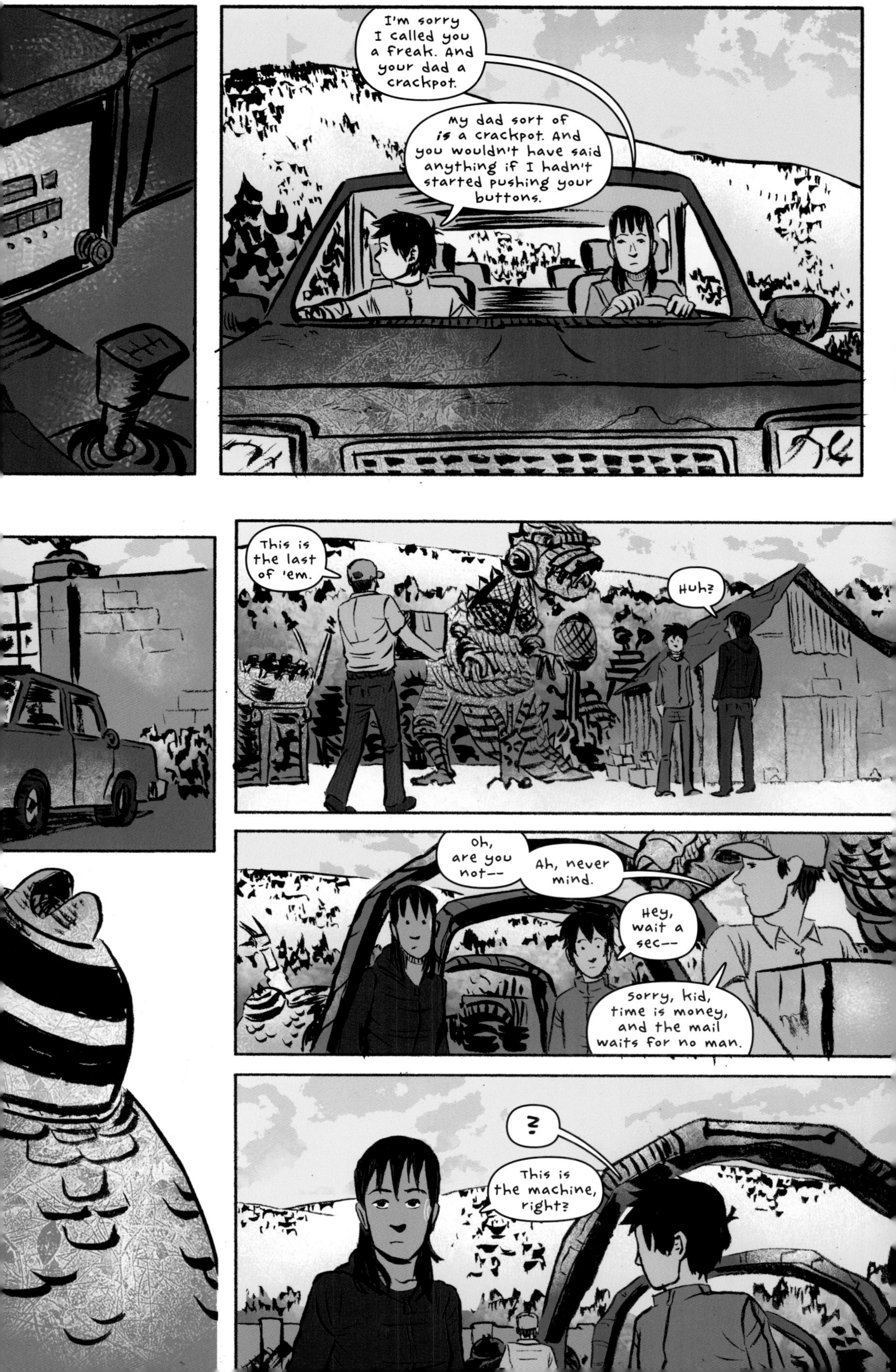
I'm sorry I called you a freak. And your dad a crackpot.
My dad sort of *is* a crackpot. And you wouldn't have said anything if I hadn't started pushing your buttons.
This is the last of 'em.
Huh?
Oh, are you not--
Ah, never mind.
Hey, wait a sec--
Sorry, kid, time is money, and the mail waits for no man.
?
This is the machine, right?

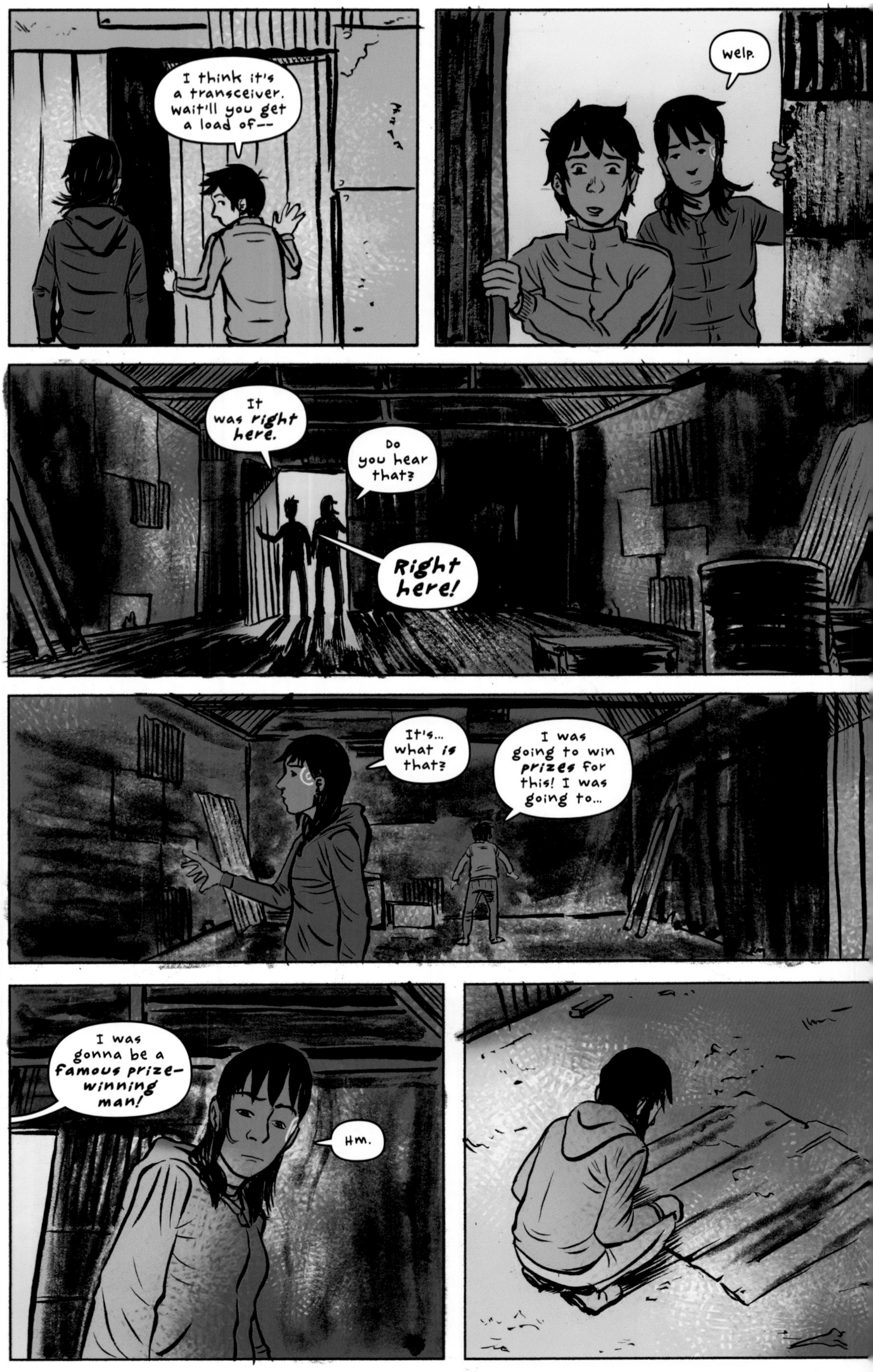
I think it's a transceiver. Wait'll you get a load of--
Welp.
It was *right* here.
Do you hear that?
Right here!
It's... what *is* that?
I was going to win *prizes* for this! I was going to...
I was gonna be a *famous prize-winning man!*
Hm.

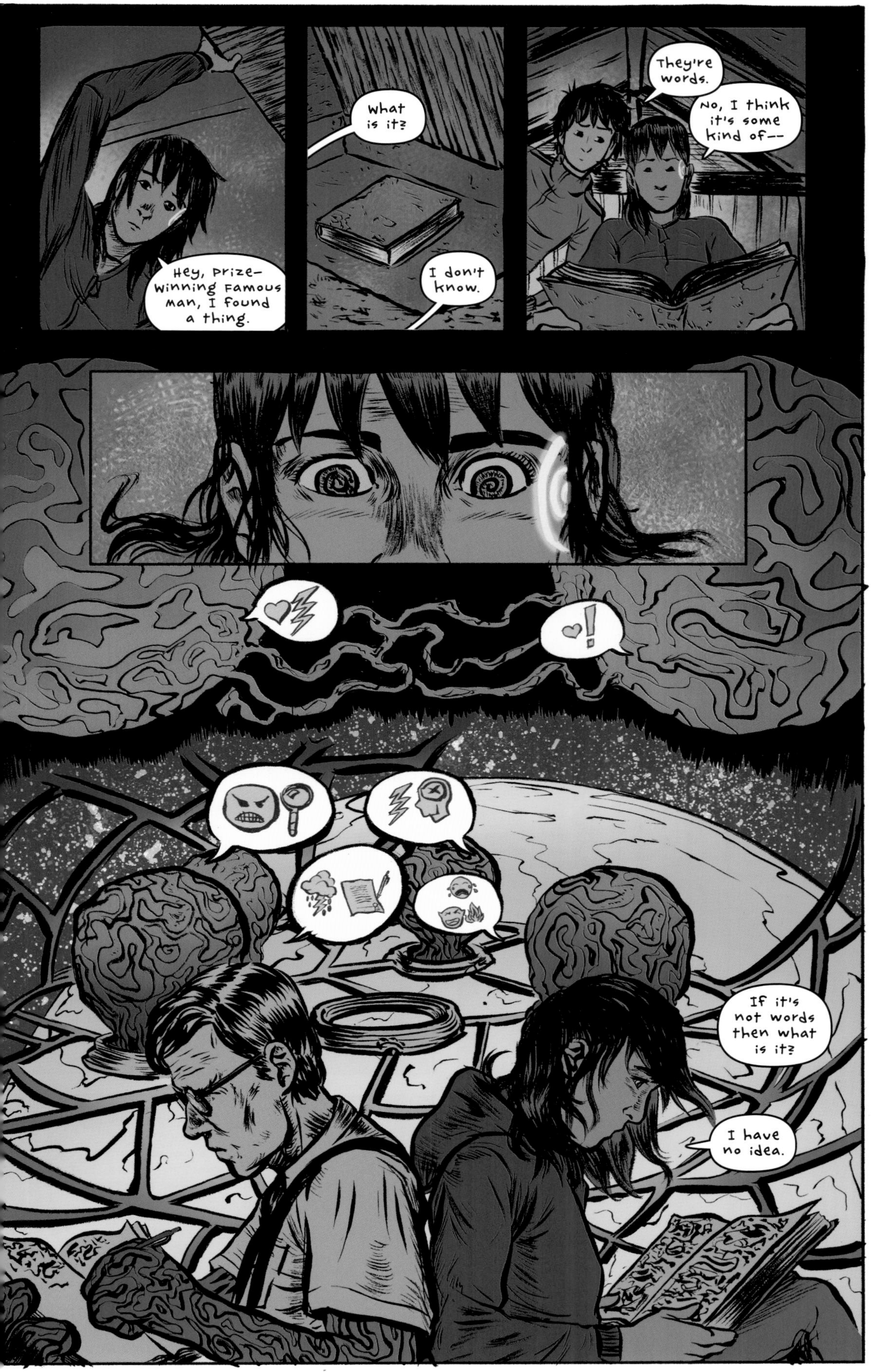
Hey, prize-winning famous man, I found a thing.
What is it?
I don't know.
They're words.
No, I think it's some kind of--
If it's not words then what is it?
I have no idea.

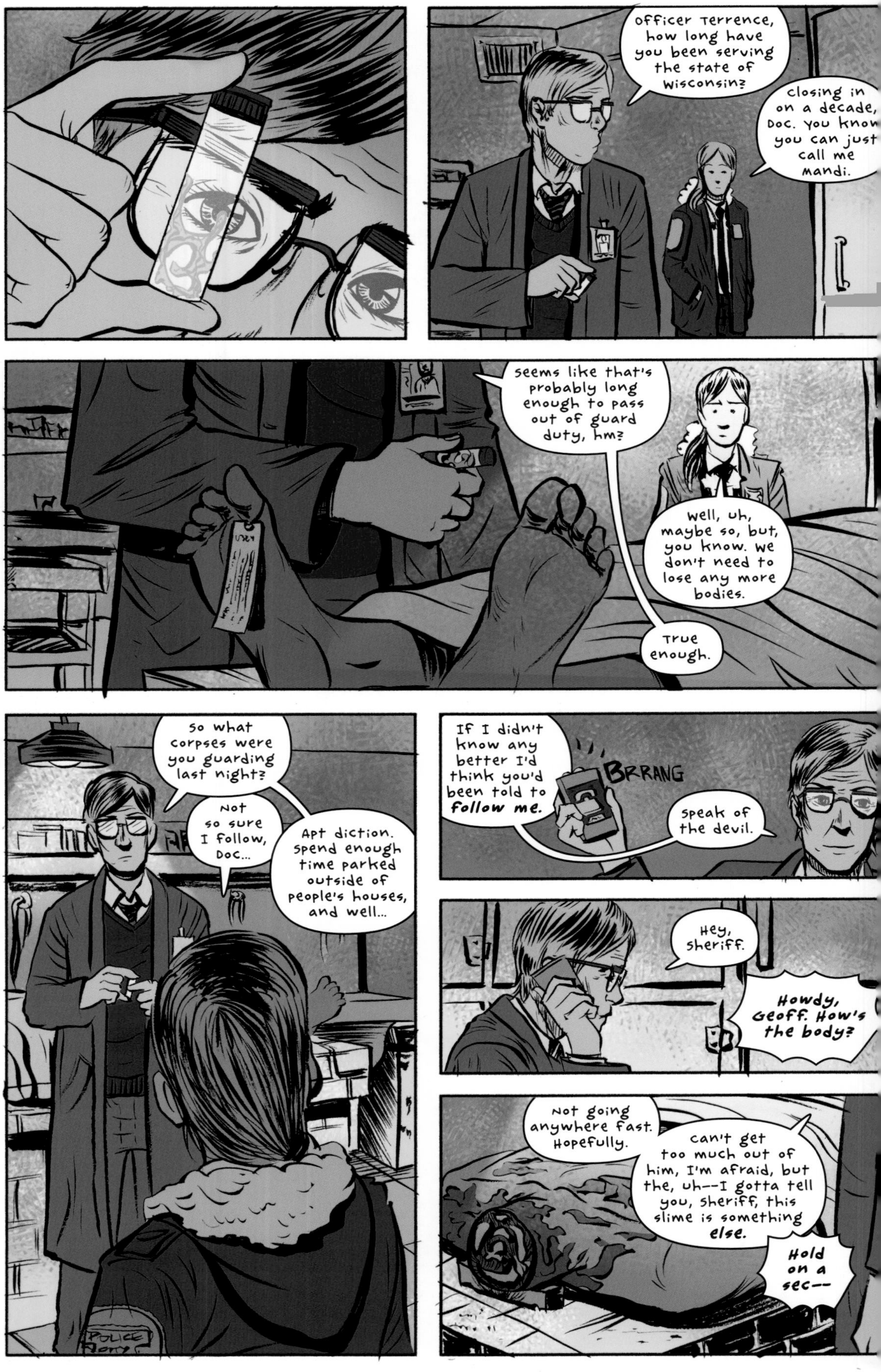
Officer Terrence, how long have you been serving the state of Wisconsin?
Closing in on a decade, Doc. You know you can just call me Mandi.
Seems like that's probably long enough to pass out of guard duty, hm?
Well, uh, maybe so, but, you know. We don't need to lose any more bodies.
True enough.
So what corpses were you guarding last night?
Not so sure I follow, Doc...
Apt diction. Spend enough time parked outside of people's houses, and well...
If I didn't know any better I'd think you'd been told to follow me.
BRRANG
Speak of the devil.
Hey, Sheriff.
Howdy, Geoff. How's the body?
Not going anywhere fast. Hopefully.
Can't get too much out of him, I'm afraid, but the, uh--I gotta tell you, Sheriff, this slime is something else.
Hold on a sec--
POLICE

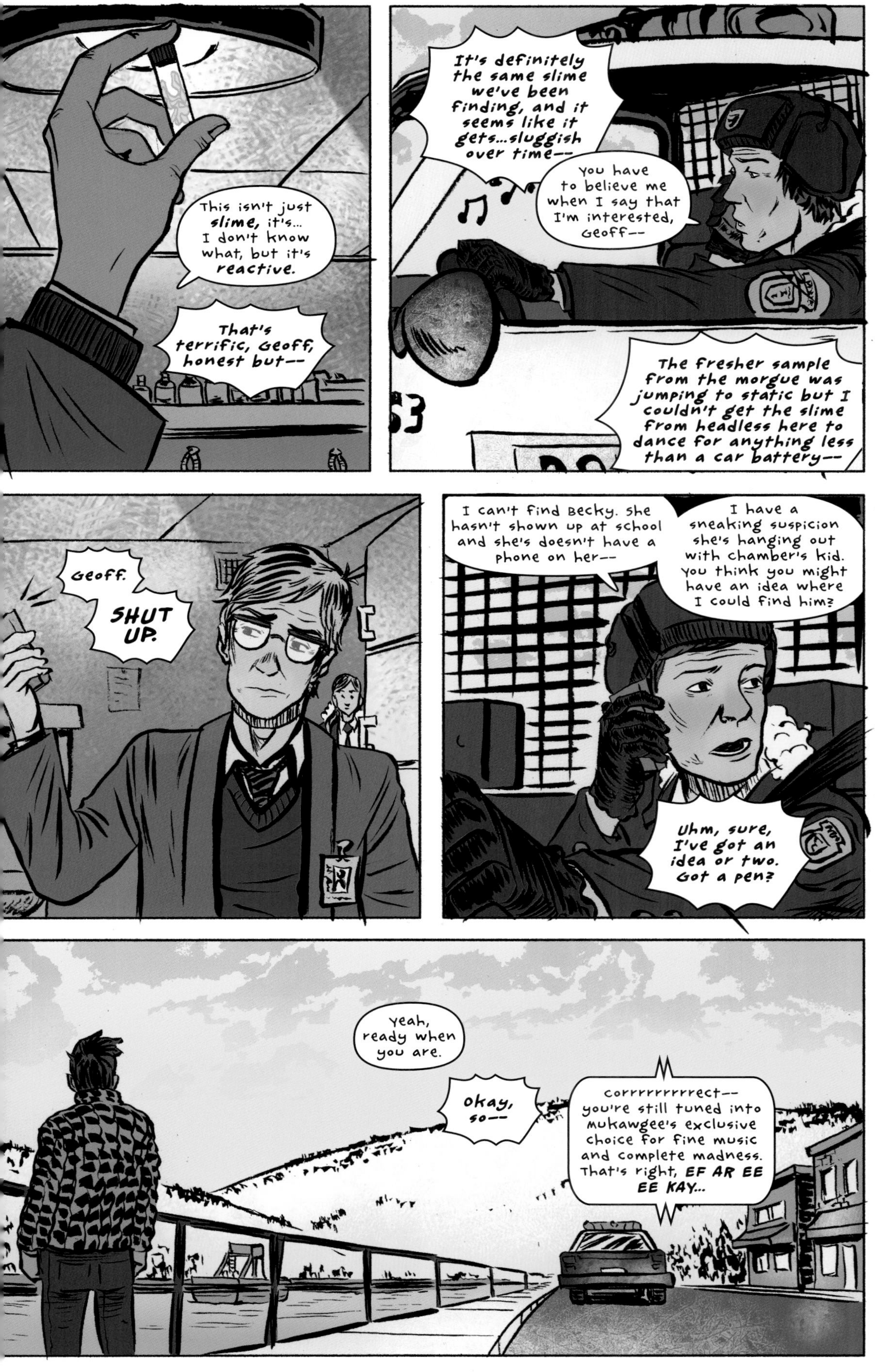

This isn't just slime, it's... I don't know what, but it's reactive.
That's terrific, Geoff, honest but--
It's definitely the same slime we've been finding, and it seems like it gets...sluggish over time--
You have to believe me when I say that I'm interested, Geoff--
The fresher sample from the morgue was jumping to static but I couldn't get the slime from headless here to dance for anything less than a car battery--
Geoff.
SHUT UP.
I can't find Becky. She hasn't shown up at school and she's doesn't have a phone on her--
I have a sneaking suspicion she's hanging out with Chamber's kid. You think you might have an idea where I could find him?
Uhm, sure, I've got an idea or two. Got a pen?
Yeah, ready when you are.
Okay, so--
Corrrrrrrrrect-- you're still tuned into Mukawgee's exclusive choice for fine music and complete madness. That's right, EF AR EE EE KAY...

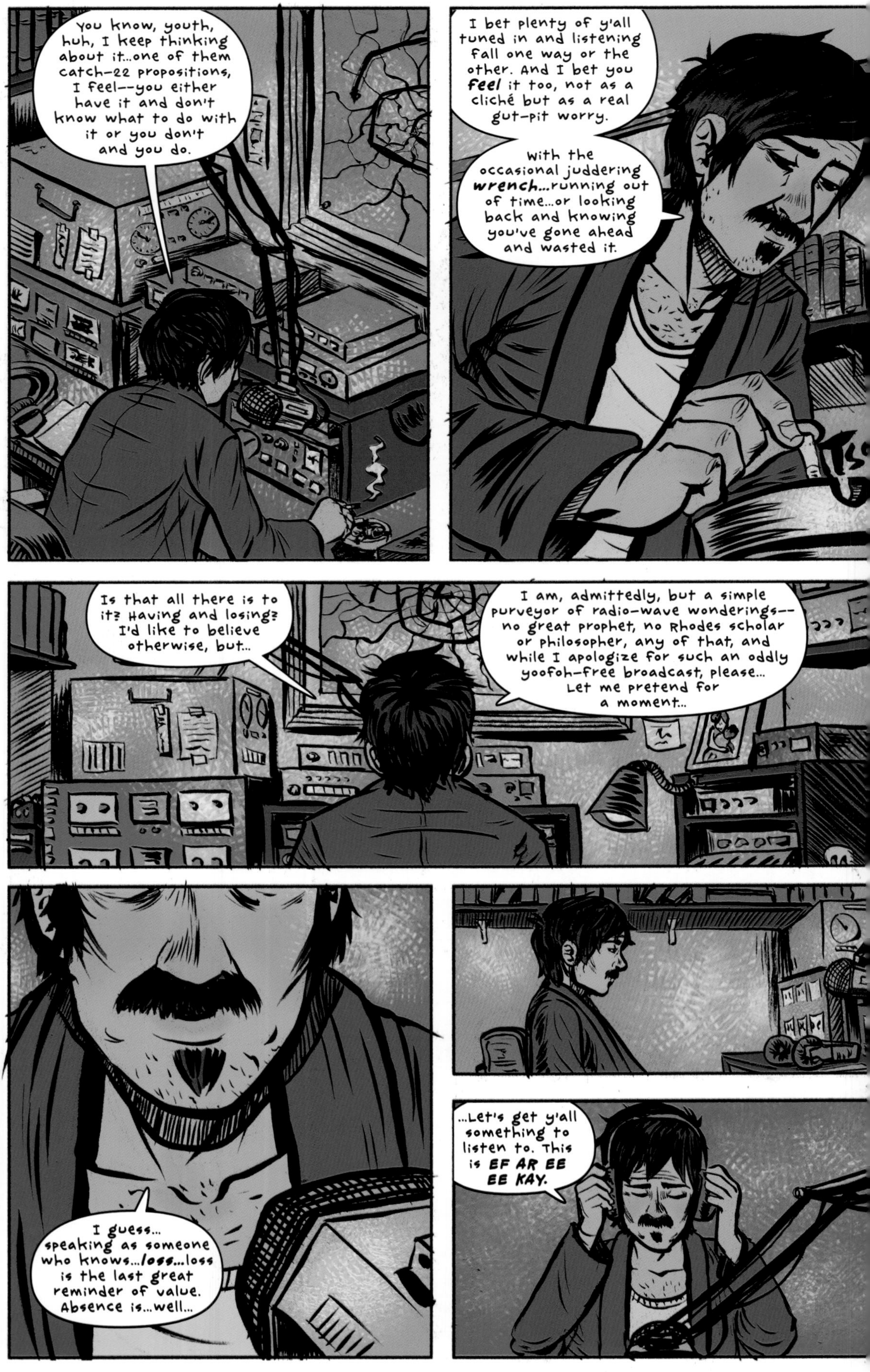
You know, youth, huh, I keep thinking about it...one of them catch-22 propositions, I feel--you either have it and don't know what to do with it or you don't and you do.
I bet plenty of y'all tuned in and listening fall one way or the other. And I bet you **feel** it too, not as a cliché but as a real gut-pit worry.
With the occasional juddering **wrench**...running out of time...or looking back and knowing you've gone ahead and wasted it.
Is that all there is to it? Having and losing? I'd like to believe otherwise, but...
I am, admittedly, but a simple purveyor of radio-wave wonderings--no great prophet, no Rhodes scholar or philosopher, any of that, and while I apologize for such an oddly yoofoh-free broadcast, please... Let me pretend for a moment...
I guess... speaking as someone who knows...**loss**...loss is the last great reminder of value. Absence is...well...
...Let's get y'all something to listen to. This is **EF AR EE EE KAY.**

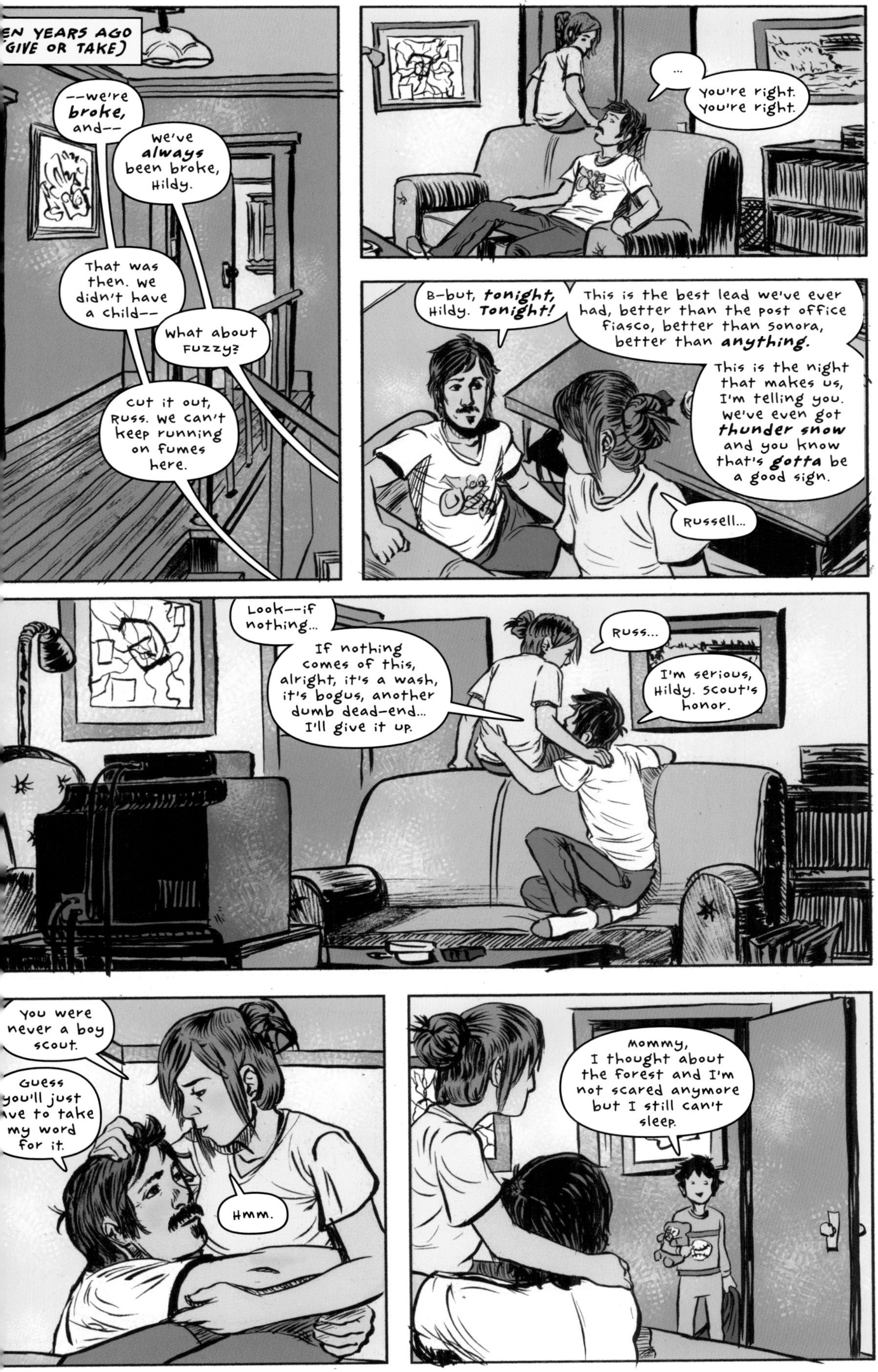

EN YEARS AGO (GIVE OR TAKE)
--we're broke, and--
We've always been broke, Hildy.
That was then. We didn't have a child--
What about Fuzzy?
Cut it out, Russ. We can't keep running on fumes here.
...
You're right. You're right.
B-but, tonight, Hildy. Tonight!
This is the best lead we've ever had, better than the post office fiasco, better than Sonora, better than anything.
This is the night that makes us, I'm telling you. We've even got thunder snow and you know that's gotta be a good sign.
Russell...
Look--if nothing...
If nothing comes of this, alright, it's a wash, it's bogus, another dumb dead-end... I'll give it up.
Russ...
I'm serious, Hildy. Scout's honor.
You were never a boy scout.
Guess you'll just ave to take my word for it.
Hmm.
Mommy, I thought about the forest and I'm not scared anymore but I still can't sleep.

Wait, how did E.T. give you nightmares?

It doesn't now!

Attaboy.

I should stay—

He did fine on his own when the babysitter canceled. I need you on this.

...Go warm up the car.

You want me to put on a tape for you?

I wanna watch...*the scariest movie.*

The *scariest* one, huh...

I'm ready! I can watch 'em!

Oooo, here a good on Just starti too. Real sc promise.

CLIK... CLIK... CLIK...

Love you, baby.

Anytime you want to tell me anything, I'm right here, don't worry.

A hint, a nudge.

Anything, really. I'm all ears.

Come on, Becky.

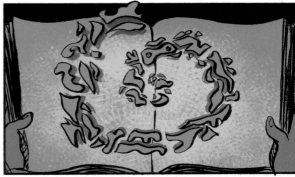

Becky?

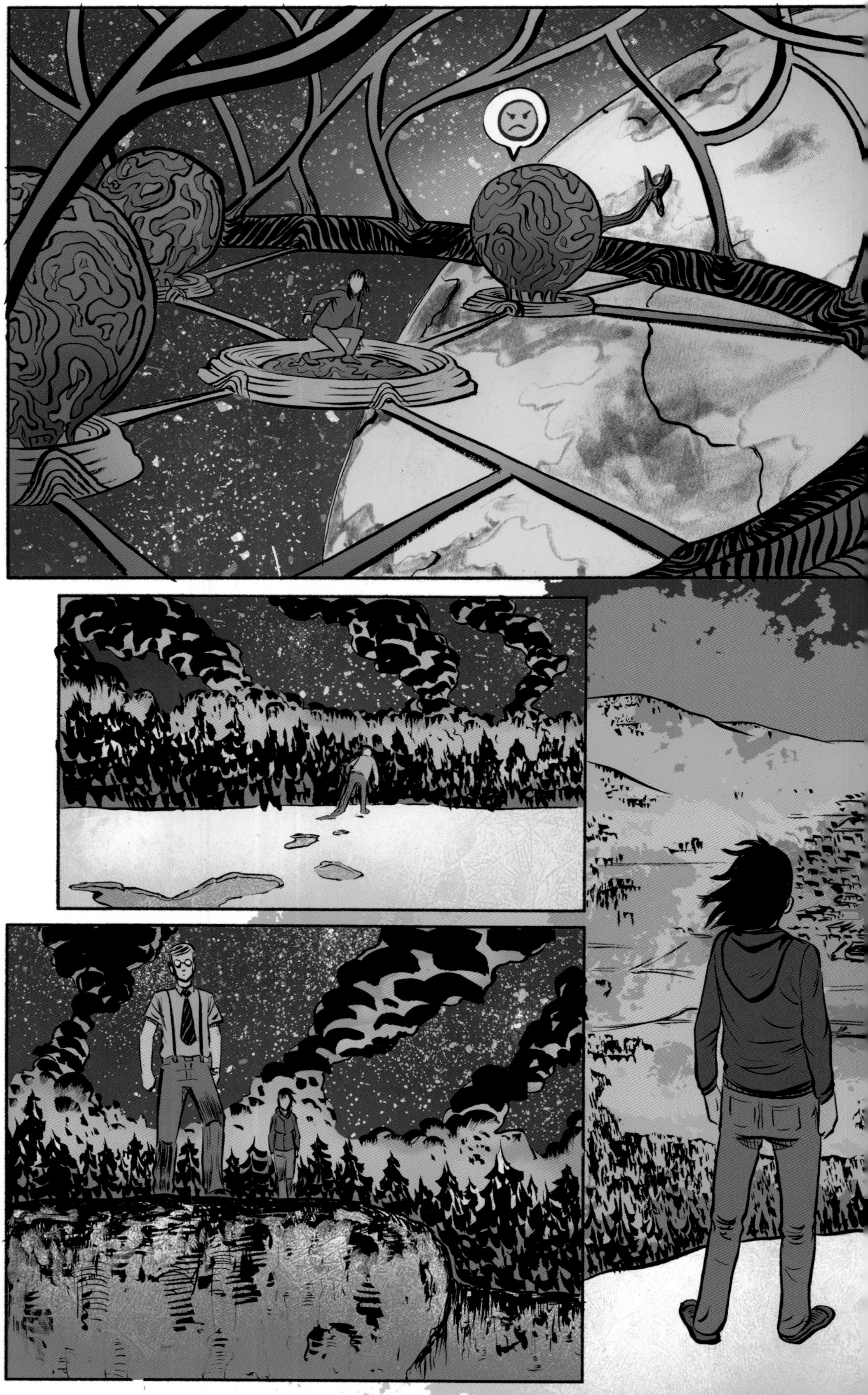

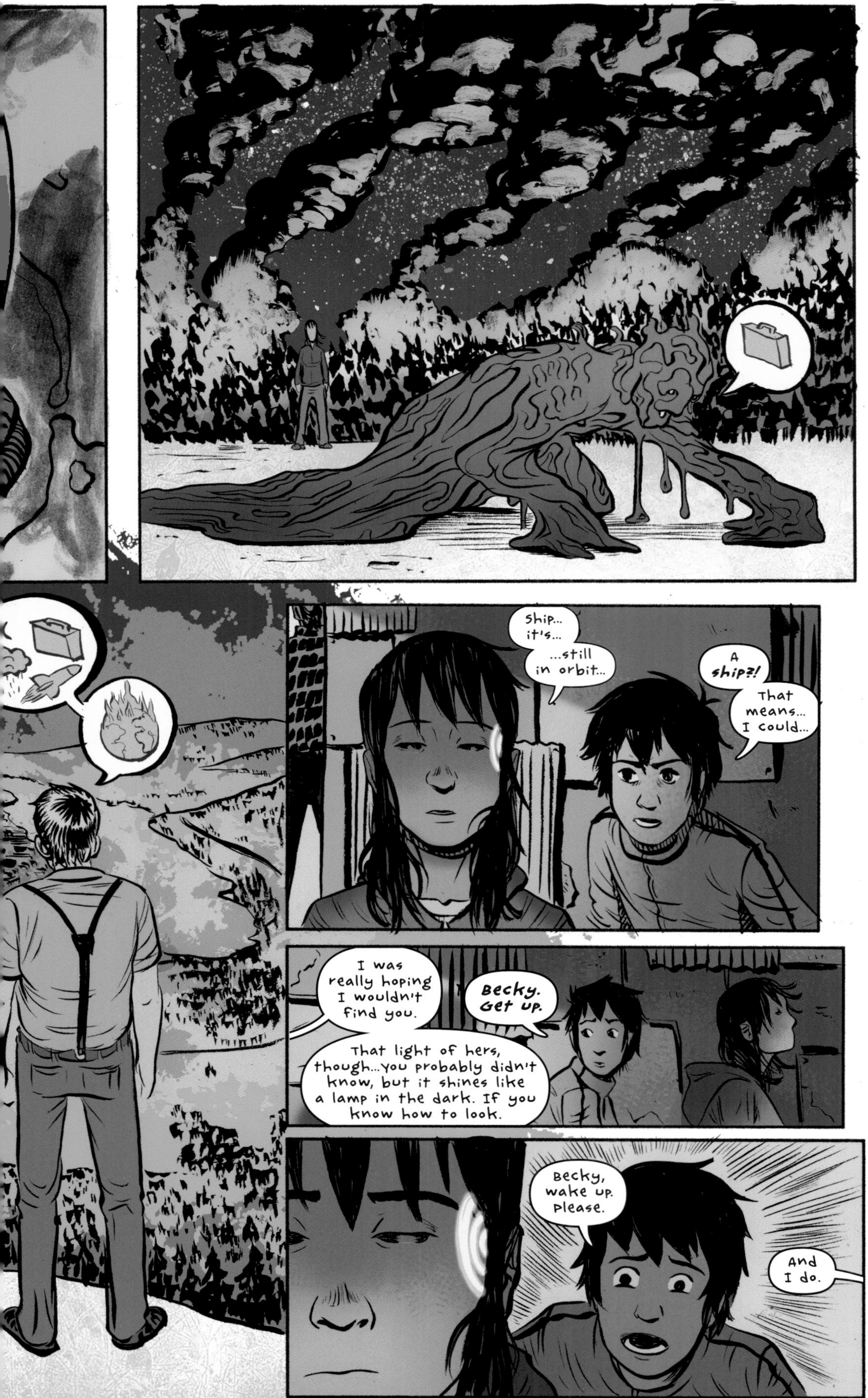
Ship... it's...
...still in orbit...
A ship?!
That means... I could...
I was really hoping I wouldn't find you.
Becky. Get up.
That light of hers, though... you probably didn't know, but it shines like a lamp in the dark. If you know how to look.
Becky, wake up. Please.
And I do.

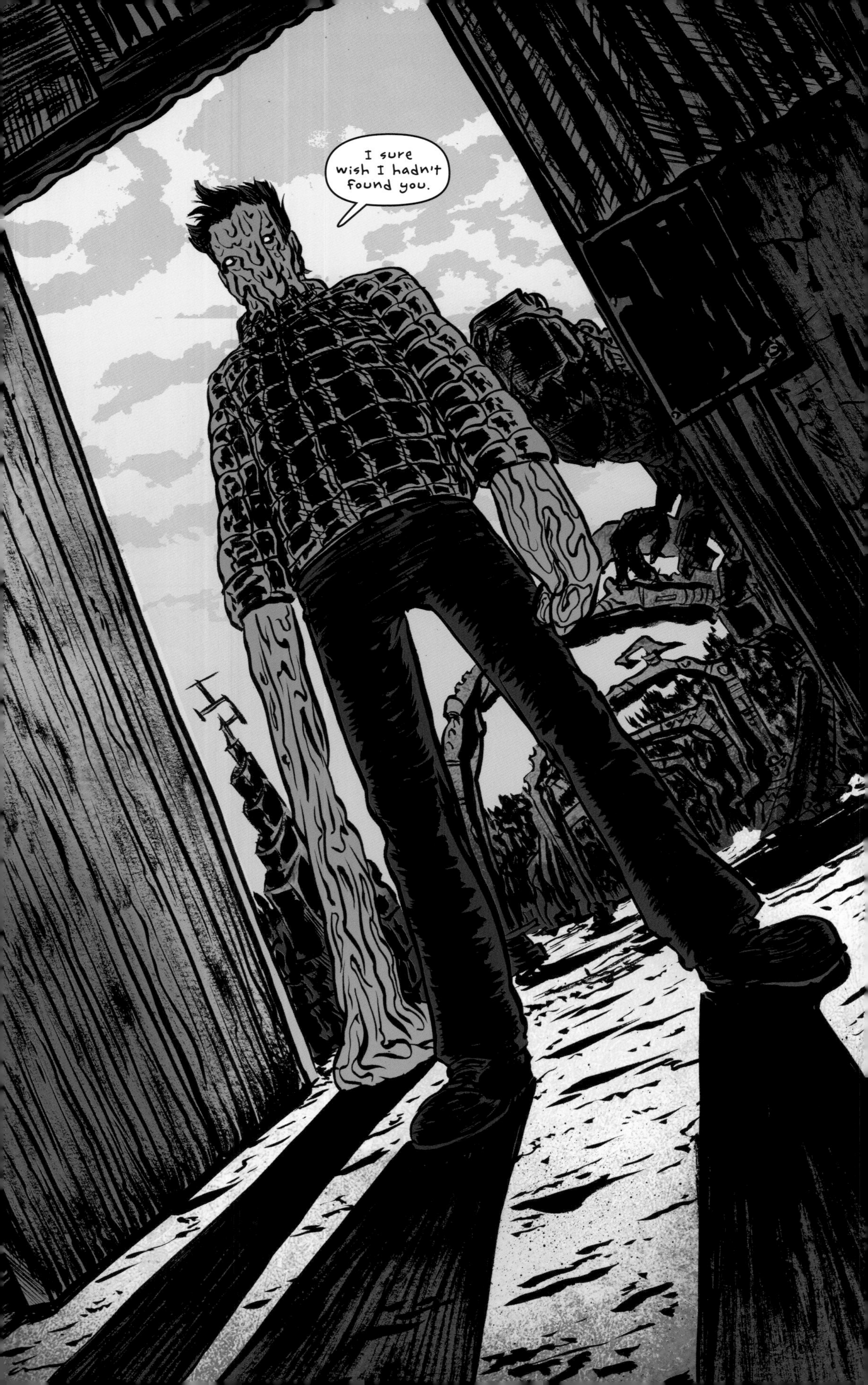
I sure wish I hadn't found you.

f·i·v·e

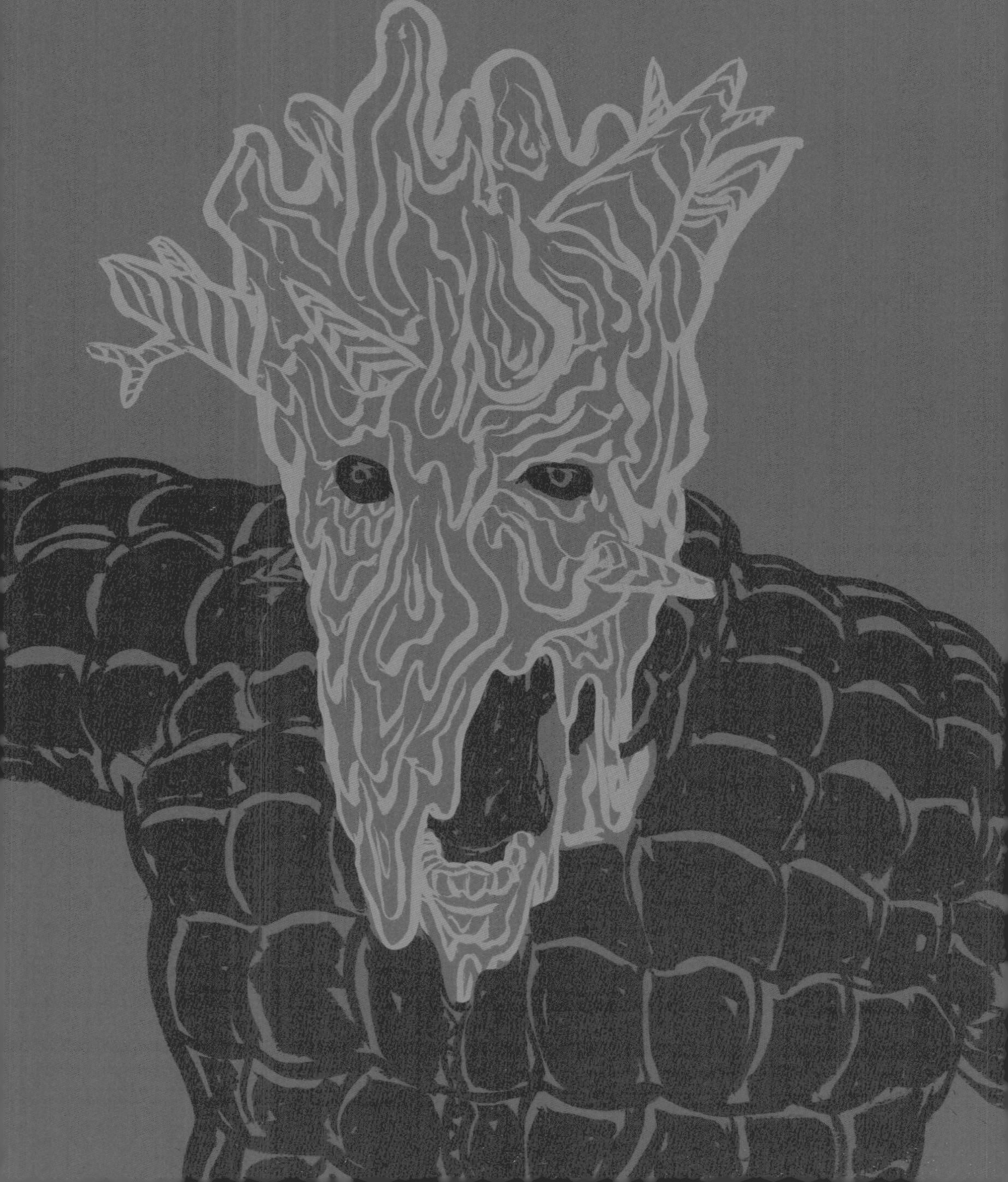

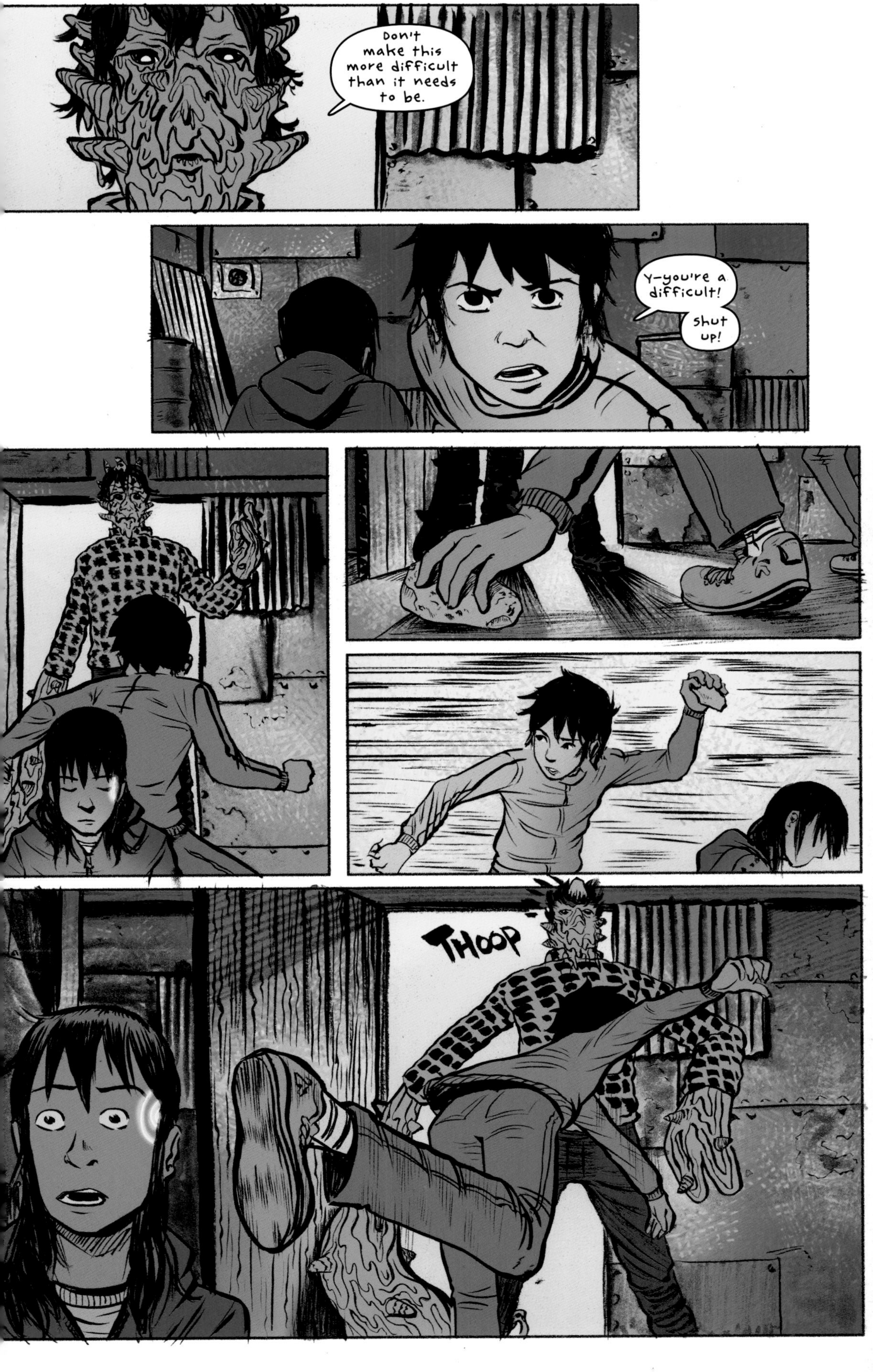
Don't make this more difficult than it needs to be.
Y-you're a difficult!
shut up!
THOOP

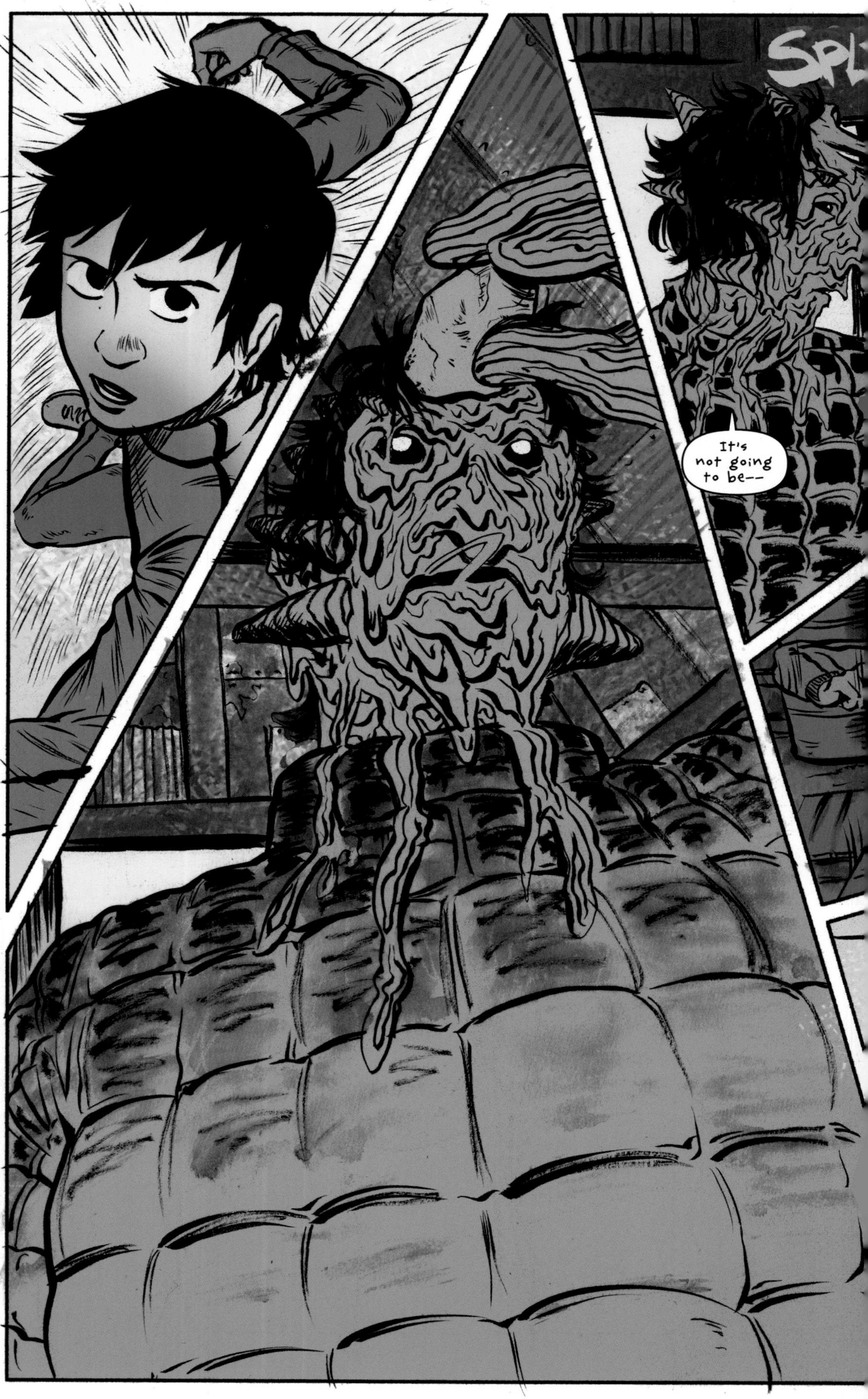
SPL
It's not going to be--

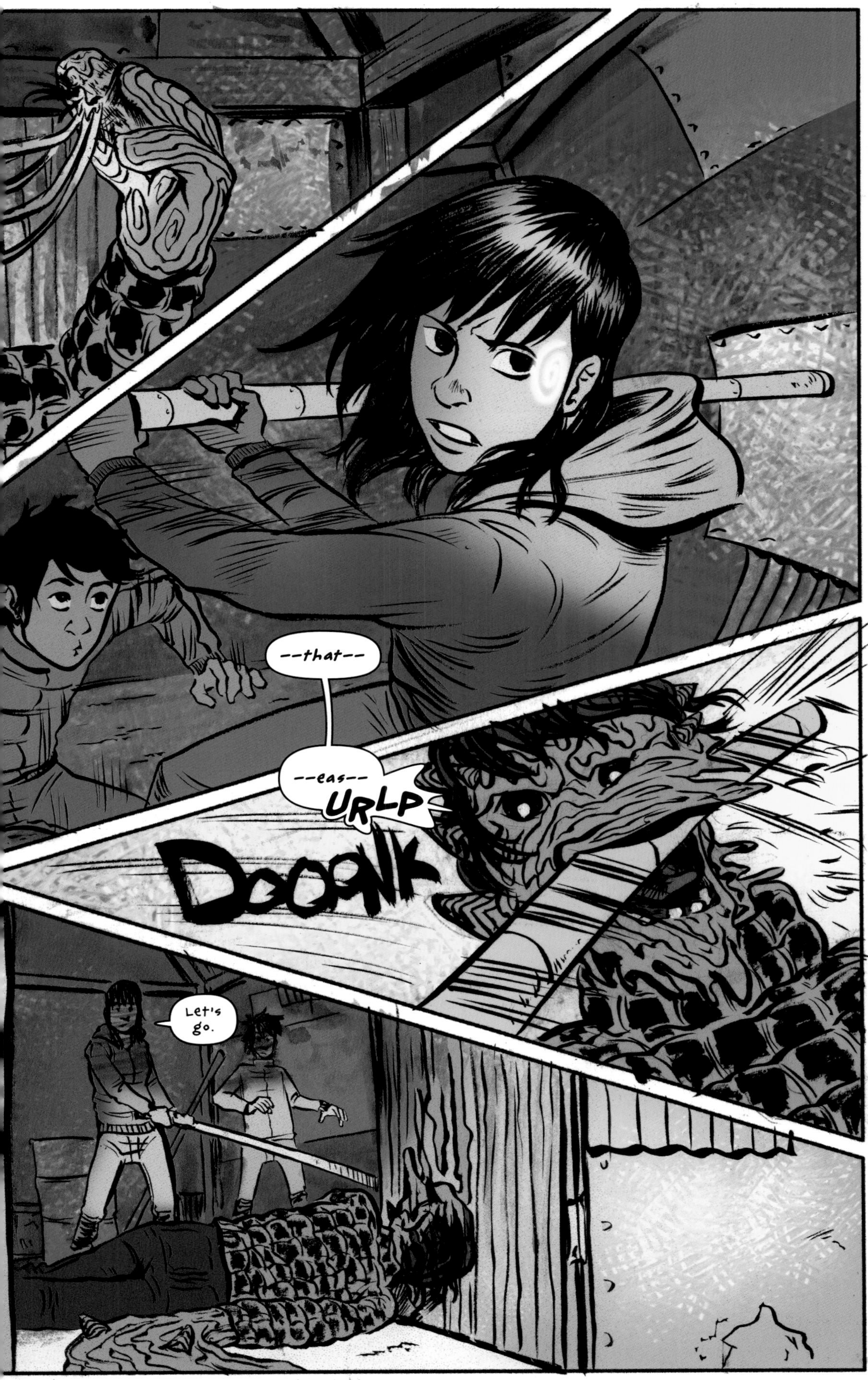
--that--
--eas--
URLP
DOOONK
Let's go.

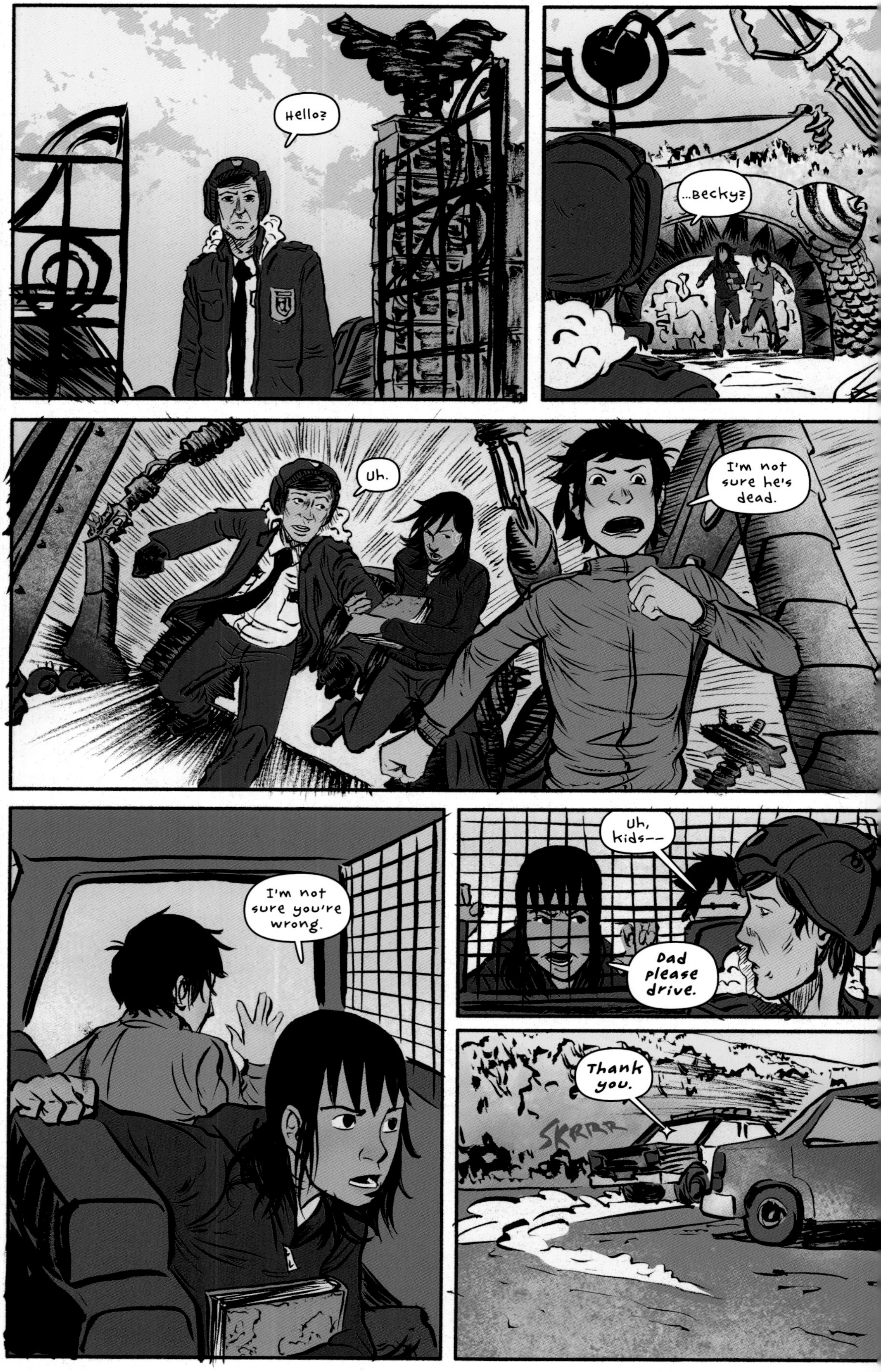
Hello?
...Becky?
Uh.
I'm not sure he's dead.
I'm not sure you're wrong.
Uh, kids--
Dad please drive.
Thank you.
SKRRR

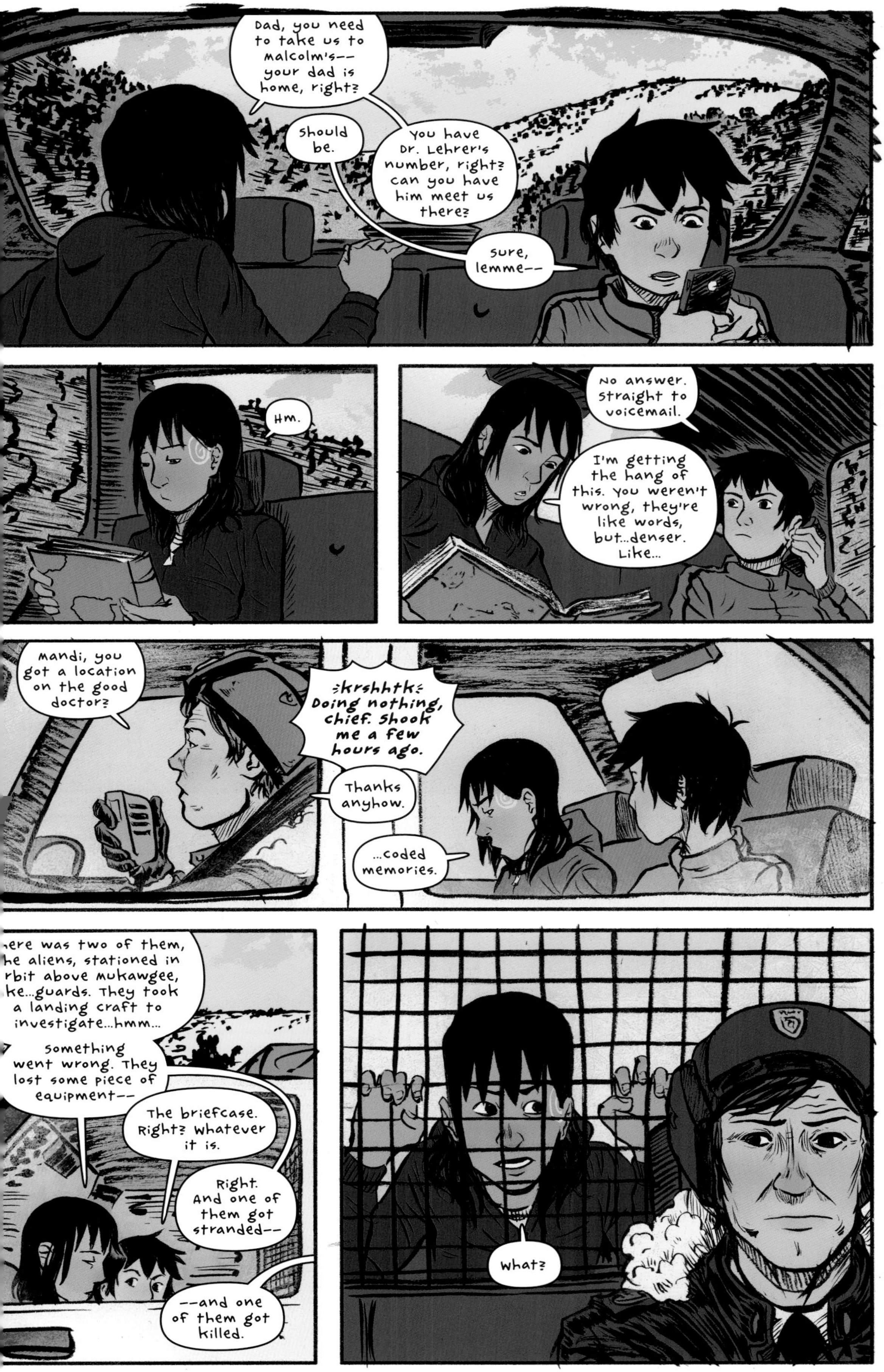

Dad, you need to take us to Malcolm's-- your dad is home, right?
Should be.
You have Dr. Lehrer's number, right? Can you have him meet us there?
Sure, lemme--
Hm.
No answer. Straight to voicemail.
I'm getting the hang of this. You weren't wrong, they're like words, but...denser. Like...
Mandi, you got a location on the good doctor?
krshhtk Doing nothing, chief. Shook me a few hours ago.
Thanks anyhow.
...coded memories.
ere was two of them, he aliens, stationed in rbit above Mukawgee, ke...guards. They took a landing craft to investigate...hmm...
Something went wrong. They lost some piece of equipment--
The briefcase. Right? Whatever it is.
Right. And one of them got stranded--
--and one of them got killed.
What?

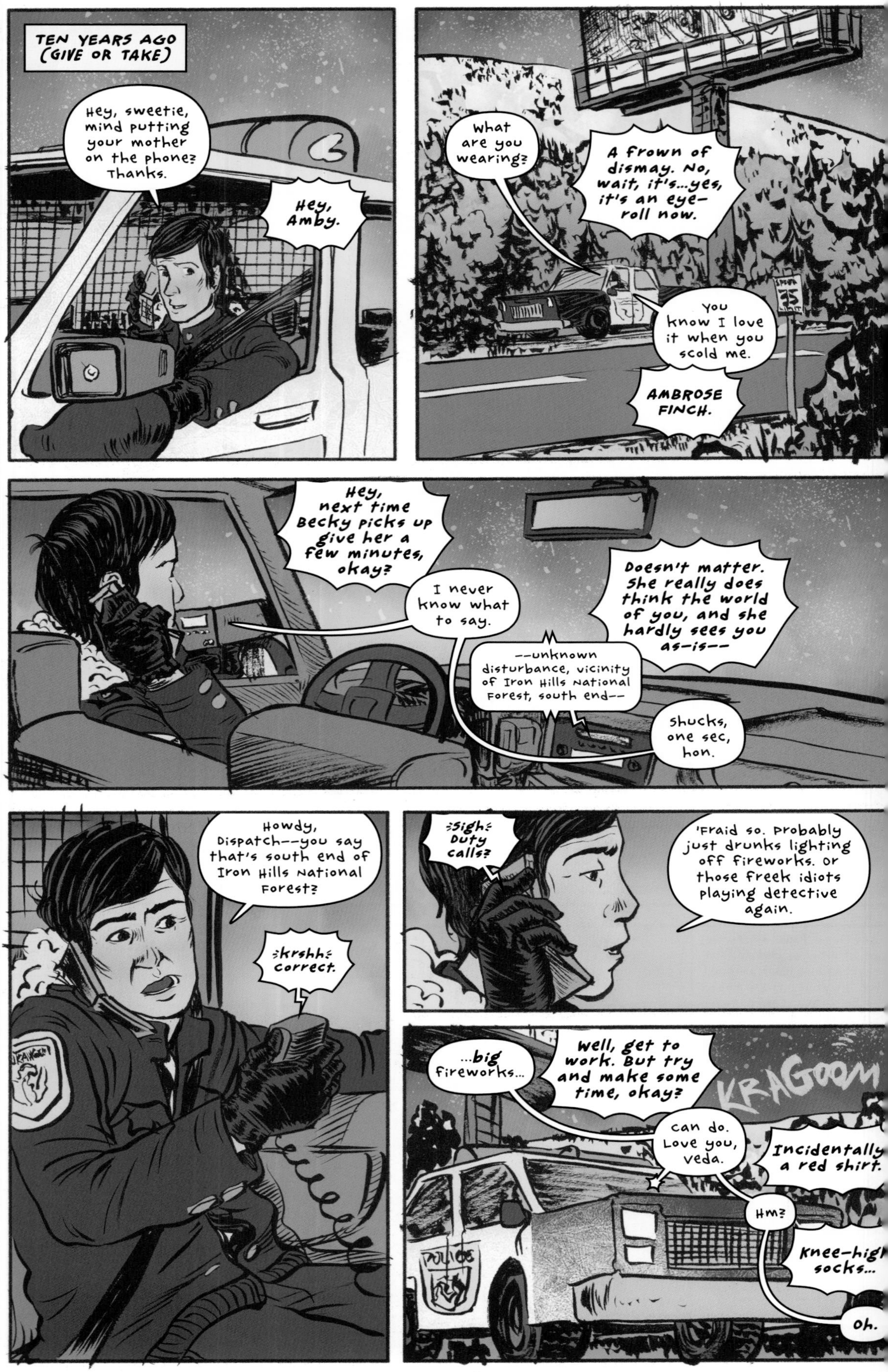
TEN YEARS AGO (GIVE OR TAKE)
Hey, sweetie, mind putting your mother on the phone? Thanks.
Hey, Amby.
What are you wearing?
A frown of dismay. No, wait, it's...yes, it's an eye-roll now.
You know I love it when you scold me.
AMBROSE FINCH.
Hey, next time Becky picks up give her a few minutes, okay?
I never know what to say.
Doesn't matter. She really does think the world of you, and she hardly sees you as-is--
--unknown disturbance, vicinity of Iron Hills National Forest, south end--
Shucks, one sec, hon.
Howdy, Dispatch--you say that's south end of Iron Hills National Forest?
krshh correct.
Sigh Duty calls?
'Fraid so. Probably just drunks lighting off fireworks. Or those freek idiots playing detective again.
...big fireworks...
Well, get to work. But try and make some time, okay?
KRAGOOM
Can do. Love you, Veda.
Incidentally a red shirt.
Hm?
Knee-high socks...
Oh.

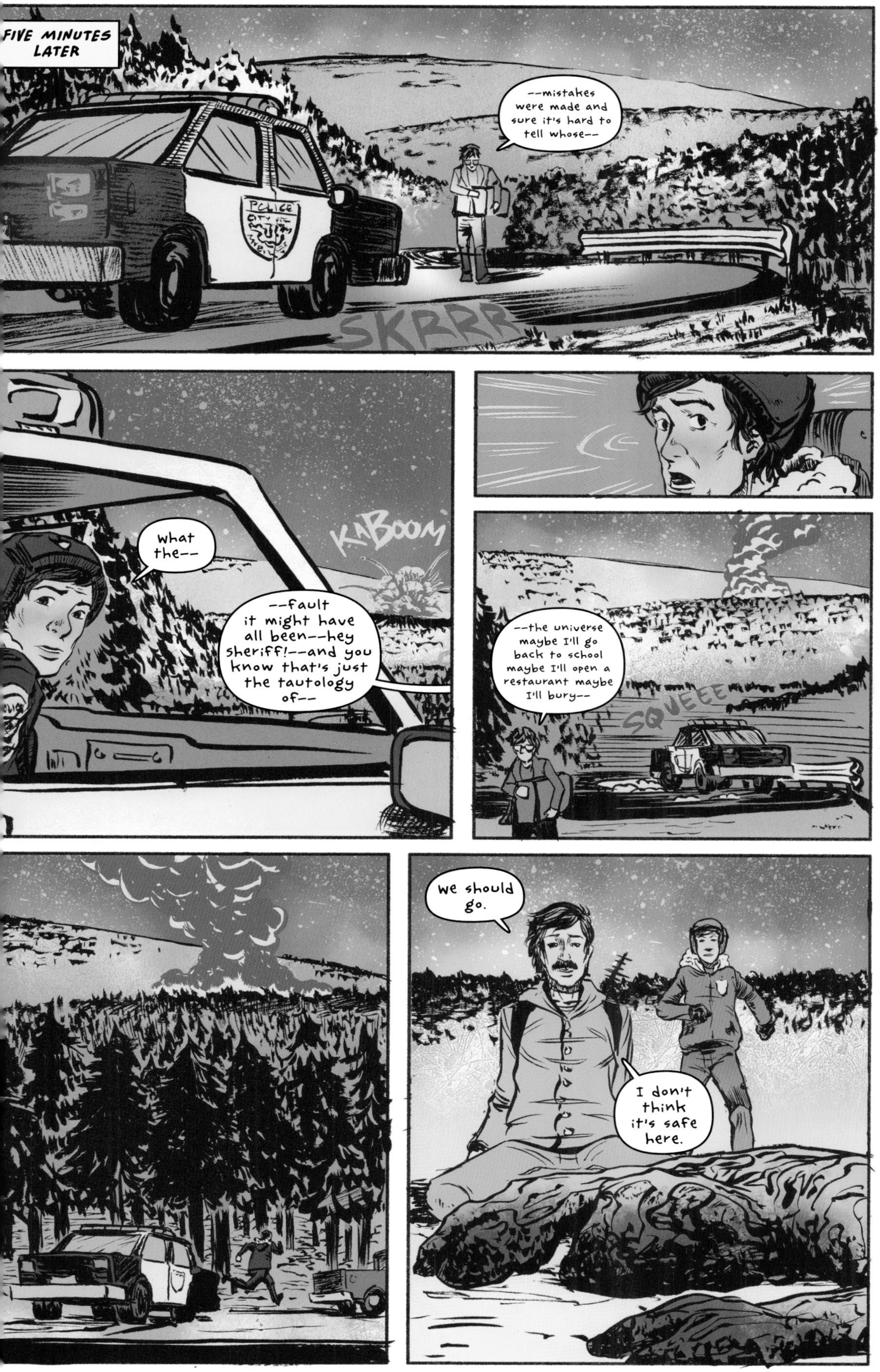
FIVE MINUTES LATER
--mistakes were made and sure it's hard to tell whose--
SKRRR
what the--
KABOOM
--fault it might have all been--hey sheriff!--and you know that's just the tautology of--
--the universe maybe I'll go back to school maybe I'll open a restaurant maybe I'll bury--
SQUEEE
We should go.
I don't think it's safe here.

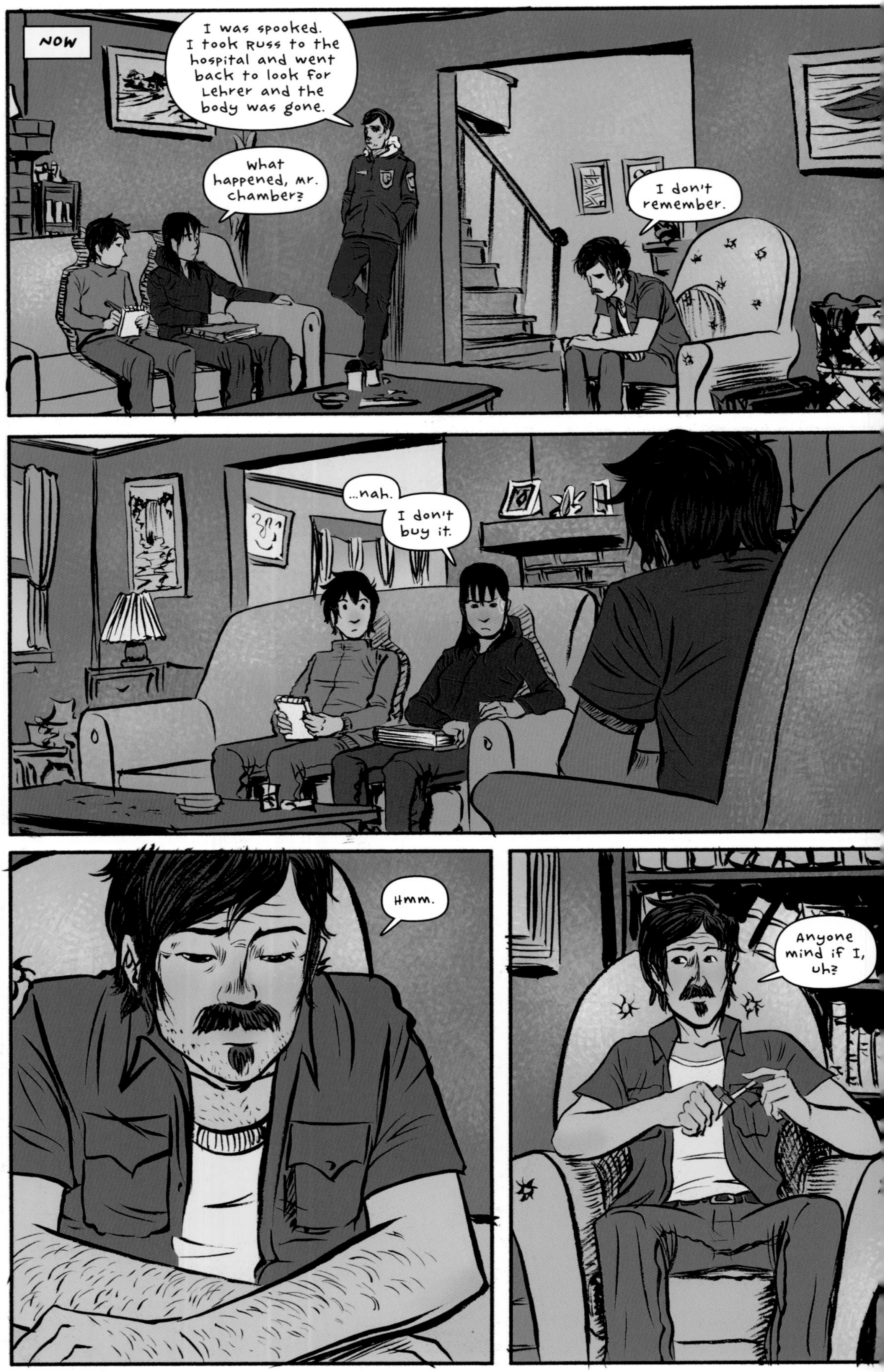
NOW
I was spooked. I took Russ to the hospital and went back to look for Lehrer and the body was gone.
What happened, mr. chamber?
I don't remember.
...nah.
I don't buy it.
Hmm.
Anyone mind if I, uh?

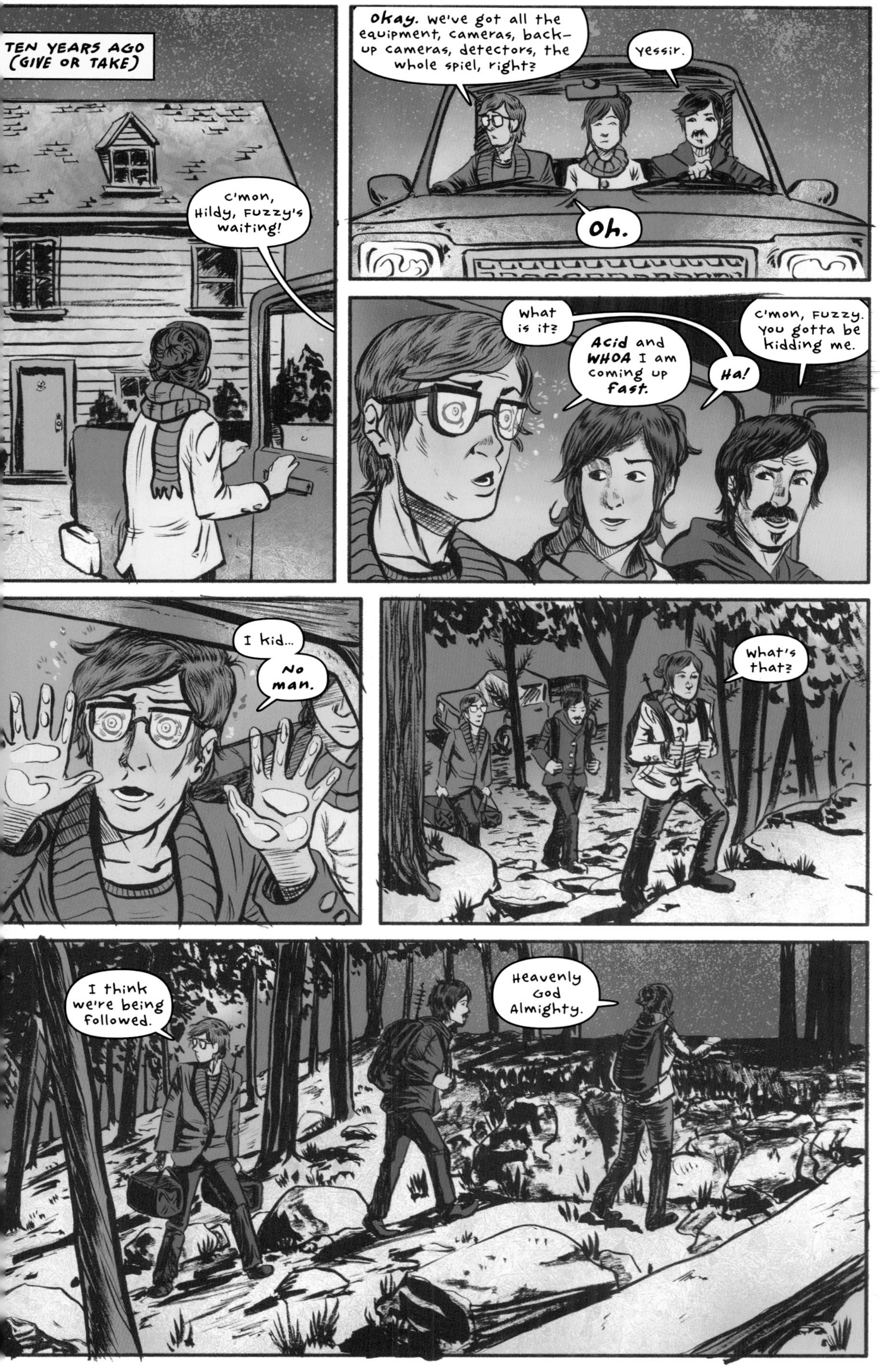
TEN YEARS AGO (GIVE OR TAKE)
C'mon, Hildy, Fuzzy's waiting!
Okay. We've got all the equipment, cameras, back-up cameras, detectors, the whole spiel, right?
Yessir.
Oh.
What is it?
Acid and WHOA I am coming up fast.
Ha!
C'mon, Fuzzy. You gotta be kidding me.
I kid...
No man.
What's that?
I think we're being followed.
Heavenly God Almighty.

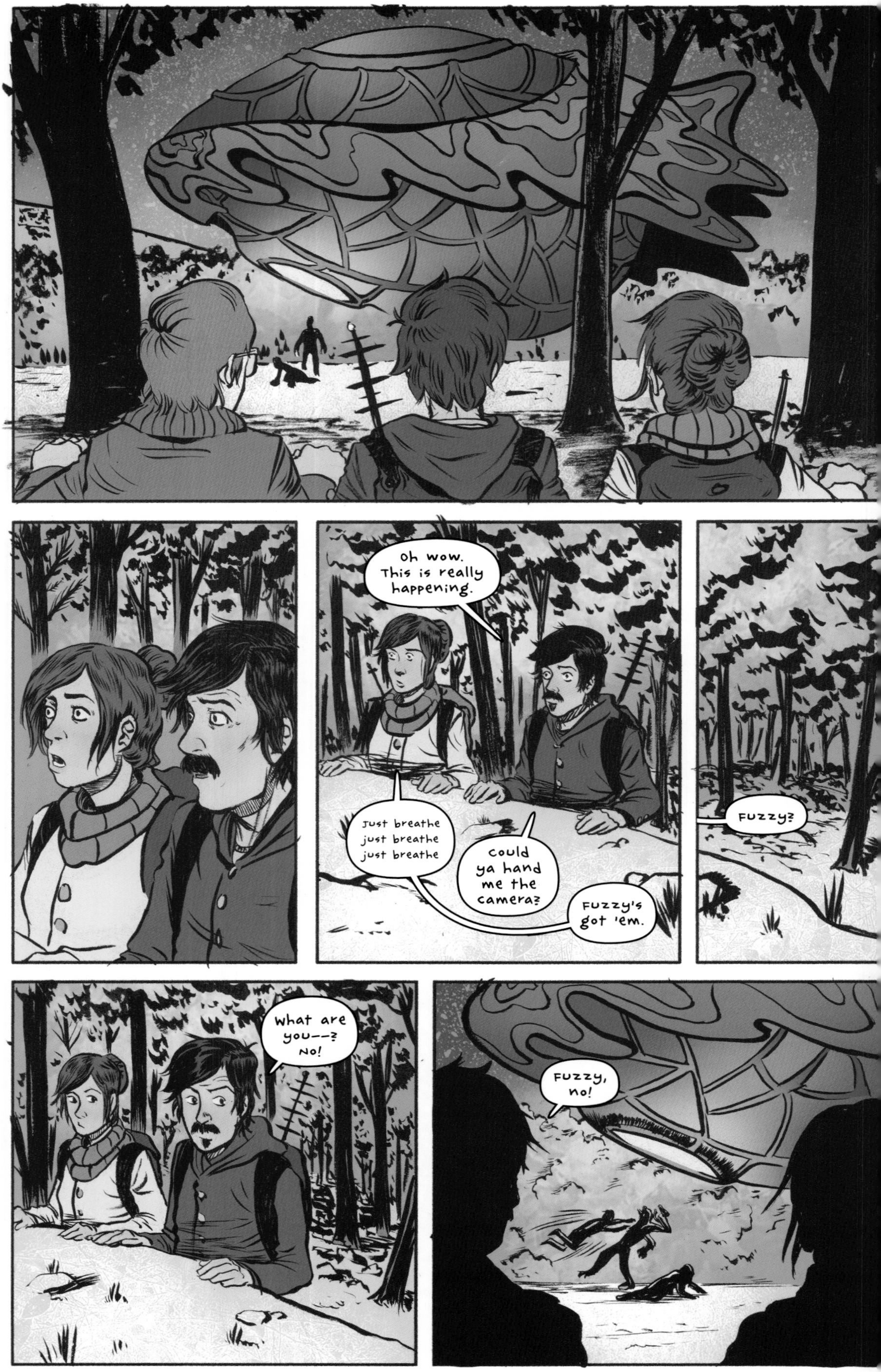
Oh wow. This is really happening.
Just breathe just breathe just breathe
Could ya hand me the camera?
Fuzzy's got 'em.
Fuzzy?
What are you--? No!
Fuzzy, no!

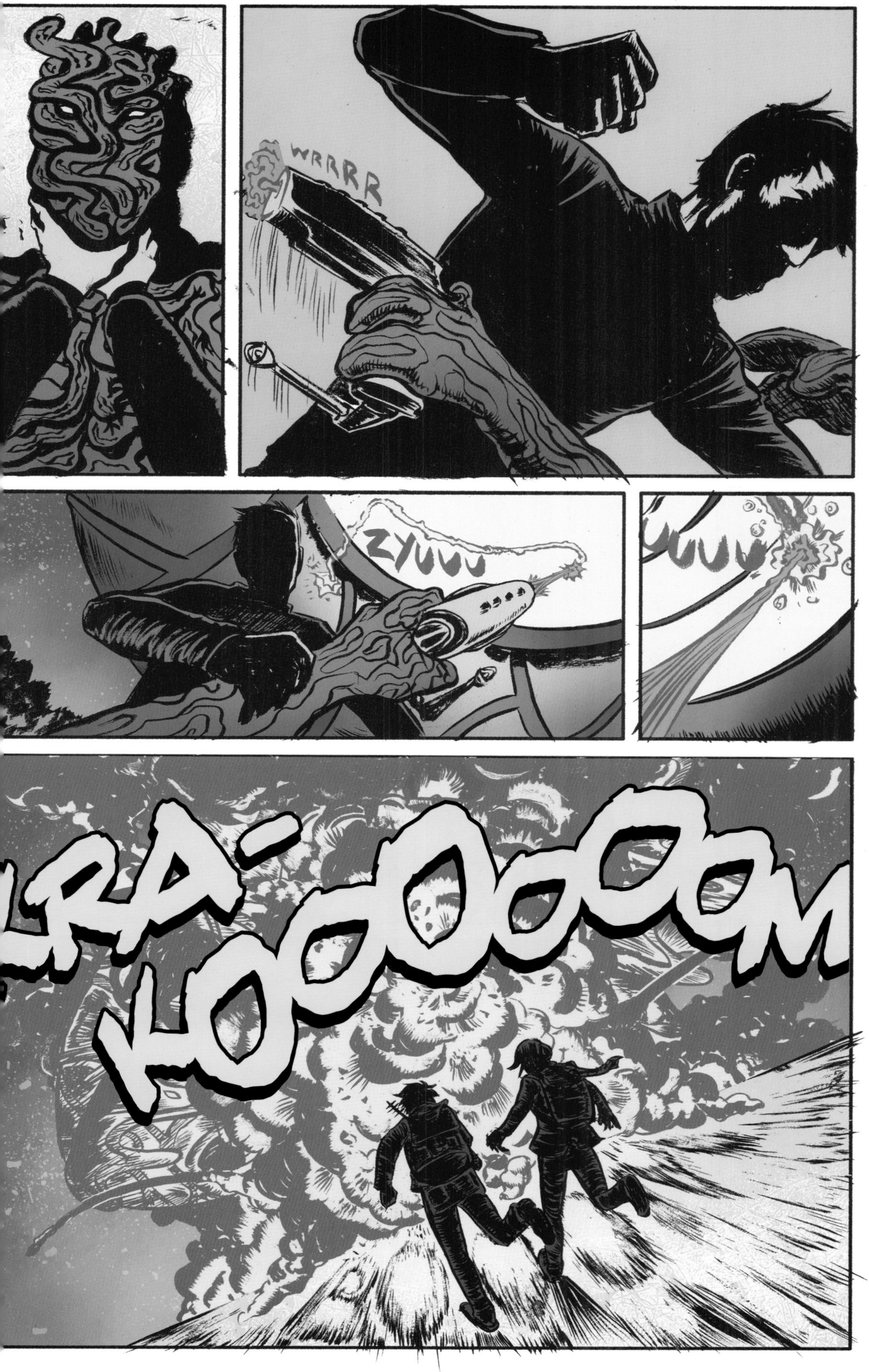
WRRRRR
ZYUUU
UUUU
RA-
KOOOOOOM

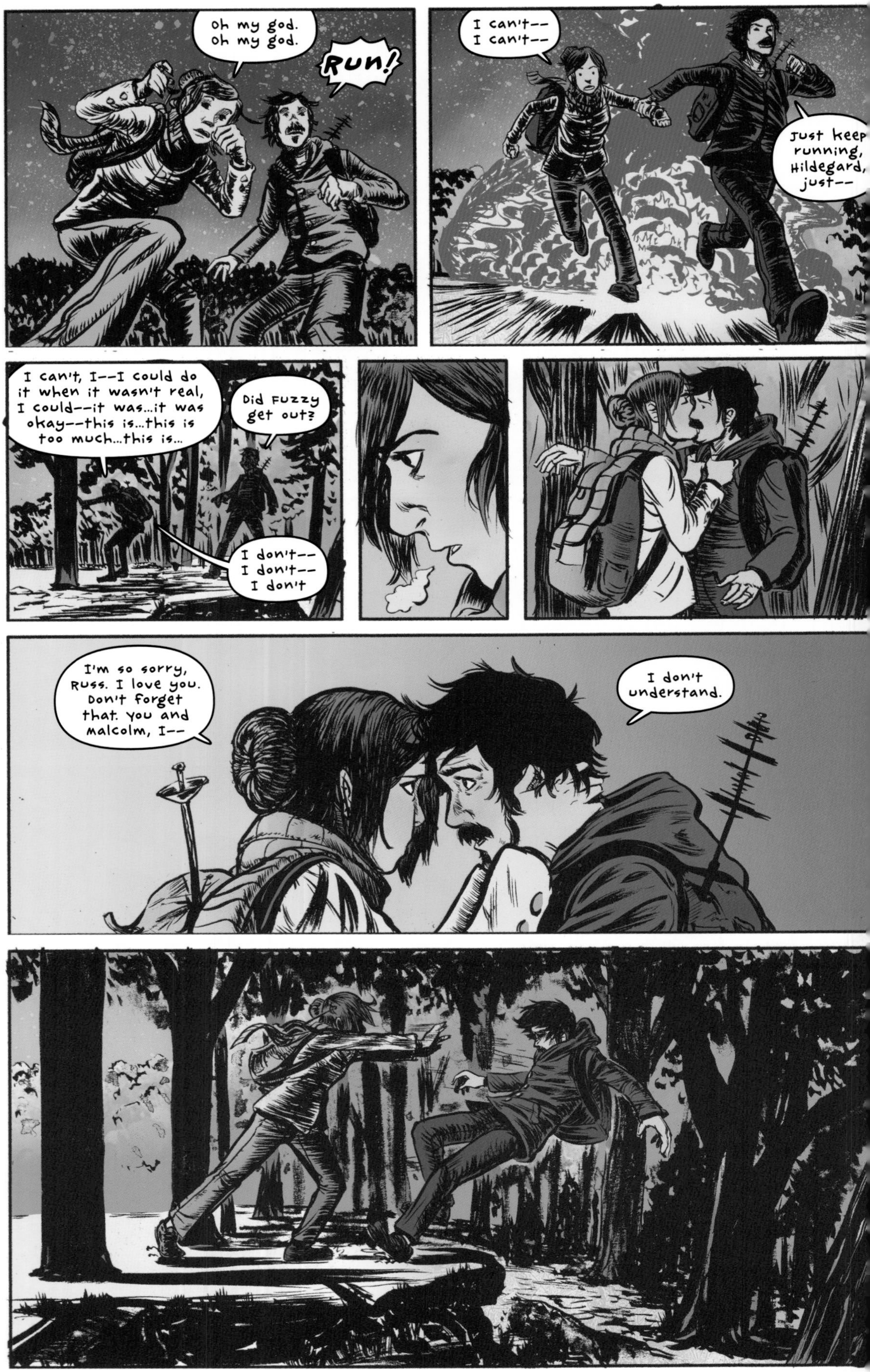
Oh my god.
Oh my god.
RUN!
I can't--
I can't--
Just keep running, Hildegard, just--
I can't, I--I could do it when it wasn't real, I could--it was...it was okay--this is...this is too much...this is...
Did Fuzzy get out?
I don't--
I don't--
I don't
I'm so sorry, Russ. I love you. Don't forget that. You and Malcolm, I--
I don't understand.

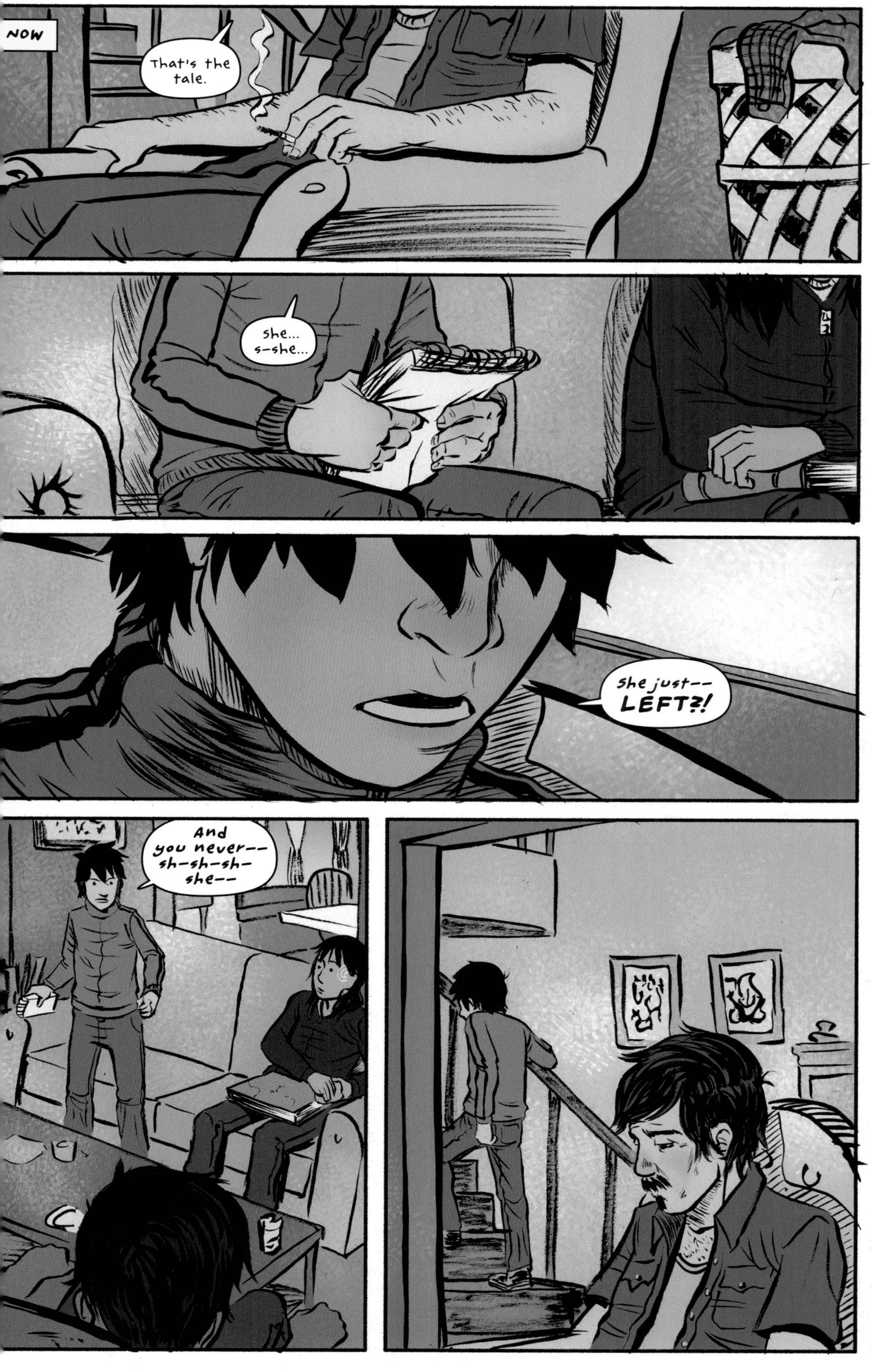
NOW
That's the tale.
She... s-she...
She just-- LEFT?!
And you never-- sh-sh-sh-she--

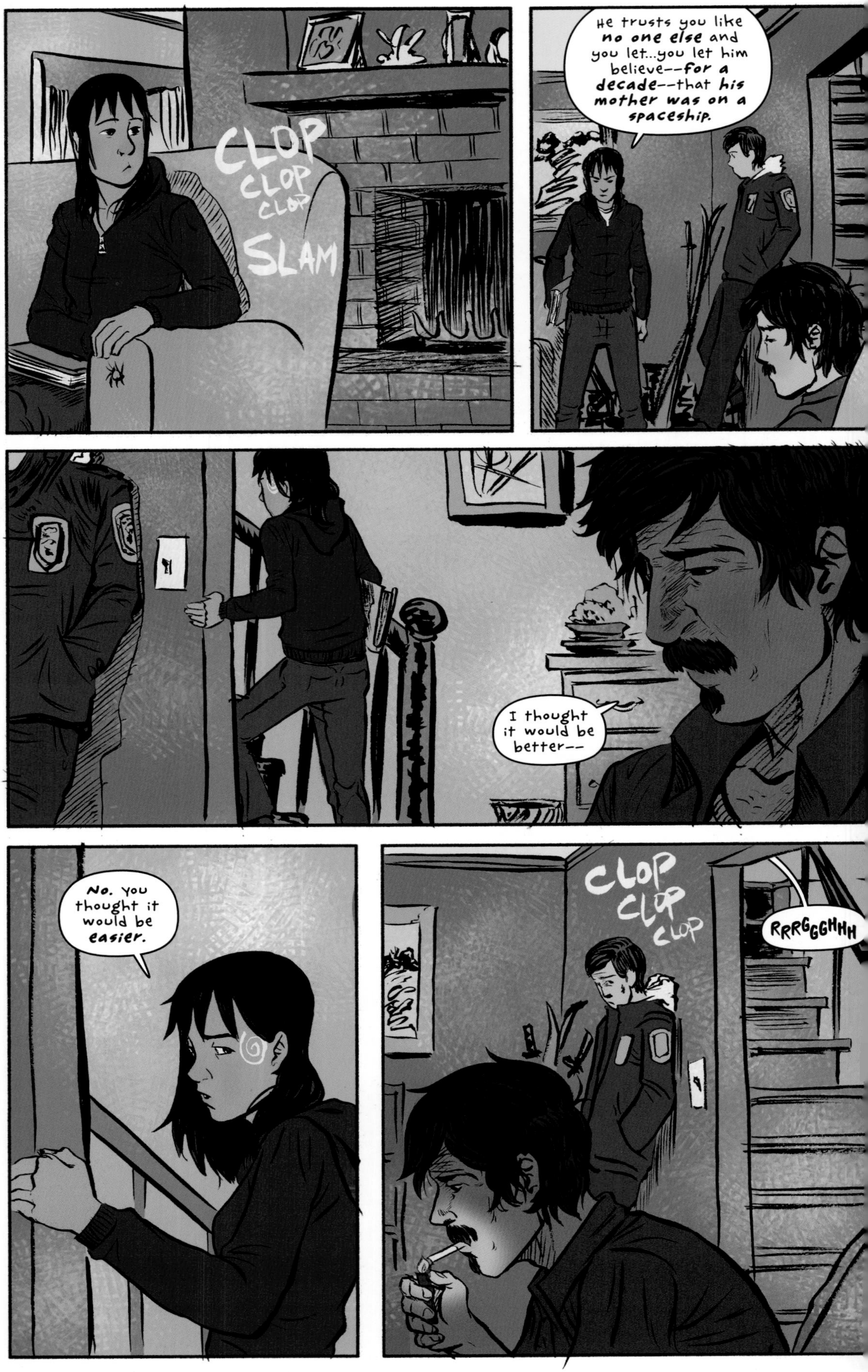
CLOP
CLOP
CLOP
SLAM
He trusts you like **no one else** and you let...you let him believe--**for a decade**--that **his mother was on a spaceship.**
I thought it would be better--
No. You thought it would be **easier.**
CLOP
CLOP
CLOP
RRRGGGHHH

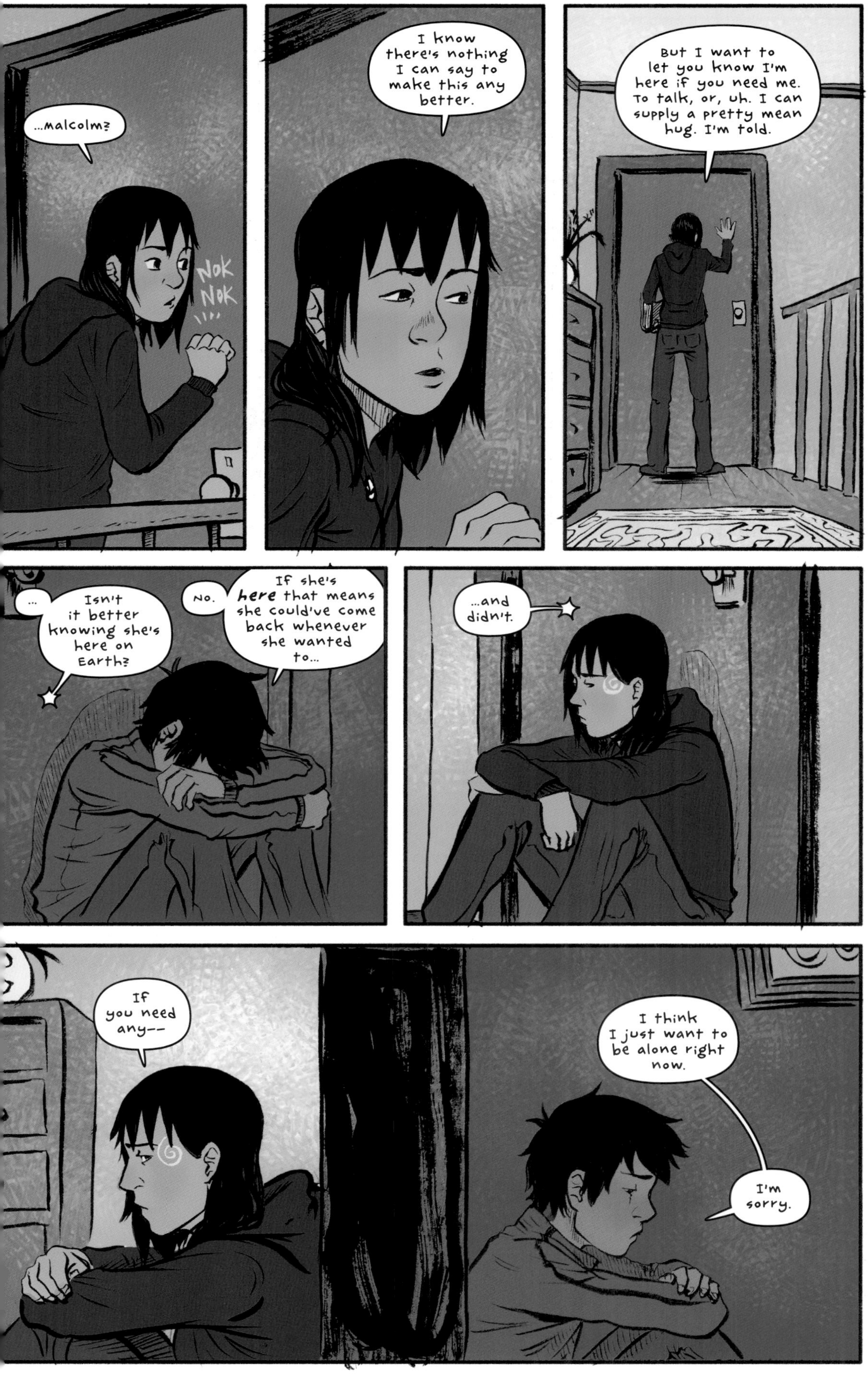
...malcolm?
NOK NOK
I know there's nothing I can say to make this any better.
But I want to let you know I'm here if you need me. To talk, or, uh. I can supply a pretty mean hug. I'm told.
...
Isn't it better knowing she's here on Earth?
No.
If she's *here* that means she could've come back whenever she wanted to...
...and didn't.
If you need any--
I think I just want to be alone right now.
I'm sorry.

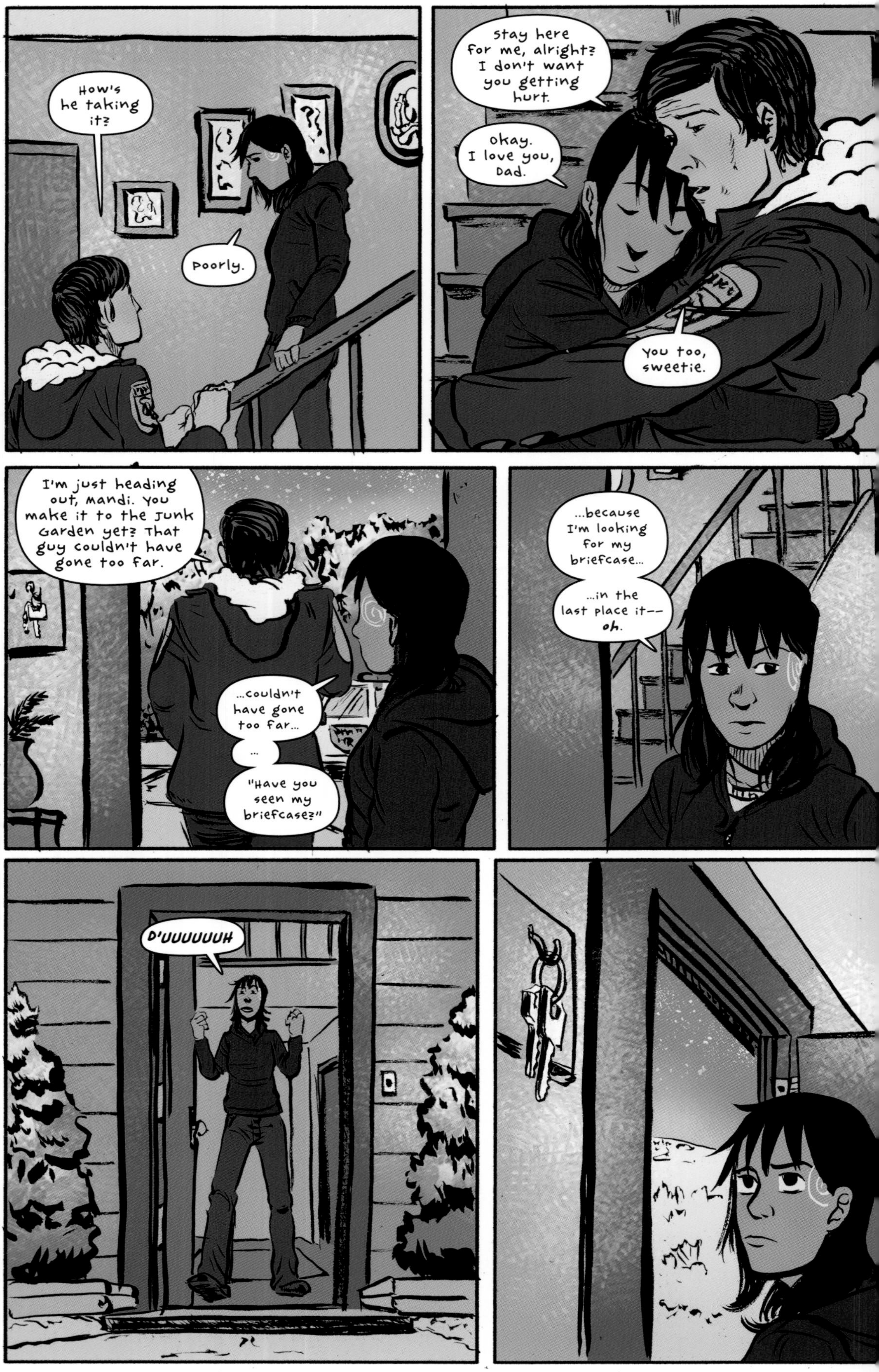
How's he taking it?
Poorly.
Stay here for me, alright? I don't want you getting hurt.
Okay. I love you, Dad.
You too, sweetie.
I'm just heading out, Mandi. You make it to the Junk Garden yet? That guy couldn't have gone too far.
...couldn't have gone too far...
...
"Have you seen my briefcase?"
...because I'm looking for my briefcase...
...in the last place it-- oh.
D'UUUUUUH

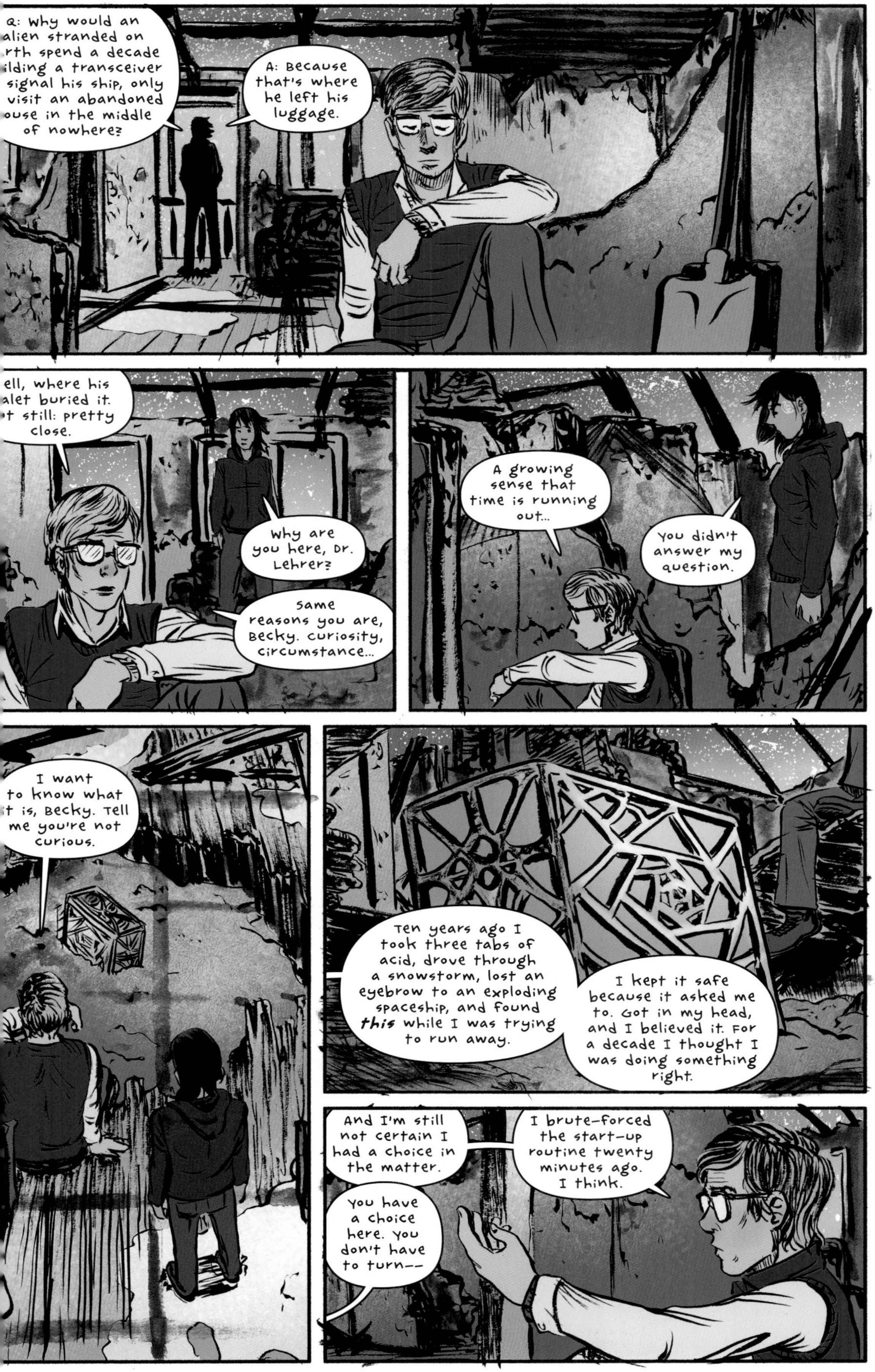
Q: Why would an alien stranded on rth spend a decade ilding a transceiver signal his ship, only visit an abandoned ouse in the middle of nowhere?
A: Because that's where he left his luggage.
ell, where his alet buried it. t still: pretty close.
Why are you here, Dr. Lehrer?
Same reasons you are, Becky. Curiosity, circumstance...
A growing sense that time is running out...
You didn't answer my question.
I want to know what t is, Becky. Tell me you're not curious.
Ten years ago I took three tabs of acid, drove through a snowstorm, lost an eyebrow to an exploding spaceship, and found *this* while I was trying to run away.
I kept it safe because it asked me to. Got in my head, and I believed it. For a decade I thought I was doing something right.
And I'm still not certain I had a choice in the matter.
I brute-forced the start-up routine twenty minutes ago. I think.
You have a choice here. You don't have to turn--

Then help me turn it off.

I won't.

But why now? Why wait?

Why not?

TSSSS

SSSS

Neat.

Anyways: why now? I waited ten years for someone to come looking for it and they're dead. And alarm bells this thing might have set off are already tripped, so why not? The spooks are already on their way.

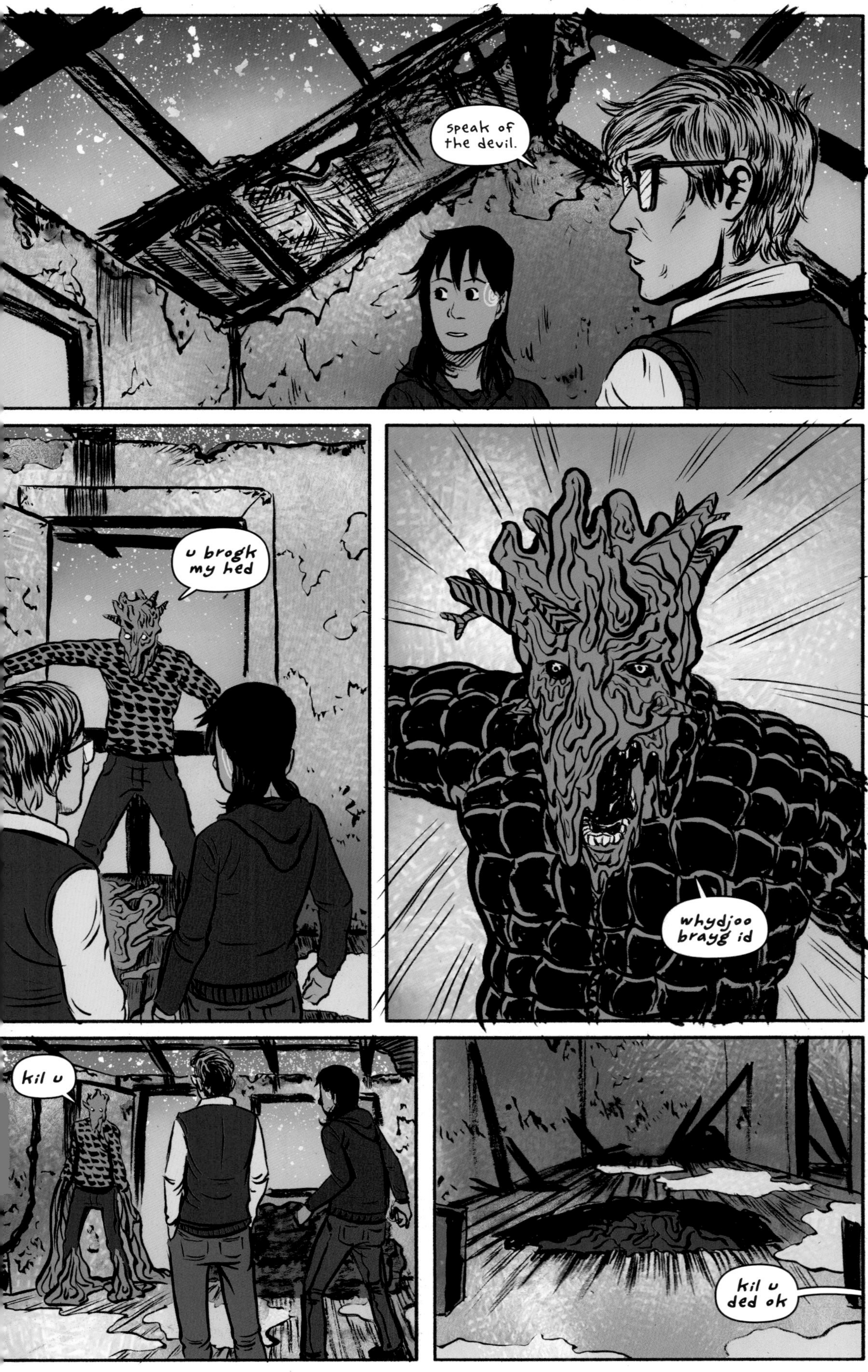
speak of the devil.
u brogk my hed
whydjoo brayg id
kil u
kil u ded ok

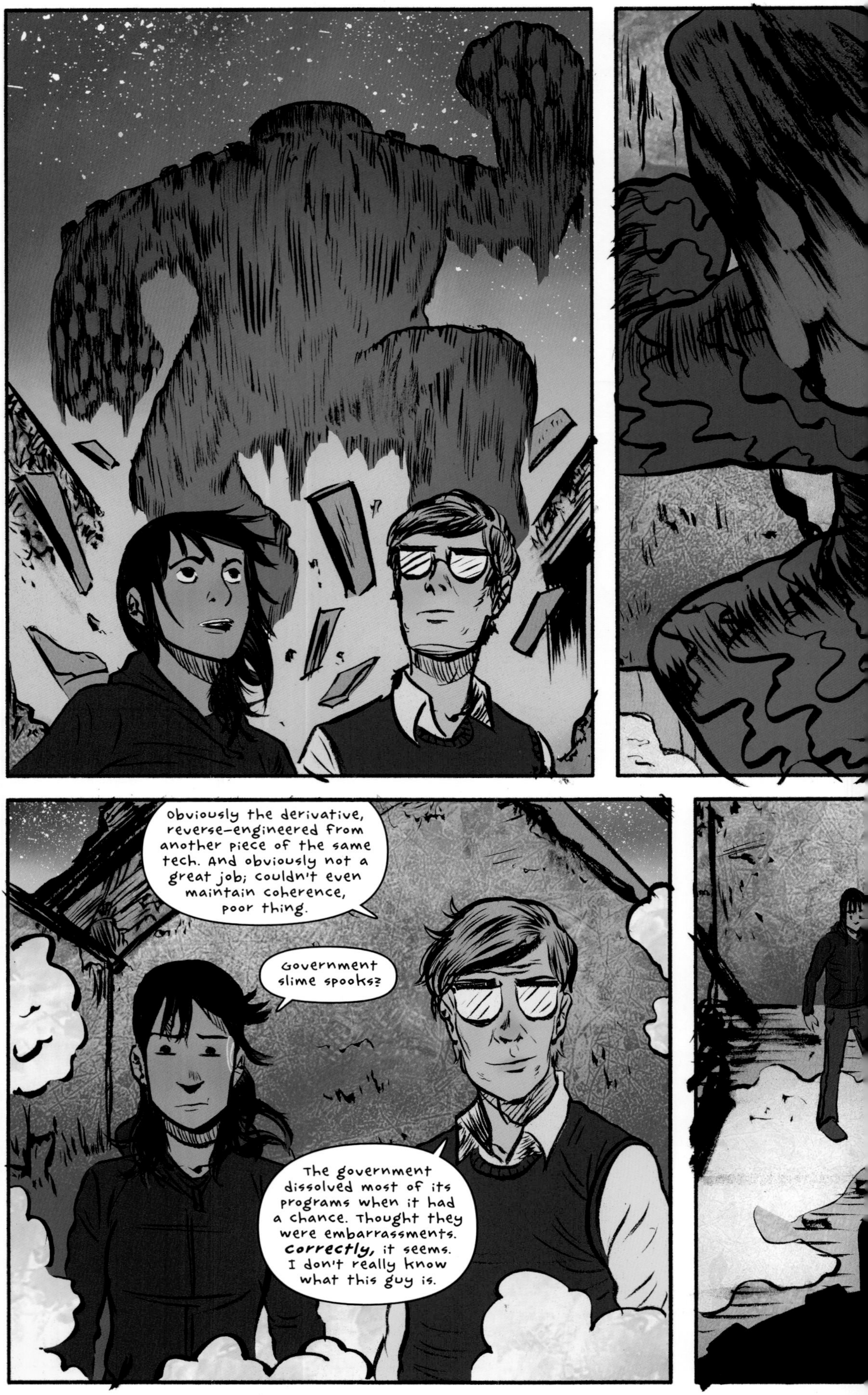

Obviously the derivative, reverse-engineered from another piece of the same tech. And obviously not a great job; couldn't even maintain coherence, poor thing.
Government slime spooks?
The government dissolved most of its programs when it had a chance. Thought they were embarrassments. *Correctly,* it seems. I don't really know what this guy is.

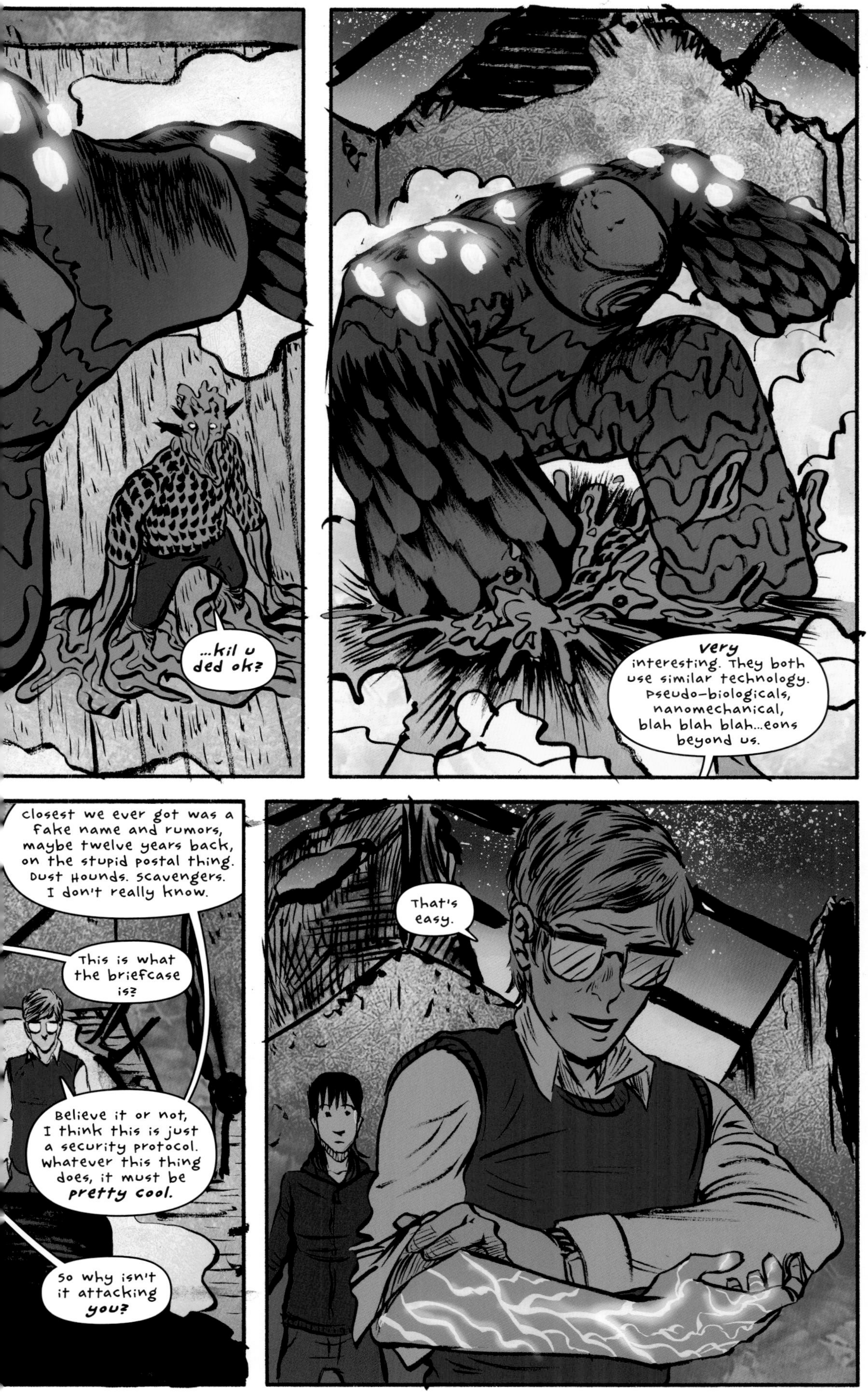
...kil u ded ok?
very interesting. They both use similar technology. Pseudo-biologicals, nanomechanical, blah blah blah...eons beyond us.
closest we ever got was a fake name and rumors, maybe twelve years back, on the stupid postal thing. Dust Hounds. Scavengers. I don't really know.
This is what the briefcase is?
Believe it or not, I think this is just a security protocol. Whatever this thing does, it must be pretty cool.
So why isn't it attacking you?
That's easy.

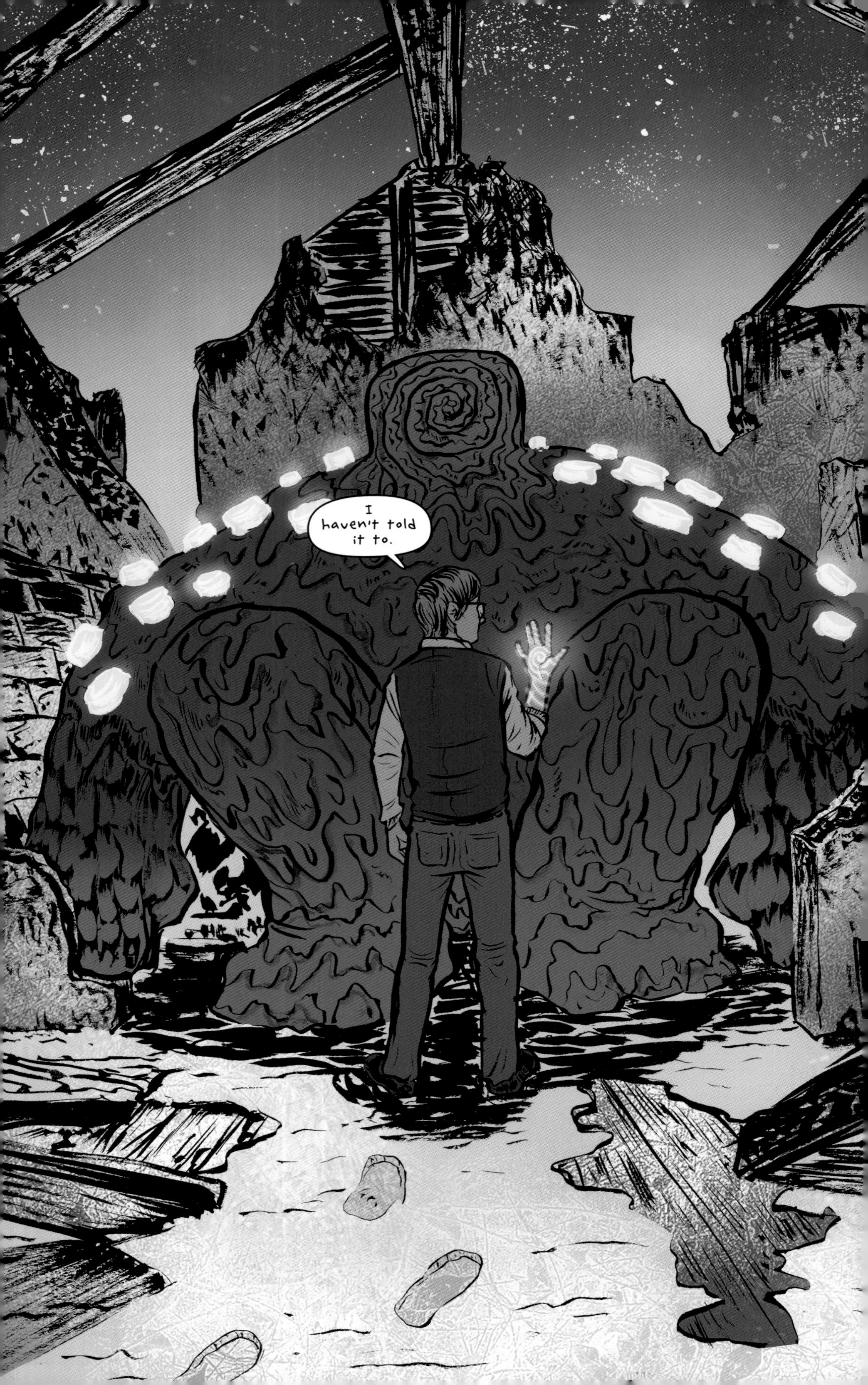
I haven't told it to.

s·i·x

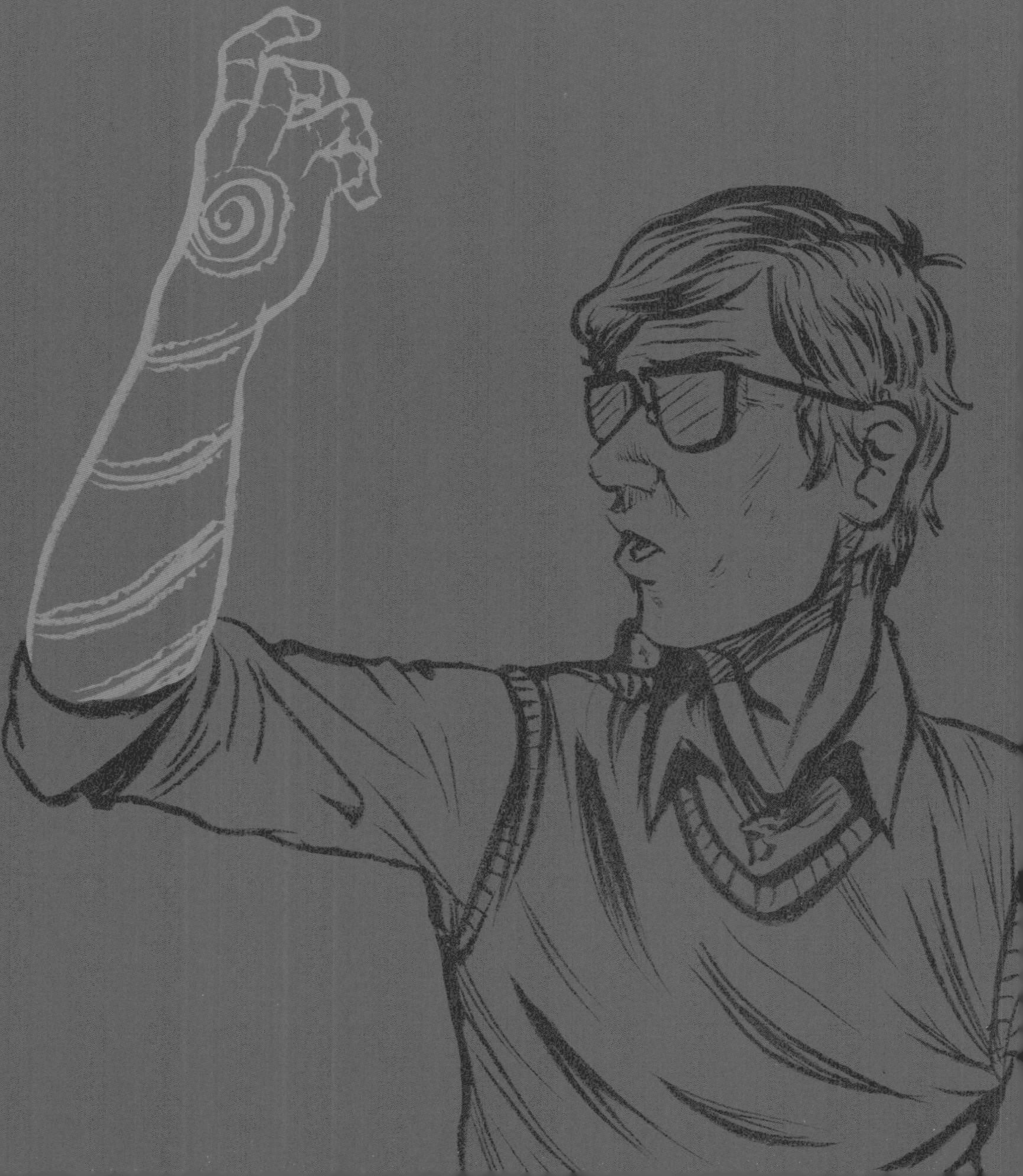

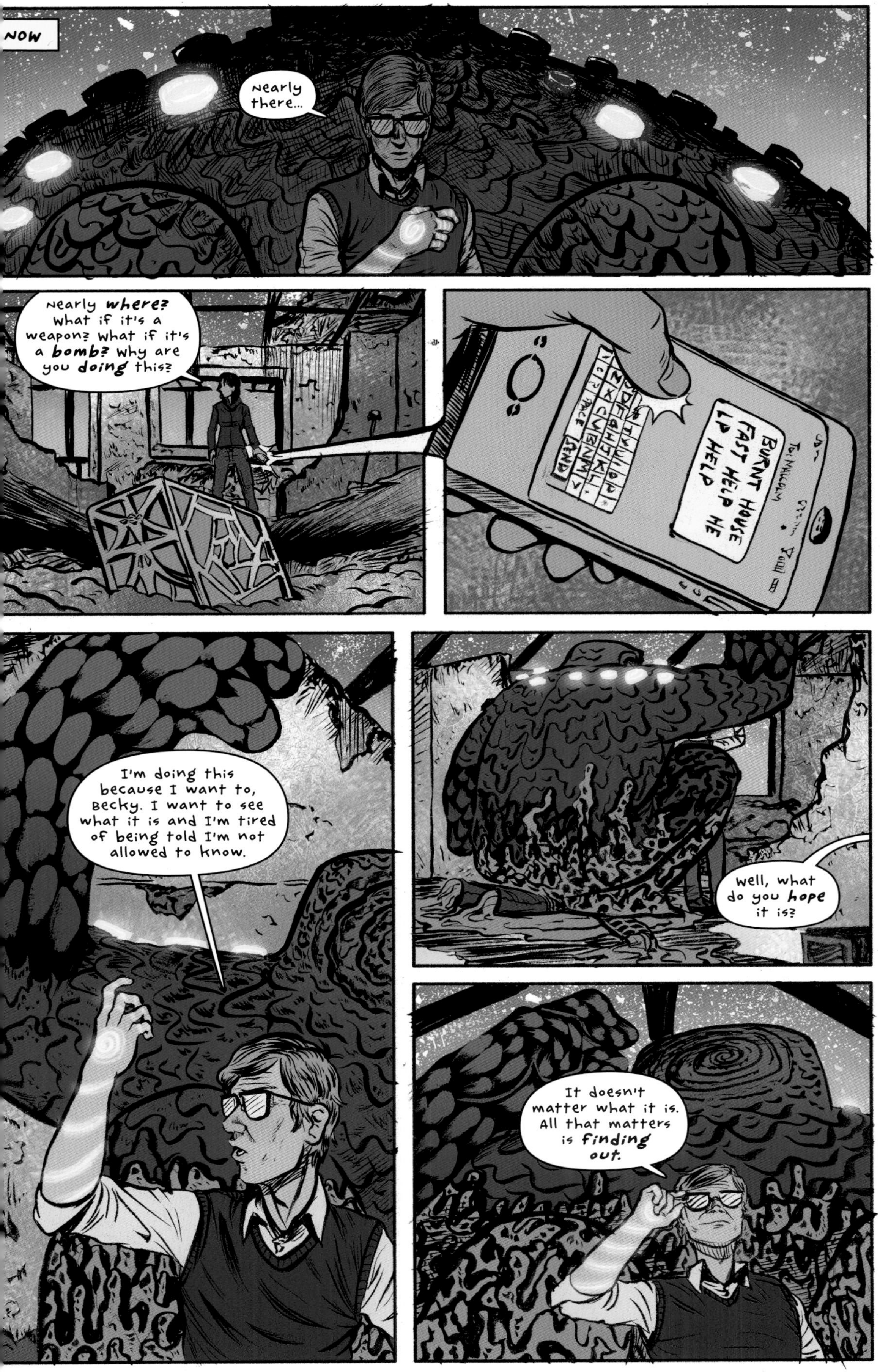
NOW
Nearly there...
Nearly **where?** What if it's a weapon? What if it's a **bomb?** Why are you **doing** this?
BURNT HOUSE FAST HELP ME LP HELP
I'm doing this because I want to, Becky. I want to see what it is and I'm tired of being told I'm not allowed to know.
Well, what do you **hope** it is?
It doesn't matter what it is. All that matters is **finding out.**

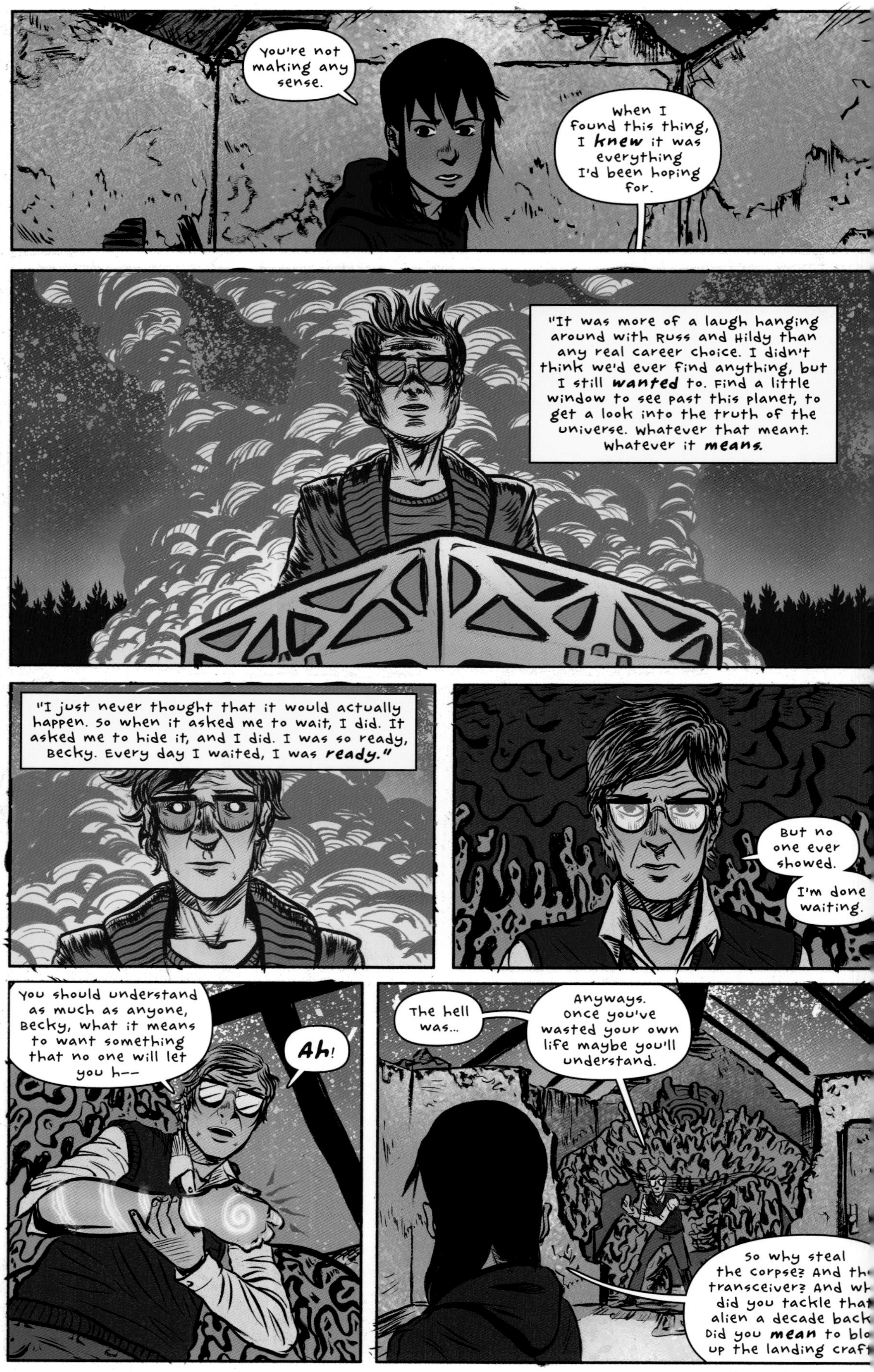
You're not making any sense.
When I found this thing, I **knew** it was everything I'd been hoping for.
"It was more of a laugh hanging around with Russ and Hildy than any real career choice. I didn't think we'd ever find anything, but I still **wanted** to. Find a little window to see past this planet, to get a look into the truth of the universe. Whatever that meant. Whatever it **means**.
"I just never thought that it would actually happen. So when it asked me to wait, I did. It asked me to hide it, and I did. I was so ready, Becky. Every day I waited, I was **ready**."
But no one ever showed.
I'm done waiting.
You should understand as much as anyone, Becky, what it means to want something that no one will let you h--
Ah!
The hell was...
Anyways. Once you've wasted your own life maybe you'll understand.
So why steal the corpse? And the transceiver? And wh did you tackle that alien a decade back Did you **mean** to blo up the landing craft

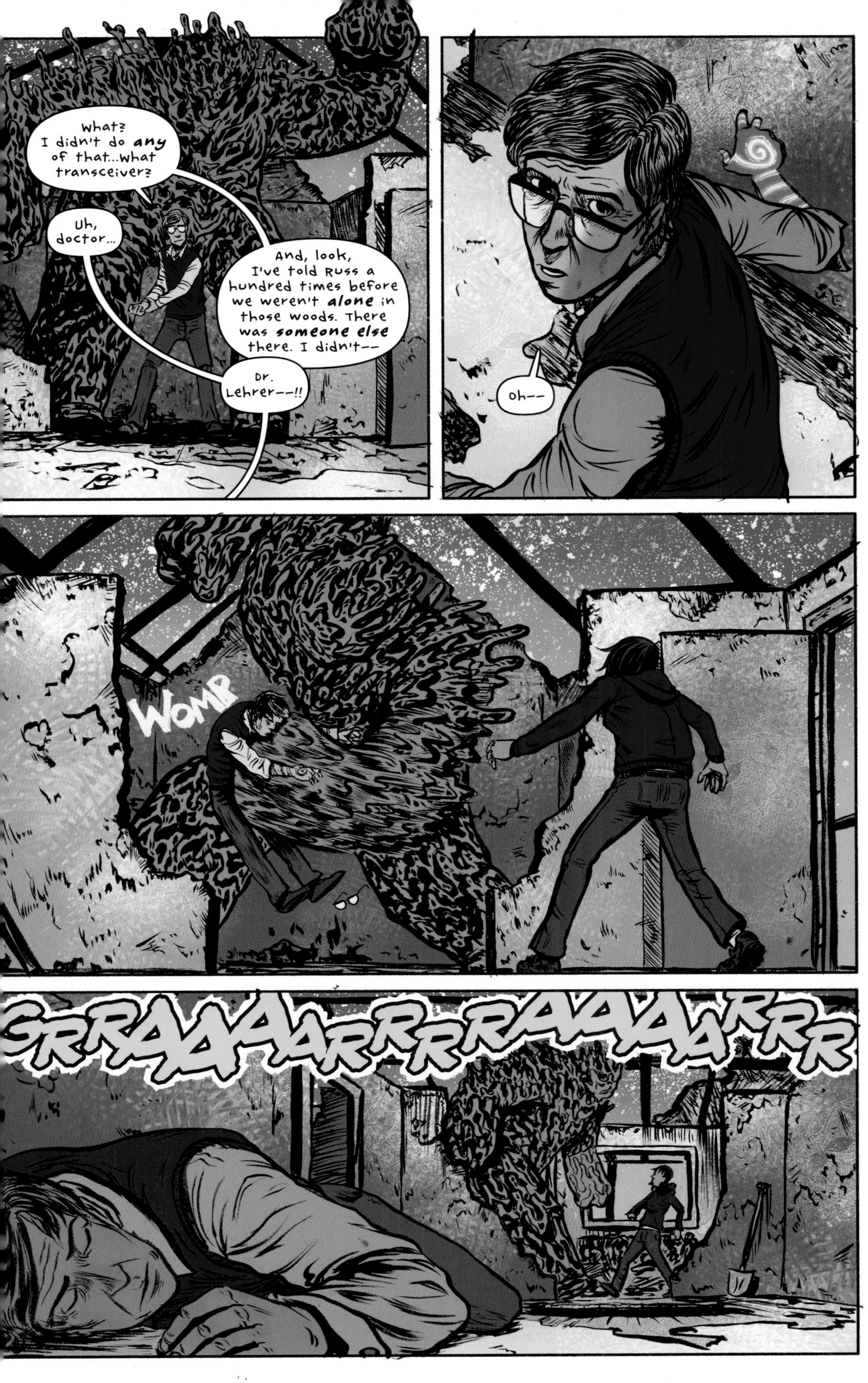
What?
I didn't do **any** of that...what transceiver?
Uh, doctor...
And, look, I've told Russ a hundred times before we weren't **alone** in those woods. There was **someone else** there. I didn't--
Dr. Lehrer--!!
Oh--
WOMP
GRRAAAARRRRAAAAARRR

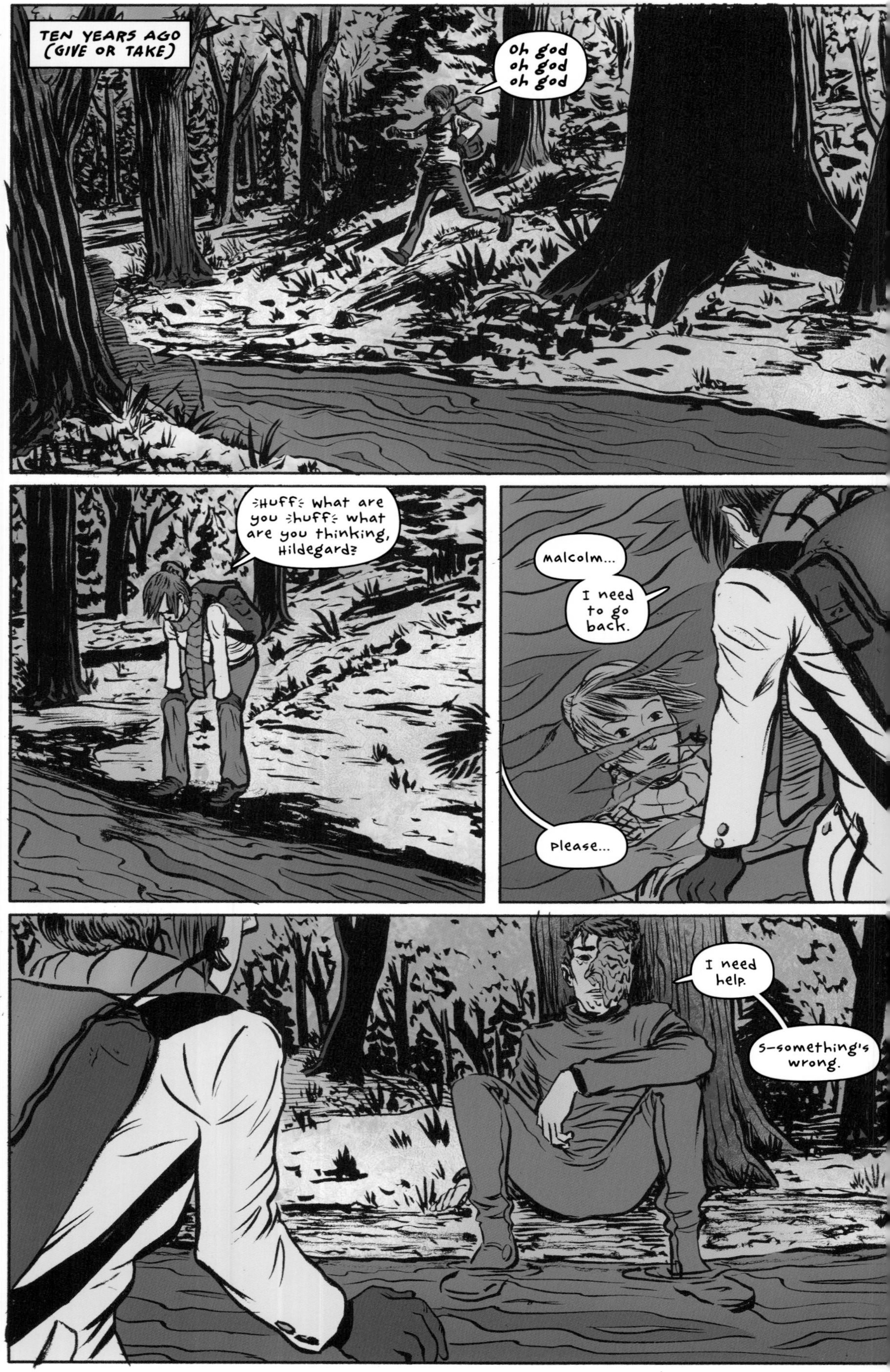
TEN YEARS AGO (GIVE OR TAKE)
Oh god oh god oh god
⸗HUFF⸗ What are you ⸗HUFF⸗ what are you thinking, Hildegard?
Malcolm...
I need to go back.
Please...
I need help.
S-something's wrong.

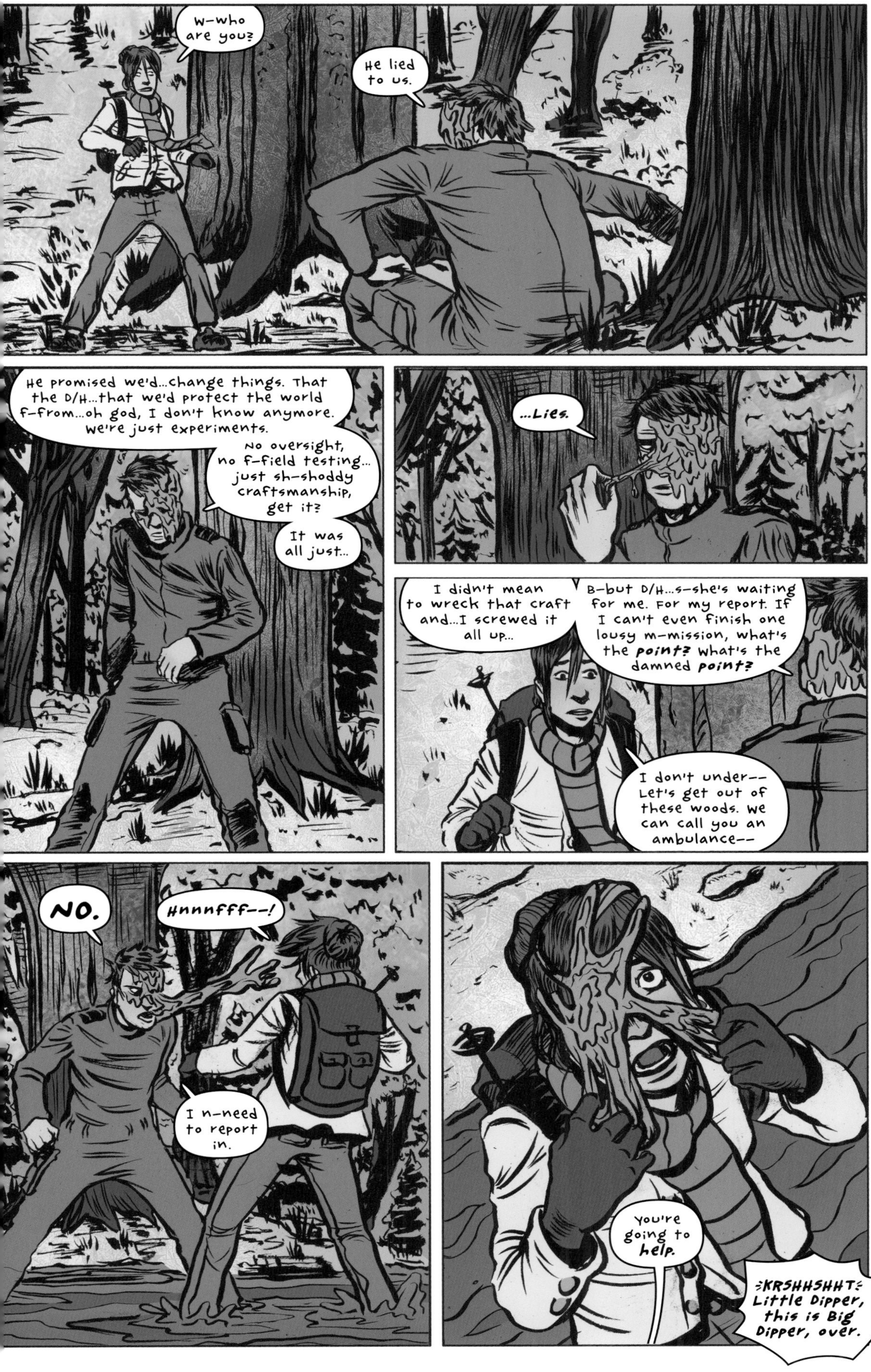
W-who are you?
He lied to us.
He promised we'd...change things. That the D/H...that we'd protect the world f-from...oh god, I don't know anymore. We're just experiments.
No oversight, no f-field testing... just sh-shoddy craftsmanship, get it?
It was all just...
...Lies.
I didn't mean to wreck that craft and...I screwed it all up...
B-but D/H...s-she's waiting for me. For my report. If I can't even finish one lousy m-mission, what's the point? What's the damned point?
I don't under-- Let's get out of these woods. We can call you an ambulance--
NO.
Hnnnfff--!
I n-need to report in.
You're going to help.
=KRSHHSHHT= Little Dipper, this is Big Dipper, over.

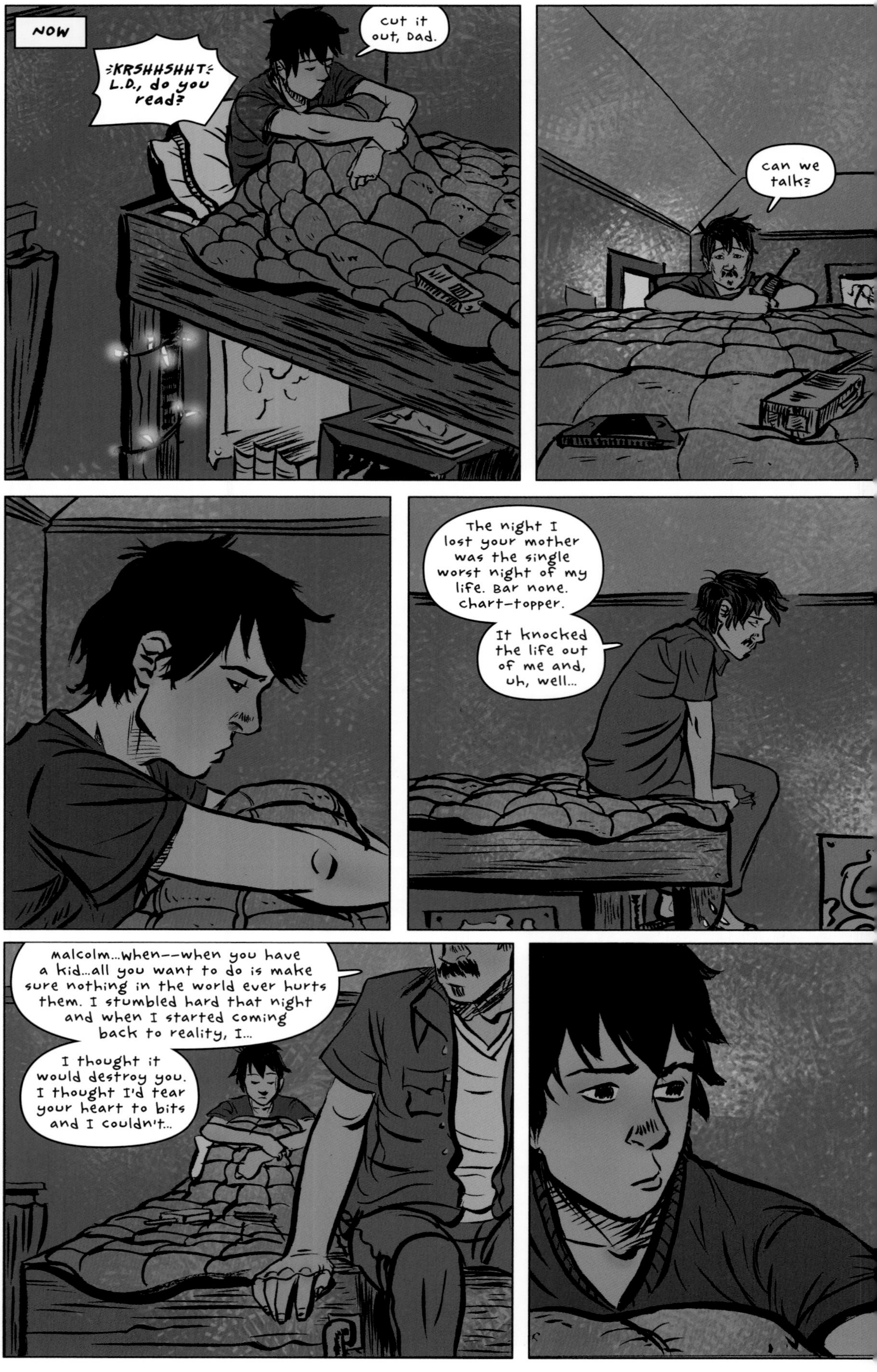
NOW
KRSHHSHHT L.D., do you read?
cut it out, Dad.
can we talk?
The night I lost your mother was the single worst night of my life. Bar none. chart-topper.
It knocked the life out of me and, uh, well...
malcolm...when--when you have a kid...all you want to do is make sure nothing in the world ever hurts them. I stumbled hard that night and when I started coming back to reality, I...
I thought it would destroy you. I thought I'd tear your heart to bits and I couldn't...

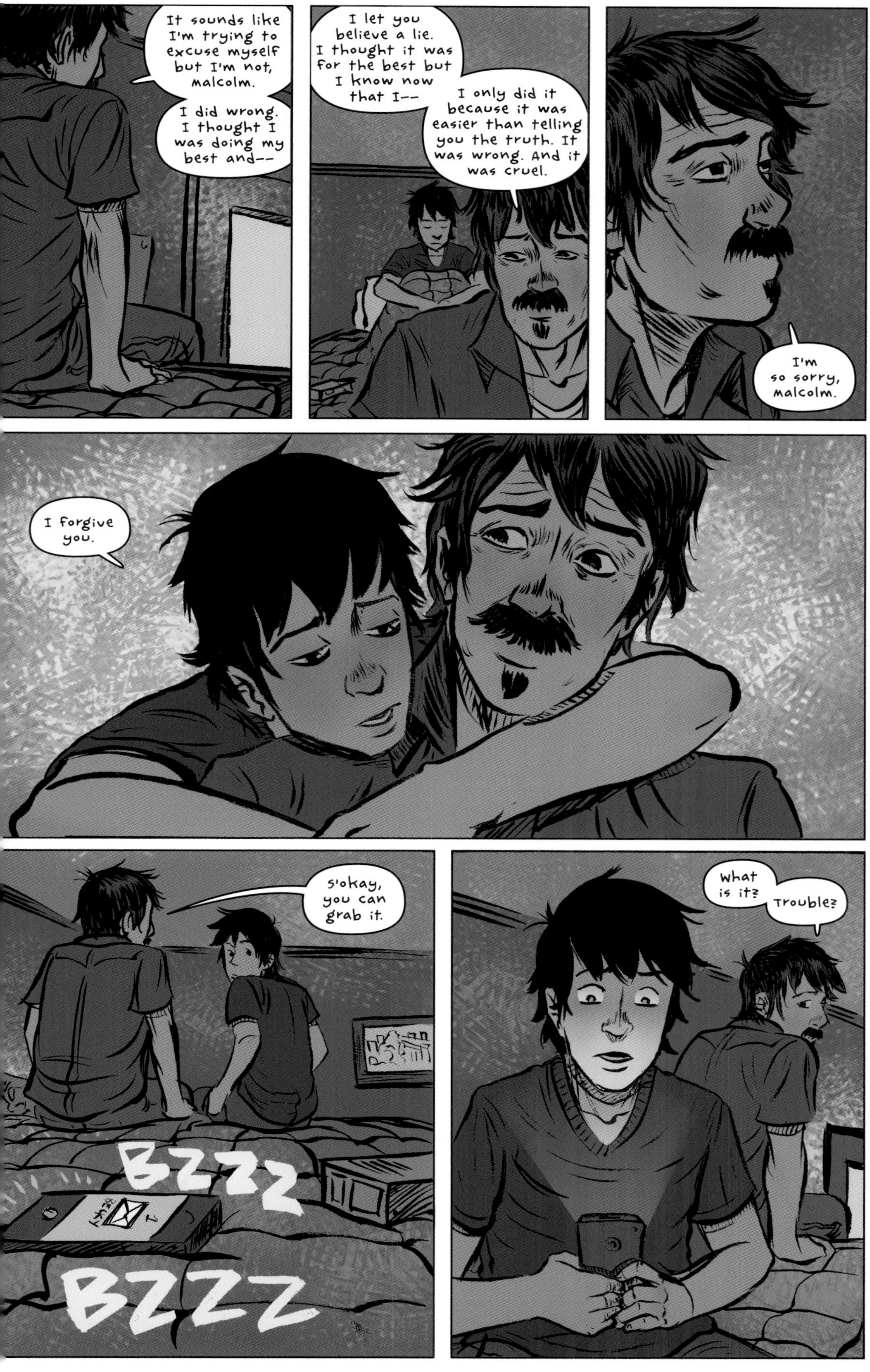
It sounds like I'm trying to excuse myself but I'm not, malcolm.
I did wrong. I thought I was doing my best and--
I let you believe a lie. I thought it was for the best but I know now that I--
I only did it because it was easier than telling you the truth. It was wrong. And it was cruel.
I'm so sorry, malcolm.
I forgive you.
s'okay, you can grab it.
BZZZ
BZZZ
What is it?
Trouble?

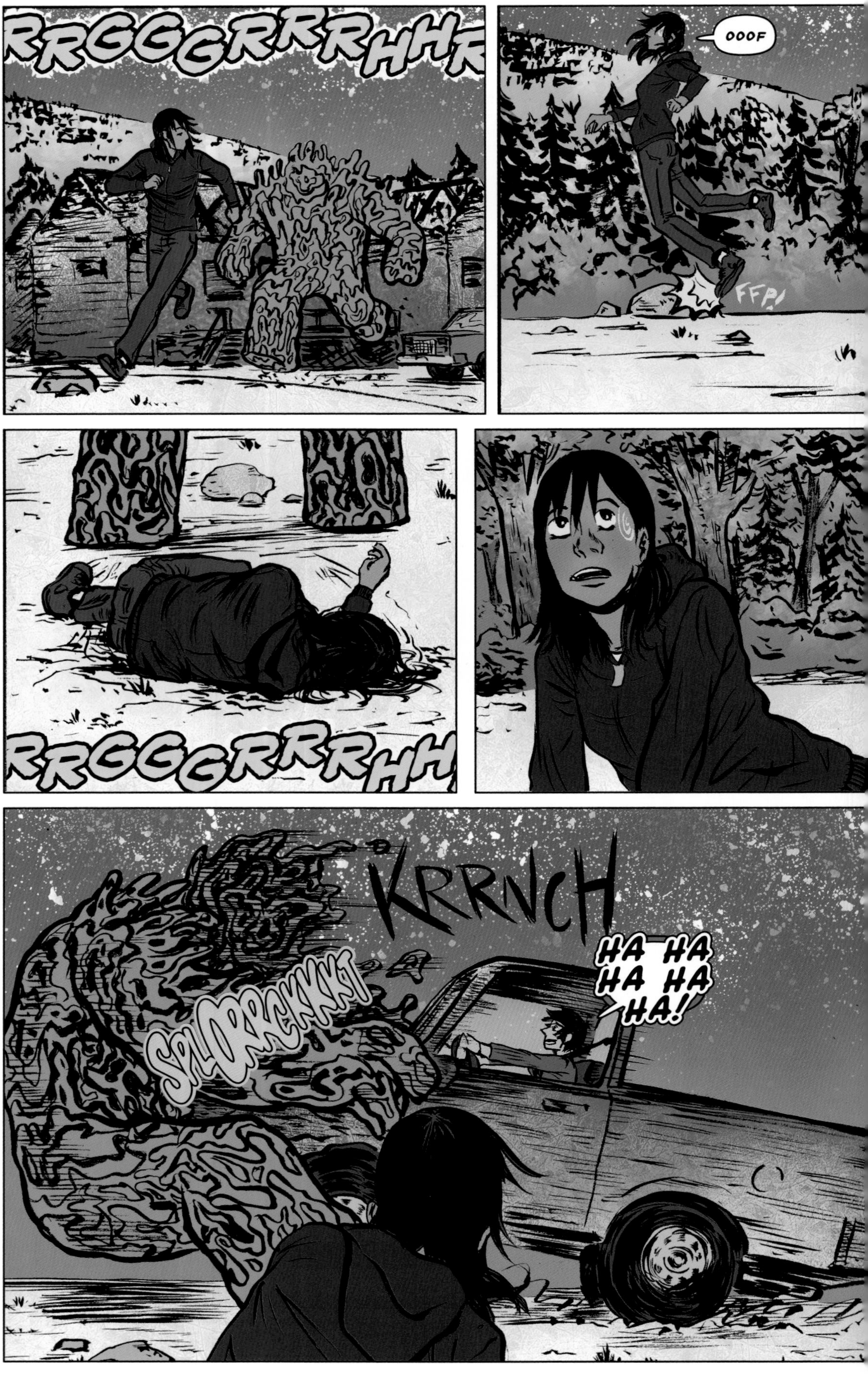
RRGGGRRRRHHR
OOOF
FFP!
RRGGGRRRRHH
KRRNCH
SPLORRCKKKT
HA HA HA HA HA!

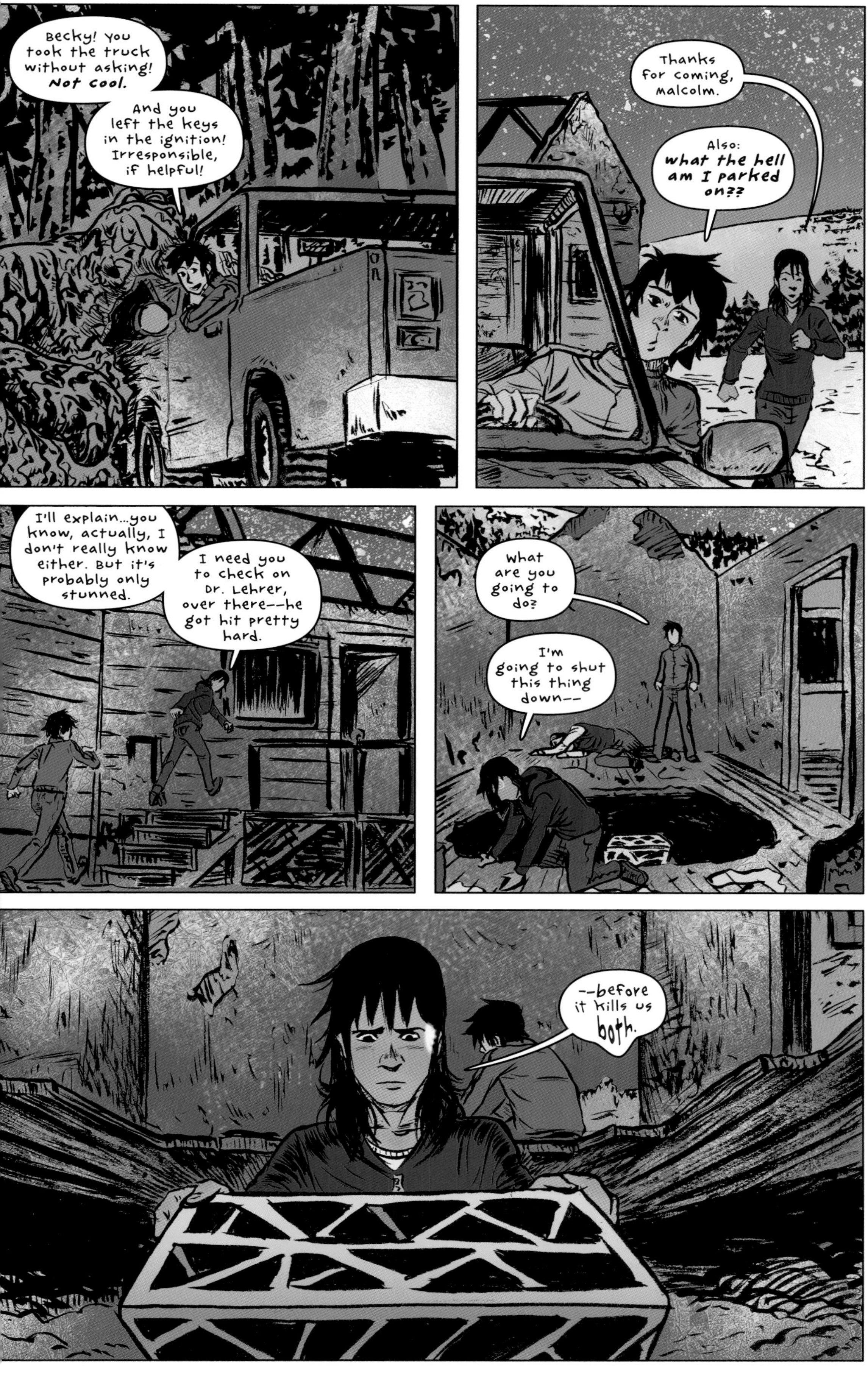
Becky! You took the truck without asking! **Not cool.**
And you left the keys in the ignition! Irresponsible, if helpful!
Thanks for coming, Malcolm.
Also: **what the hell am I parked on??**
I'll explain...you know, actually, I don't really know either. But it's probably only stunned.
I need you to check on Dr. Lehrer, over there--he got hit pretty hard.
What are you going to do?
I'm going to shut this thing down--
--before it kills us both.

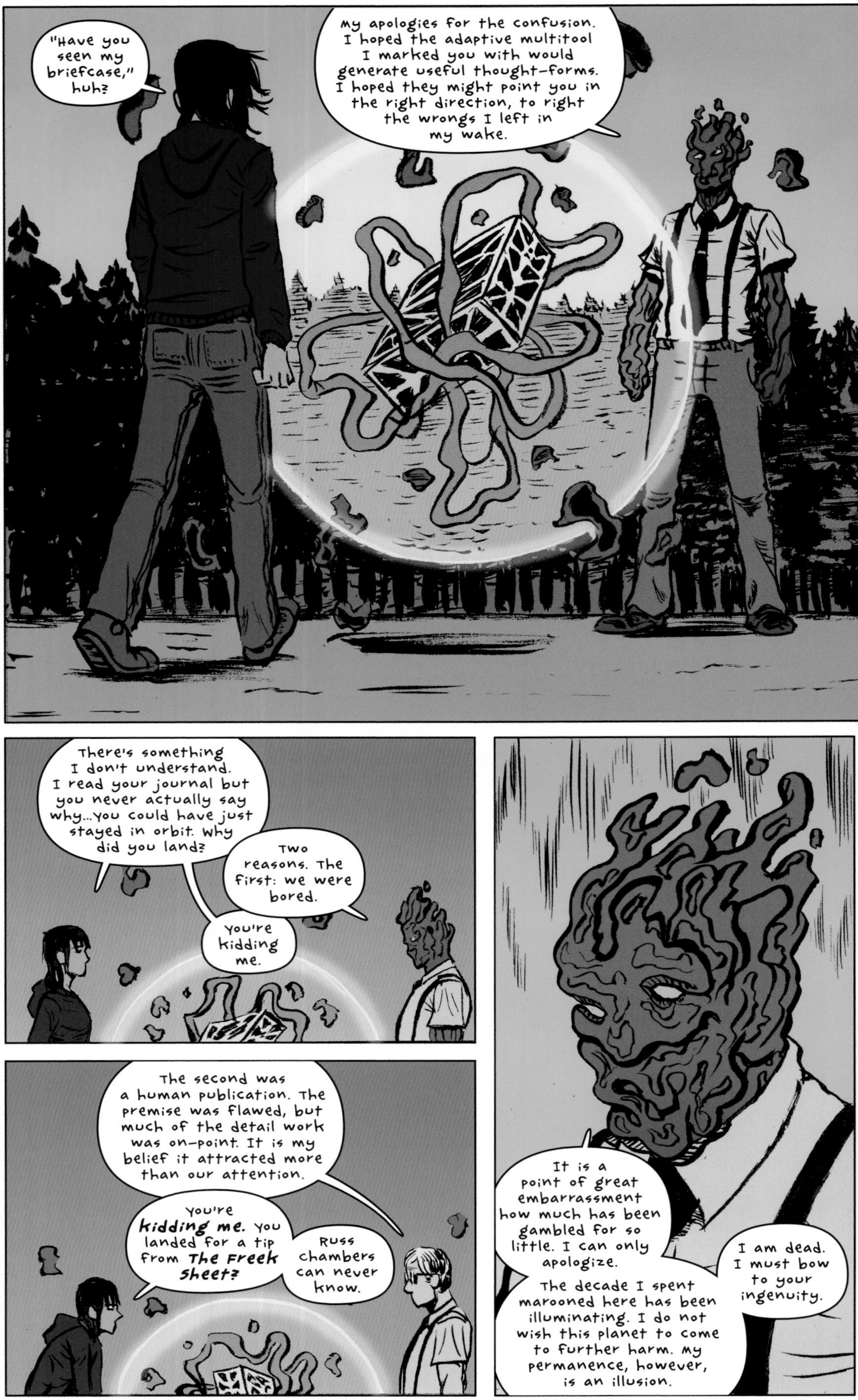
"Have you seen my briefcase," huh?
My apologies for the confusion. I hoped the adaptive multitool I marked you with would generate useful thought-forms. I hoped they might point you in the right direction, to right the wrongs I left in my wake.
There's something I don't understand. I read your journal but you never actually say why...you could have just stayed in orbit. Why did you land?
Two reasons. The first: we were bored.
You're kidding me.
The second was a human publication. The premise was flawed, but much of the detail work was on-point. It is my belief it attracted more than our attention.
You're kidding me. You landed for a tip from The Freek Sheet?
Russ Chambers can never know.
It is a point of great embarrassment how much has been gambled for so little. I can only apologize.
The decade I spent marooned here has been illuminating. I do not wish this planet to come to further harm. My permanence, however, is an illusion.
I am dead. I must bow to your ingenuity.

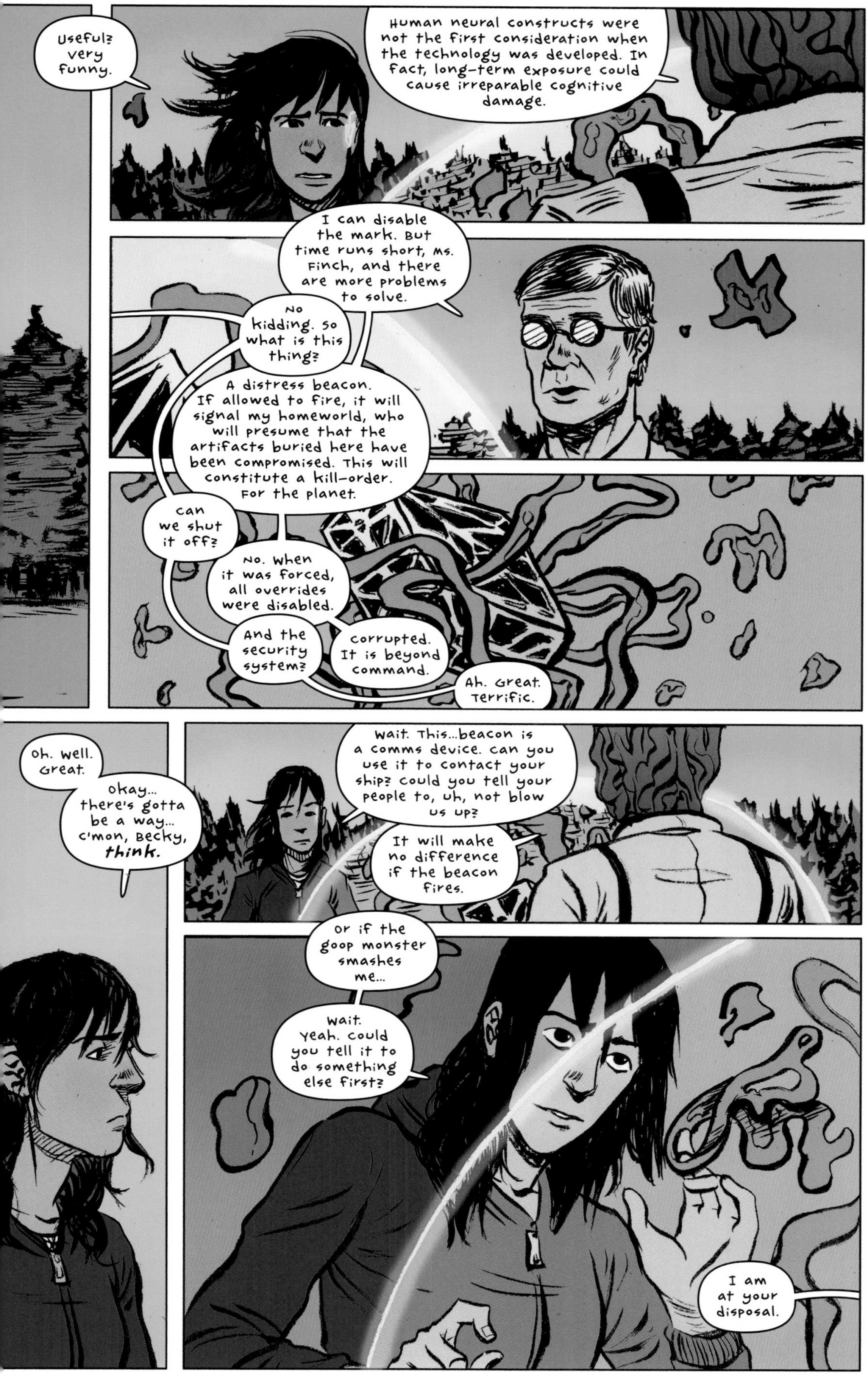
Useful? very funny.
Human neural constructs were not the first consideration when the technology was developed. In fact, long-term exposure could cause irreparable cognitive damage.
I can disable the mark. But time runs short, Ms. Finch, and there are more problems to solve.
No kidding. So what is this thing?
A distress beacon. If allowed to fire, it will signal my homeworld, who will presume that the artifacts buried here have been compromised. This will constitute a kill-order. For the planet.
Can we shut it off?
No. When it was forced, all overrides were disabled.
And the security system?
Corrupted. It is beyond command.
Ah. Great. Terrific.
Oh. Well. Great.
Okay... there's gotta be a way... c'mon, Becky, *think.*
Wait. This...beacon is a comms device. Can you use it to contact your ship? Could you tell your people to, uh, not blow us up?
It will make no difference if the beacon fires.
Or if the goop monster smashes me...
Wait. Yeah. Could you tell it to do something else first?
I am at your disposal.

C'mon, Uncle Fuzzy, wake up.

Hey, cut that out. I could have a spine injury.

Do youз

No, but--

OOF. Now, maybe. We don't have a lot of time. I need you to tell Becky that I'm sorry.

Tell her yourself, we're going to--

There's no time. I've burnt my bridges here. Your father and I...we tried. We wanted to change the world, uncover the truth, but we couldn't handle it.

I couldn't handle it. We *failed*.

I want you to have--where is it--I want you to have this.

Uncle Fuzzy...

I have to go. We thought Dust Hounds was just some kind of dead-end joke, but--I have some leads to follow up on.

THRRRRRRRRRRRRM

THRRRRRRRRRRRRMMMM

Here. This opens the basement in my house. You wanna grab the lockboxes.

They've got notes, samples and--look. Use it, or destroy it, but whatever you d be good, Malcolm. Don' lose your way.

THRRRRRRRR....RM

I don't understand--

whoa, what is *that?*

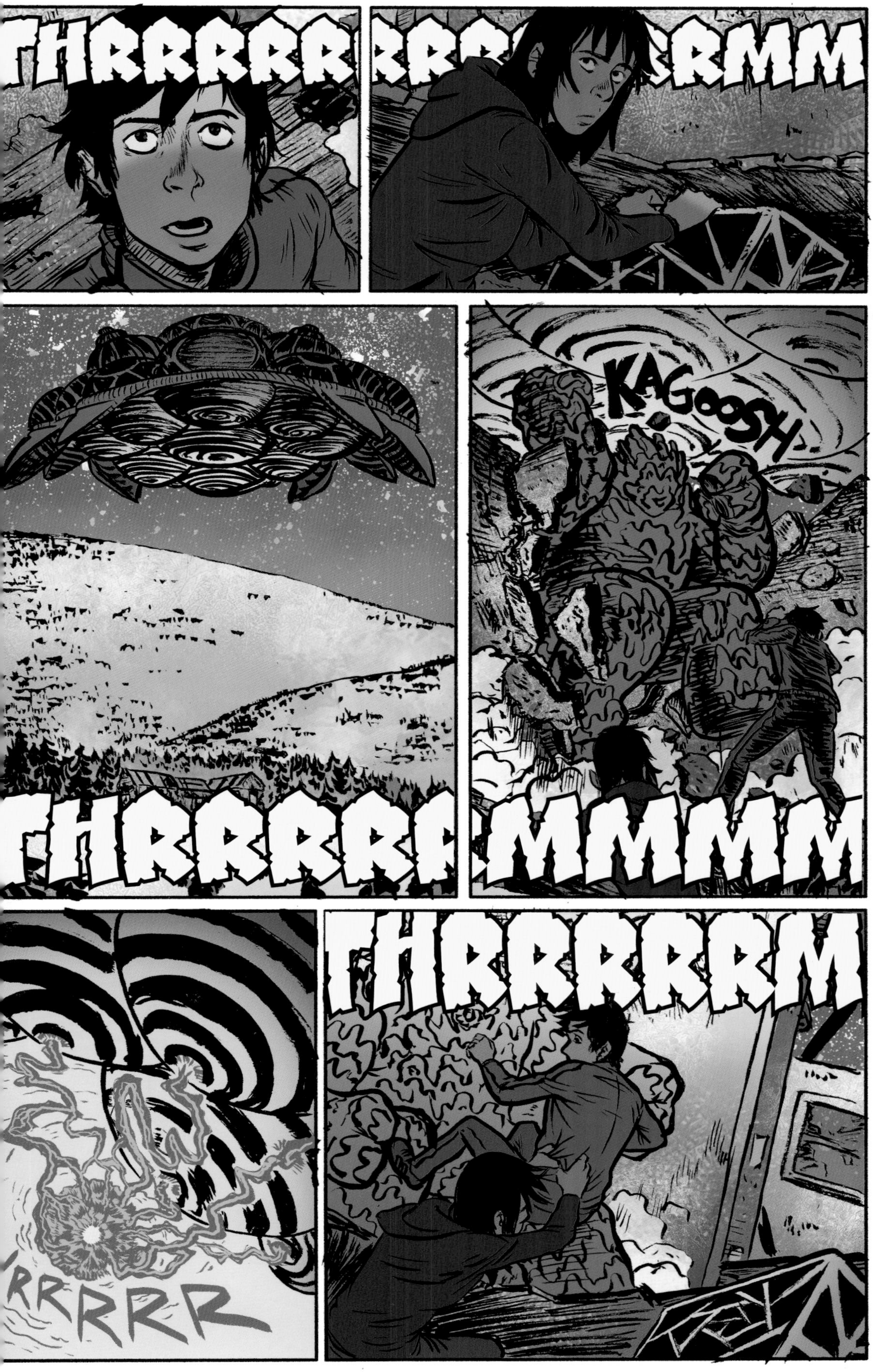
THRRRRRR
RRRRMM
KAGOOSH
THRRRRMMMMM
RRRRR
THRRRRRRM

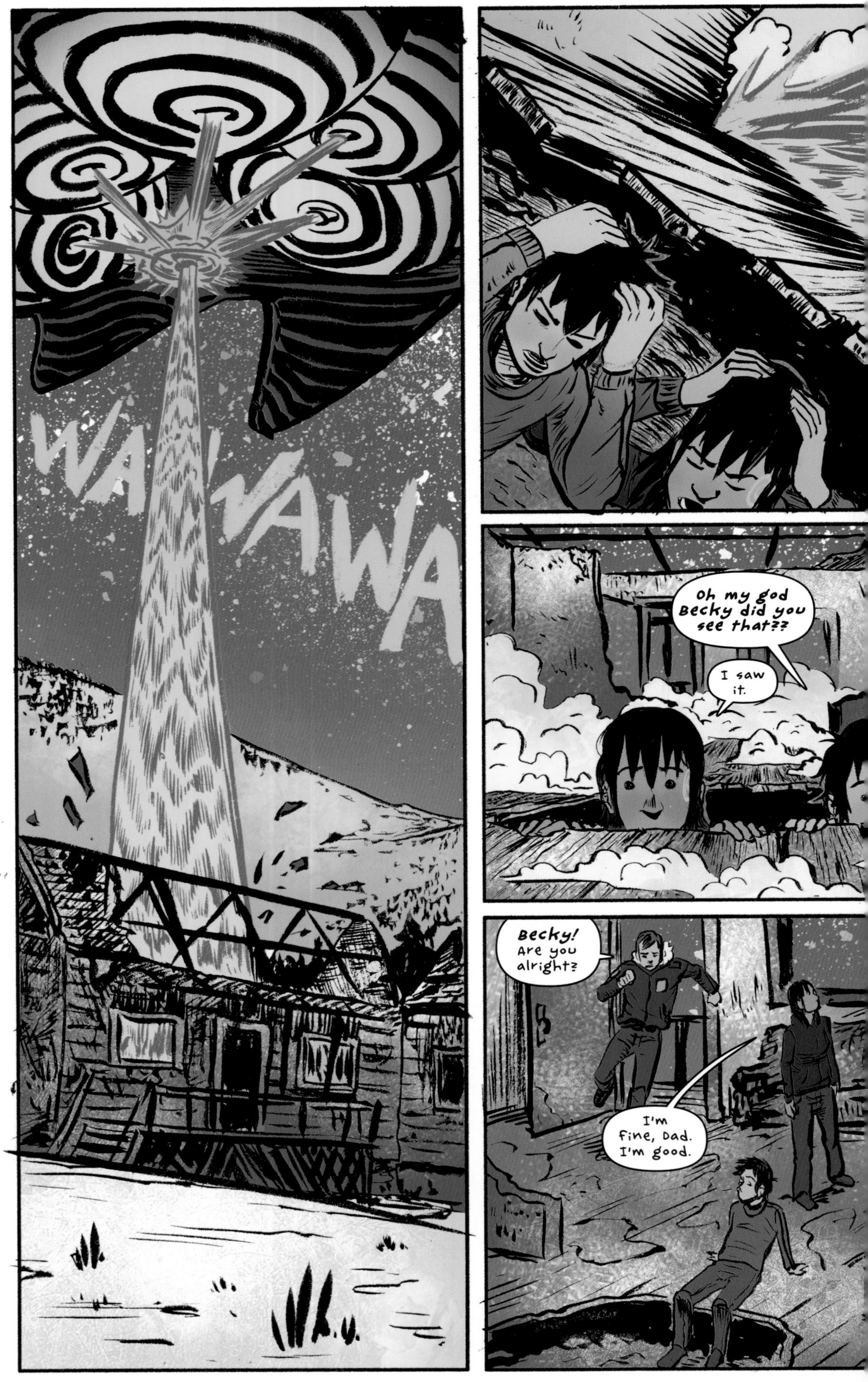
WAWAWAWA
Oh my god Becky did you see that??
I saw it.
Becky! Are you alright?
I'm fine, Dad. I'm good.

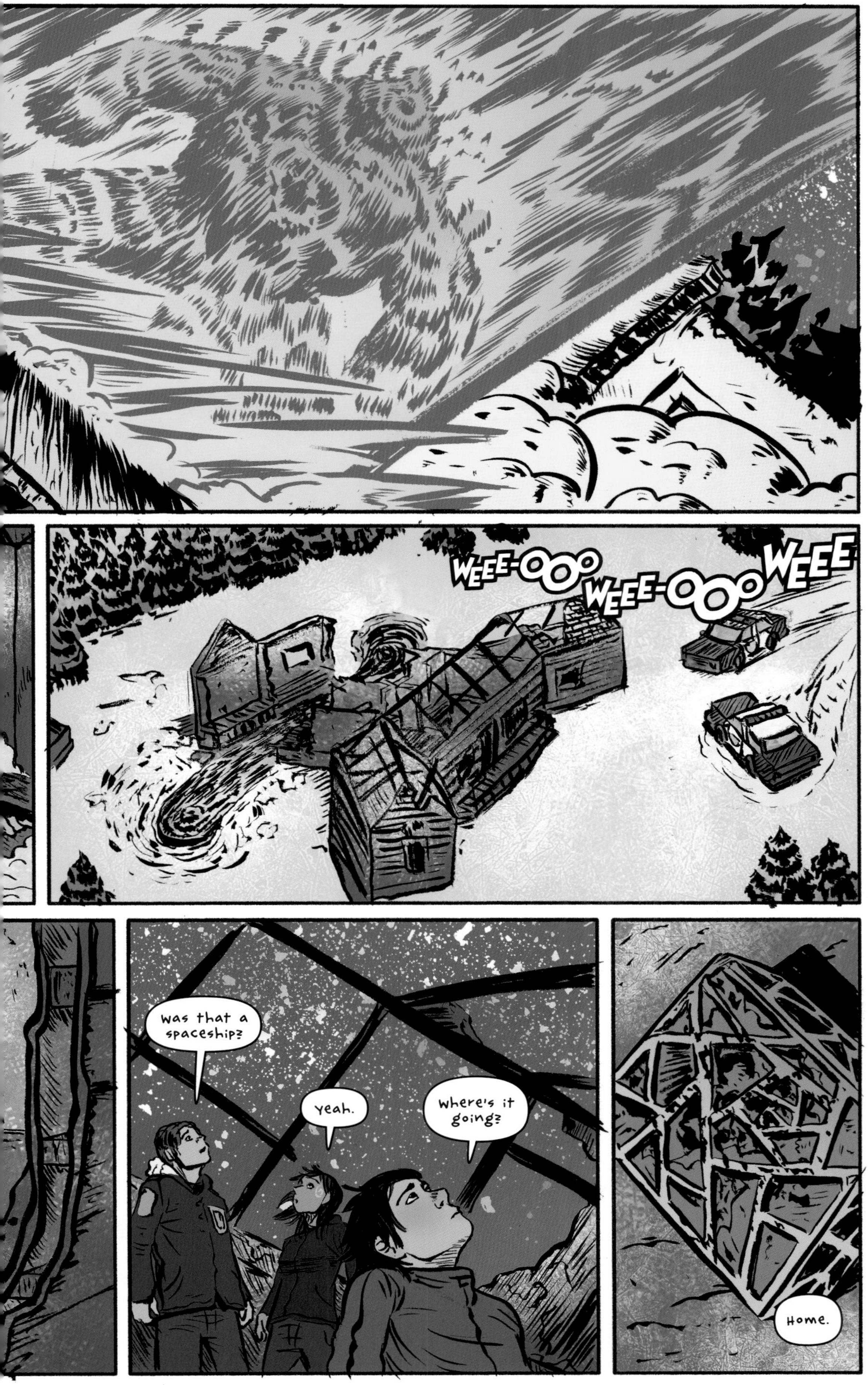
WEEE-OOO
WEEE-OOO
WEEE
Was that a spaceship?
Yeah.
Where's it going?
Home.

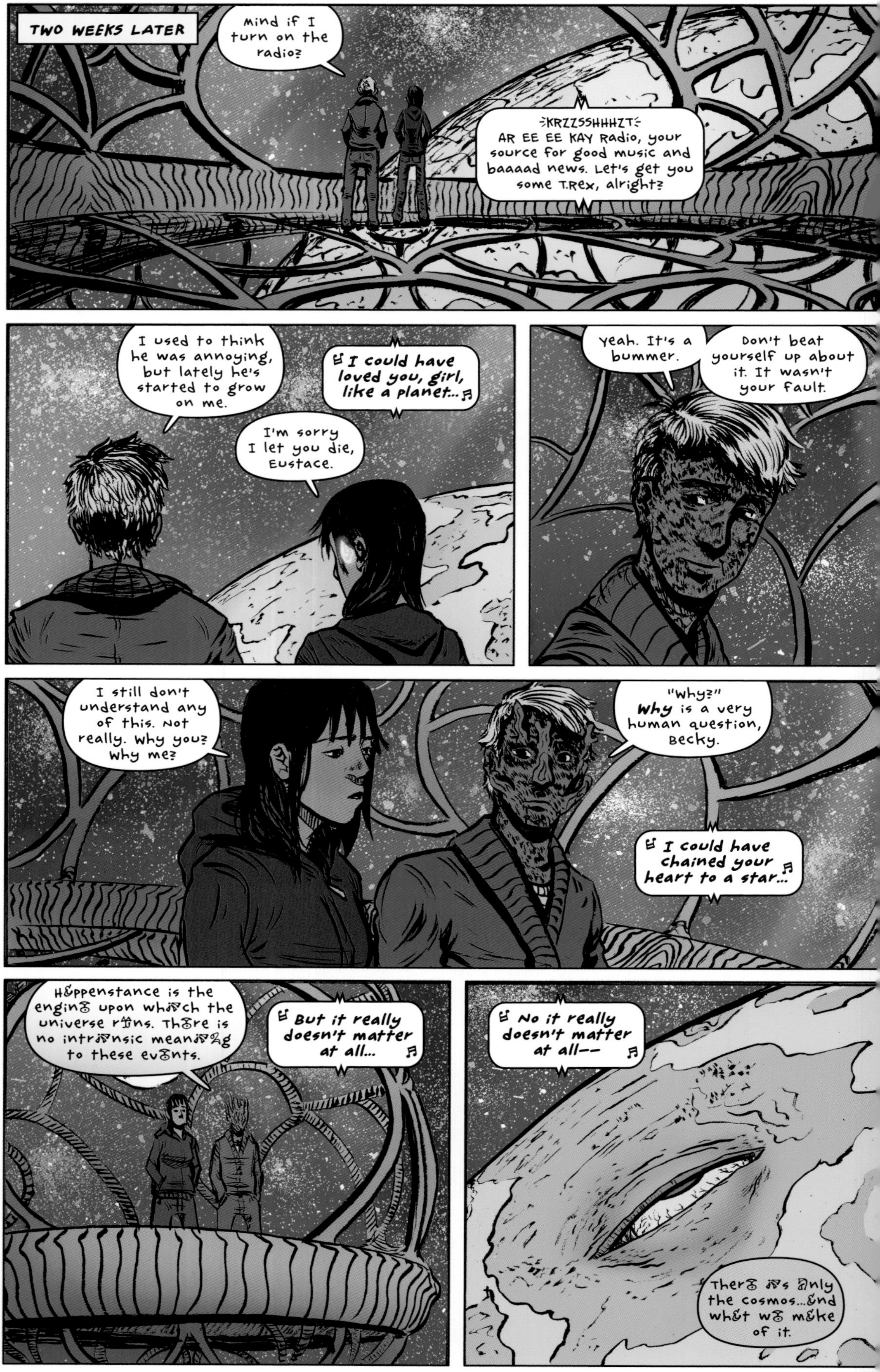
TWO WEEKS LATER
Mind if I turn on the radio?
KRZZSSHHHZT
AR EE EE KAY Radio, your source for good music and baaaad news. Let's get you some T.Rex, alright?
I used to think he was annoying, but lately he's started to grow on me.
I could have loved you, girl, like a planet...
I'm sorry I let you die, Eustace.
Yeah. It's a bummer.
Don't beat yourself up about it. It wasn't your fault.
I still don't understand any of this. Not really. Why you? Why me?
"Why?" Why is a very human question, Becky.
I could have chained your heart to a star...
Happenstance is the engine upon which the universe runs. There is no intrinsic meaning to these events.
But it really doesn't matter at all...
No it really doesn't matter at all--
There is only the cosmos...and what we make of it.

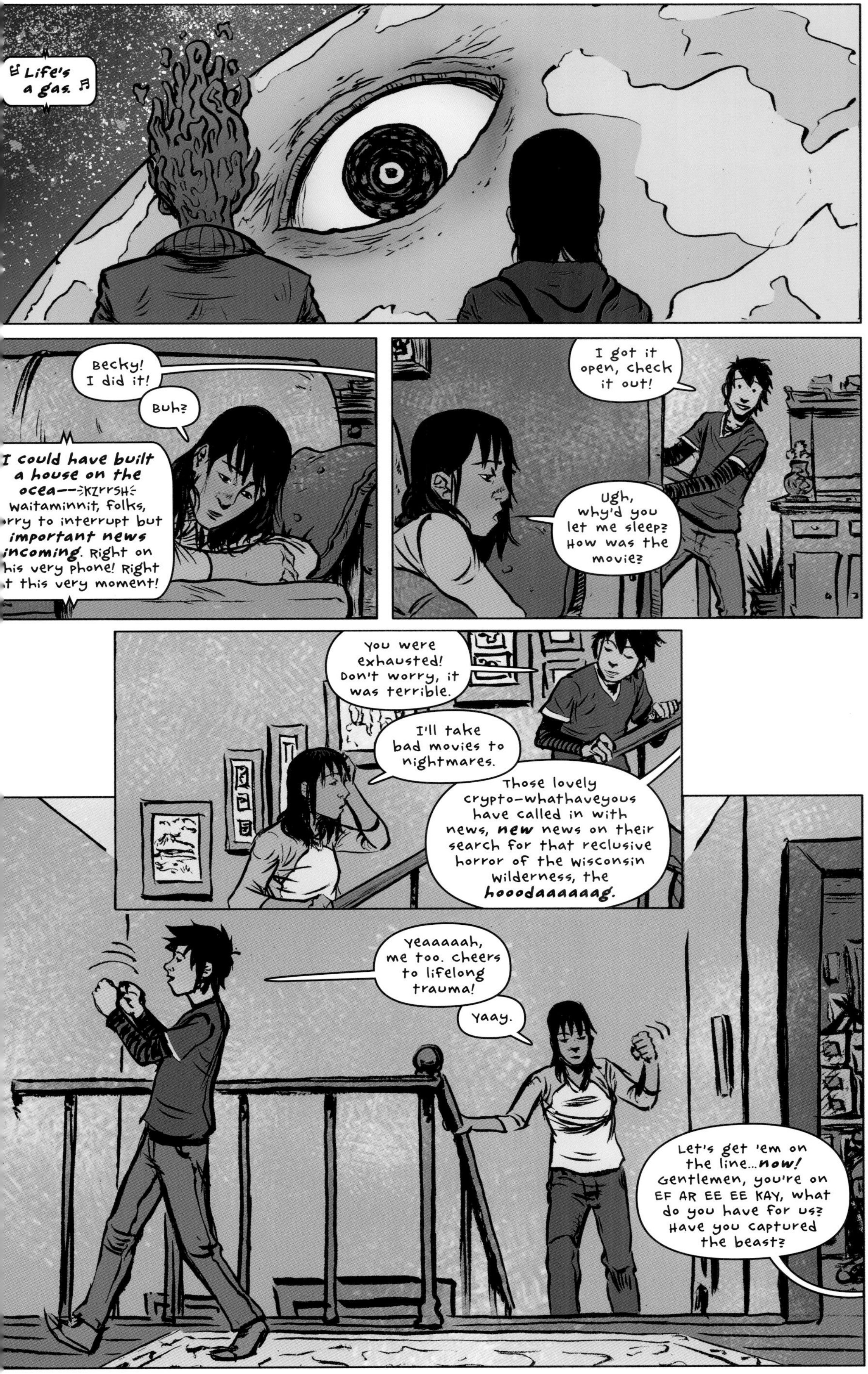
Life's a gas.
Becky! I did it!
Buh?
I could have built a house on the ocea--KZRRSH- Waitaminnit, folks, orry to interrupt but important news incoming. Right on his very phone! Right t this very moment!
I got it open, check it out!
Ugh, why'd you let me sleep? How was the movie?
You were exhausted! Don't worry, it was terrible.
I'll take bad movies to nightmares.
Those lovely crypto-whathaveyous have called in with news, new news on their search for that reclusive horror of the Wisconsin wilderness, the hooodaaaaaag.
Yeaaaaah, me too. Cheers to lifelong trauma!
Yaay.
Let's get 'em on the line...now! Gentlemen, you're on EF AR EE EE KAY, what do you have for us? Have you captured the beast?

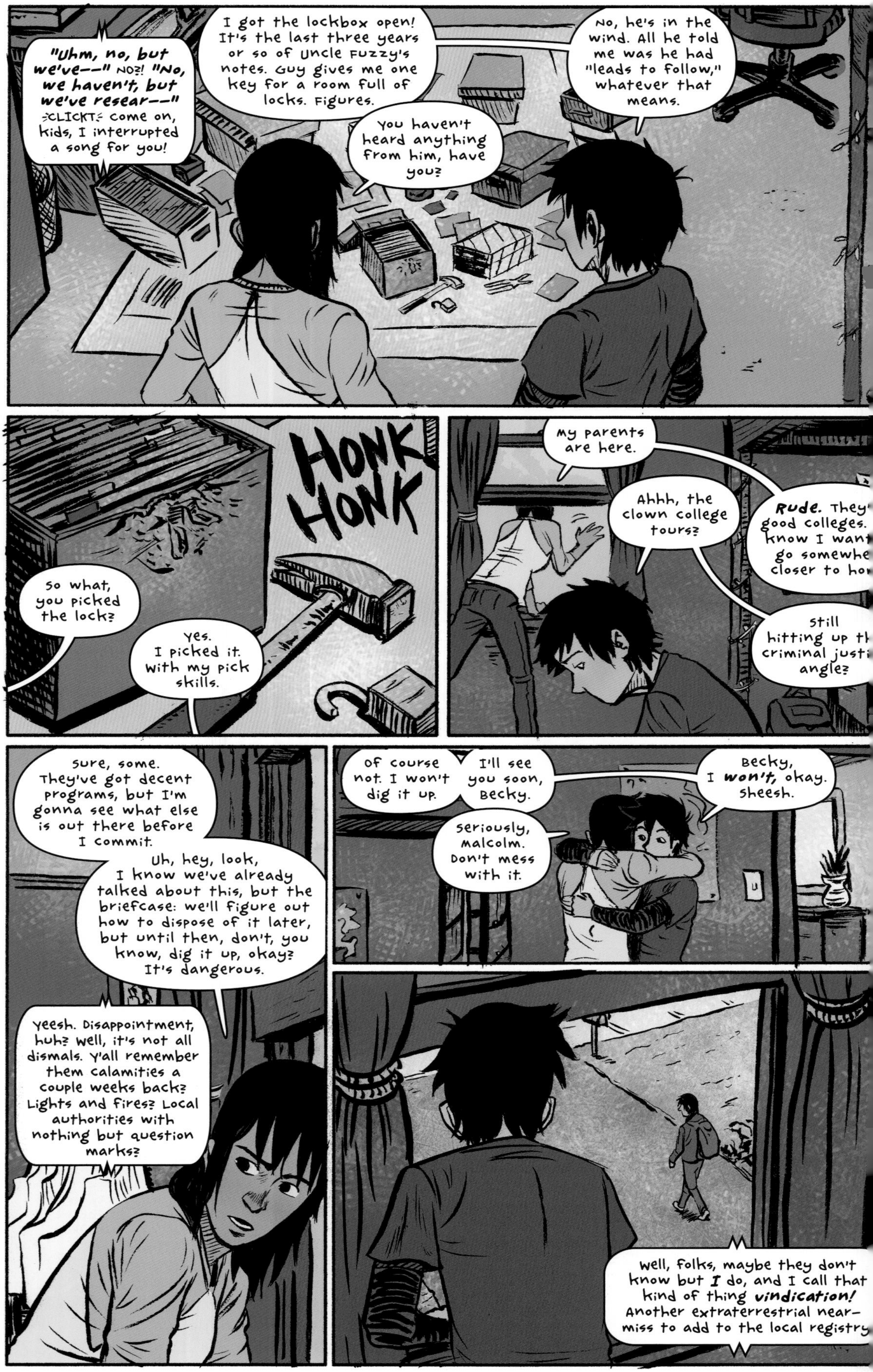
"Uhm, no, but we've--" NO?! "No, we haven't, but we've resear--" =CLICK!= come on, kids, I interrupted a song for you!
I got the lockbox open! It's the last three years or so of Uncle Fuzzy's notes. Guy gives me one key for a room full of locks. Figures.
You haven't heard anything from him, have you?
No, he's in the wind. All he told me was he had "leads to follow," whatever that means.
HONK HONK
So what, you picked the lock?
Yes. I picked it. With my pick skills.
My parents are here.
Ahhh, the clown college tours?
Rude. They
good colleges.
know I want
go somewhe
closer to ho
Still hitting up th
criminal justi
angle?
Sure, some. They've got decent programs, but I'm gonna see what else is out there before I commit.
Uh, hey, look, I know we've already talked about this, but the briefcase: we'll figure out how to dispose of it later, but until then, don't, you know, dig it up, okay? It's dangerous.
Yeesh. Disappointment, huh? Well, it's not all dismals. Y'all remember them calamities a couple weeks back? Lights and fires? Local authorities with nothing but question marks?
Of course not. I won't dig it up.
I'll see you soon, Becky.
Becky, I won't, okay. Sheesh.
Seriously, Malcolm. Don't mess with it.
Well, folks, maybe they don't know but I do, and I call that kind of thing vindication! Another extraterrestrial near-miss to add to the local registry

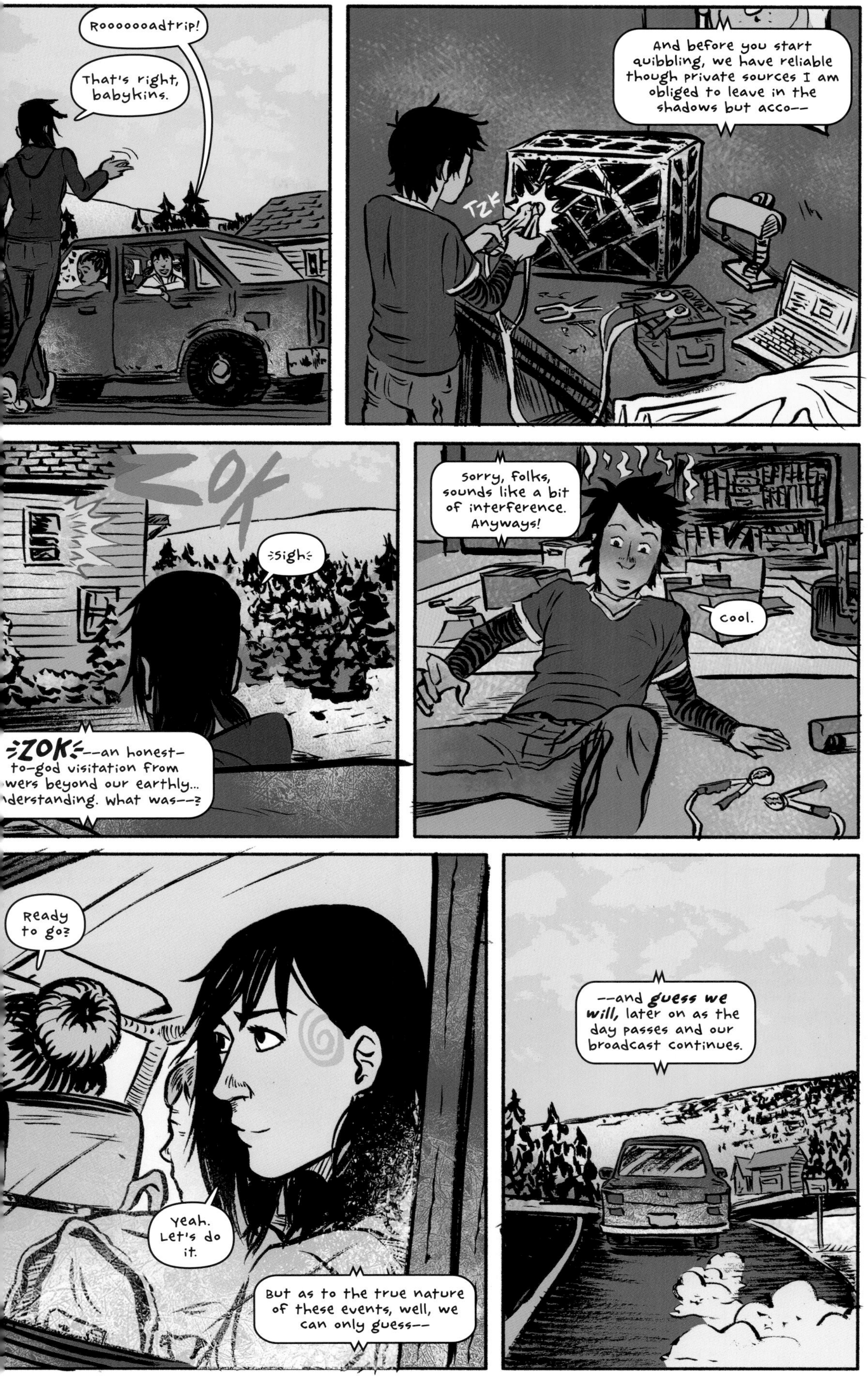
Rooooooadtrip!
That's right, babykins.
And before you start quibbling, we have reliable though private sources I am obliged to leave in the shadows but acco--
TZK
ZOK
sigh
ZOK--an honest-to-god visitation from wers beyond our earthly... derstanding. What was--?
Sorry, folks, sounds like a bit of interference. Anyways!
cool.
Ready to go?
Yeah. Let's do it.
But as to the true nature of these events, well, we can only guess--
--and guess we will, later on as the day passes and our broadcast continues.

ELSEWHERE

After all, it's just another of a million tales of the under-understood drifting around this little galaxy of ours, easy to miss if you're not looking, like most of us aren't. There's always another to consider.

♫ I COULD H@VE BUILT A HOUSE ON THE OCEAN... ♫

Hello, Lieutenant.

FSSK

♫ I COULD H4VE PLACED OUR LOVE IN THE SKYYYYYY... ♫

oh God.

Are you here to kill me?

I could. I'd *like* to. You and yours have taken quite a bit from me.

But she doesn't want you dead. She misses you.

♫ BUT It RLLY DOESN'T M4TTER @ ALL... ♫

she——?

And, for the moment, I need you as well.

Two weeks after the mukawgee incide there was a very br sort of signal with broken encryption. M organizations with t equipment to liste wrote it off as noise.

♫ NO It RLLY DOESN'T M4TTER @ ALL... ♫

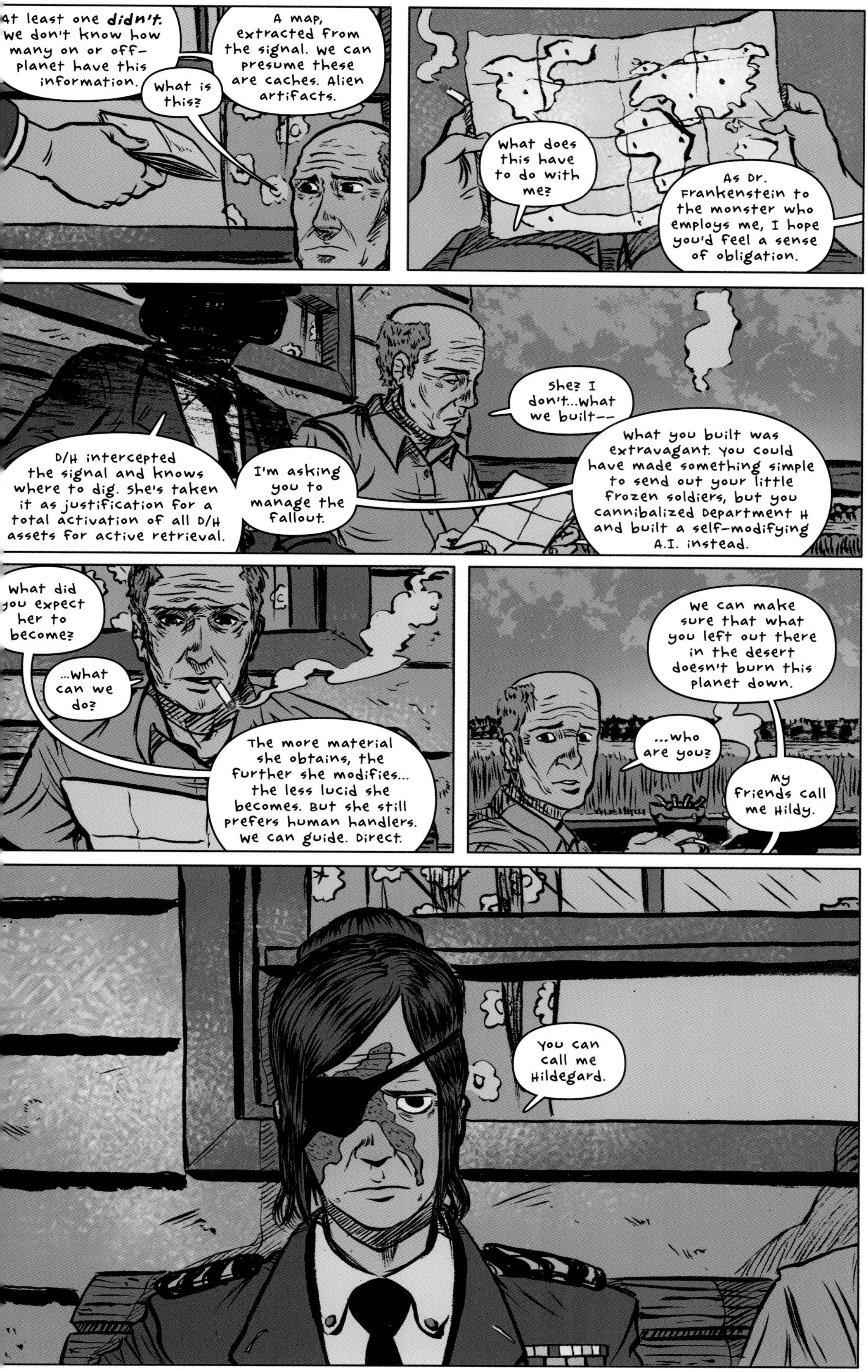
At least one didn't. We don't know how many on or off-planet have this information.
What is this?
A map, extracted from the signal. We can presume these are caches. Alien artifacts.
What does this have to do with me?
As Dr. Frankenstein to the monster who employs me, I hope you'd feel a sense of obligation.
D/H intercepted the signal and knows where to dig. She's taken it as justification for a total activation of all D/H assets for active retrieval.
I'm asking you to manage the fallout.
She? I don't...what we built--
What you built was extravagant. You could have made something simple to send out your little frozen soldiers, but you cannibalized Department H and built a self-modifying A.I. instead.
...What can we do?
What did you expect her to become?
The more material she obtains, the further she modifies... the less lucid she becomes. But she still prefers human handlers. We can guide. Direct.
We can make sure that what you left out there in the desert doesn't burn this planet down.
...Who are you?
My friends call me Hildy.
You can call me Hildegard.

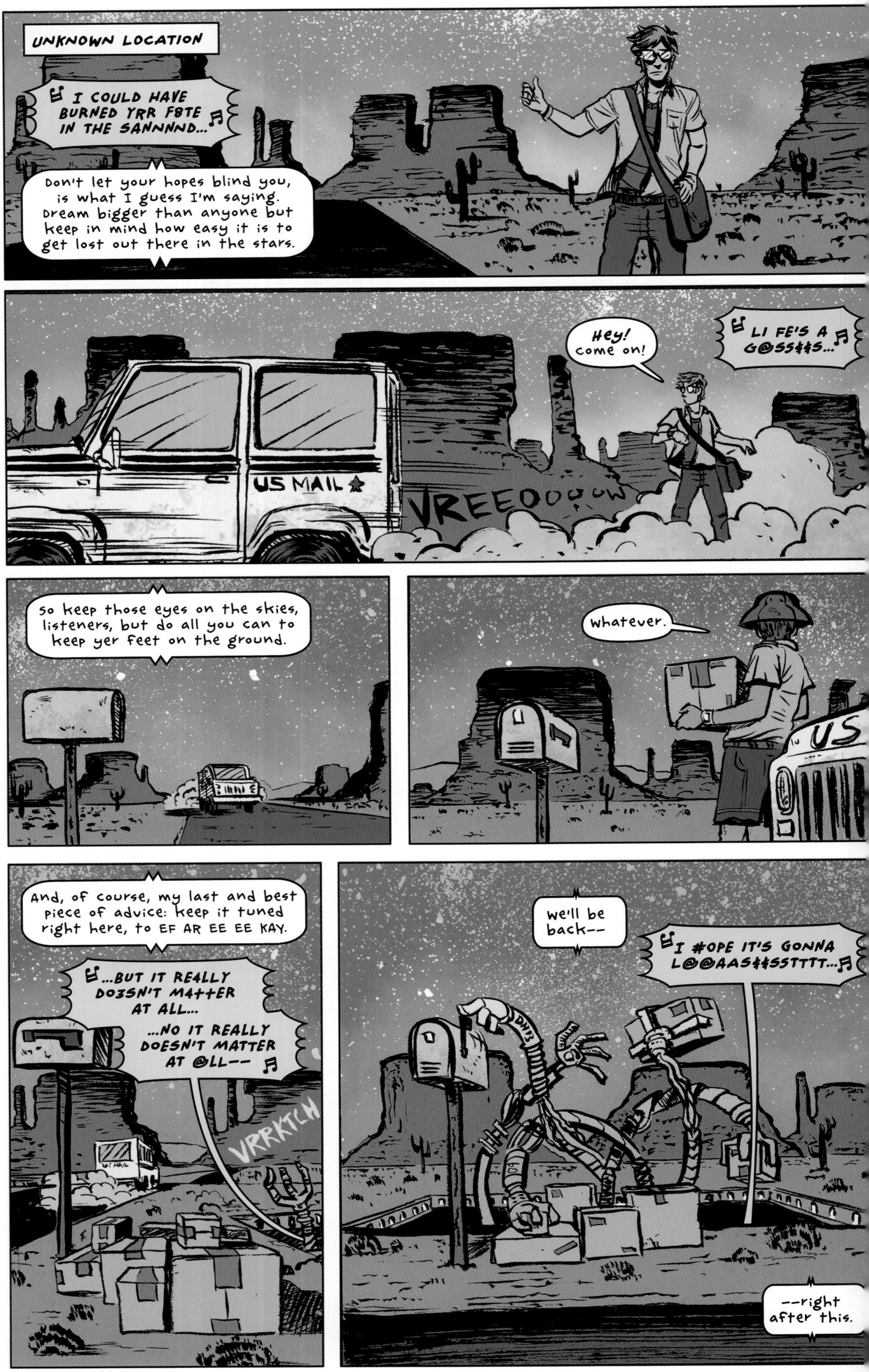
UNKNOWN LOCATION
I COULD HAVE BURNED YRR F8TE IN THE SANNNND...
Don't let your hopes blind you, is what I guess I'm saying. Dream bigger than anyone but keep in mind how easy it is to get lost out there in the stars.
Hey! Come on!
LI FE'S A G@SS$$S...
US MAIL
VREEOOOOW
So keep those eyes on the skies, listeners, but do all you can to keep yer feet on the ground.
Whatever.
And, of course, my last and best piece of advice: keep it tuned right here, to EF AR EE EE KAY.
...BUT IT RE4LLY DO3SN'T M4TTER AT ALL...
...NO IT REALLY DOESN'T MATTER AT @LL--
VRRKTCH
We'll be back--
I #OPE IT'S GONNA L@@AAS$$SSTTTT...
--right after this.

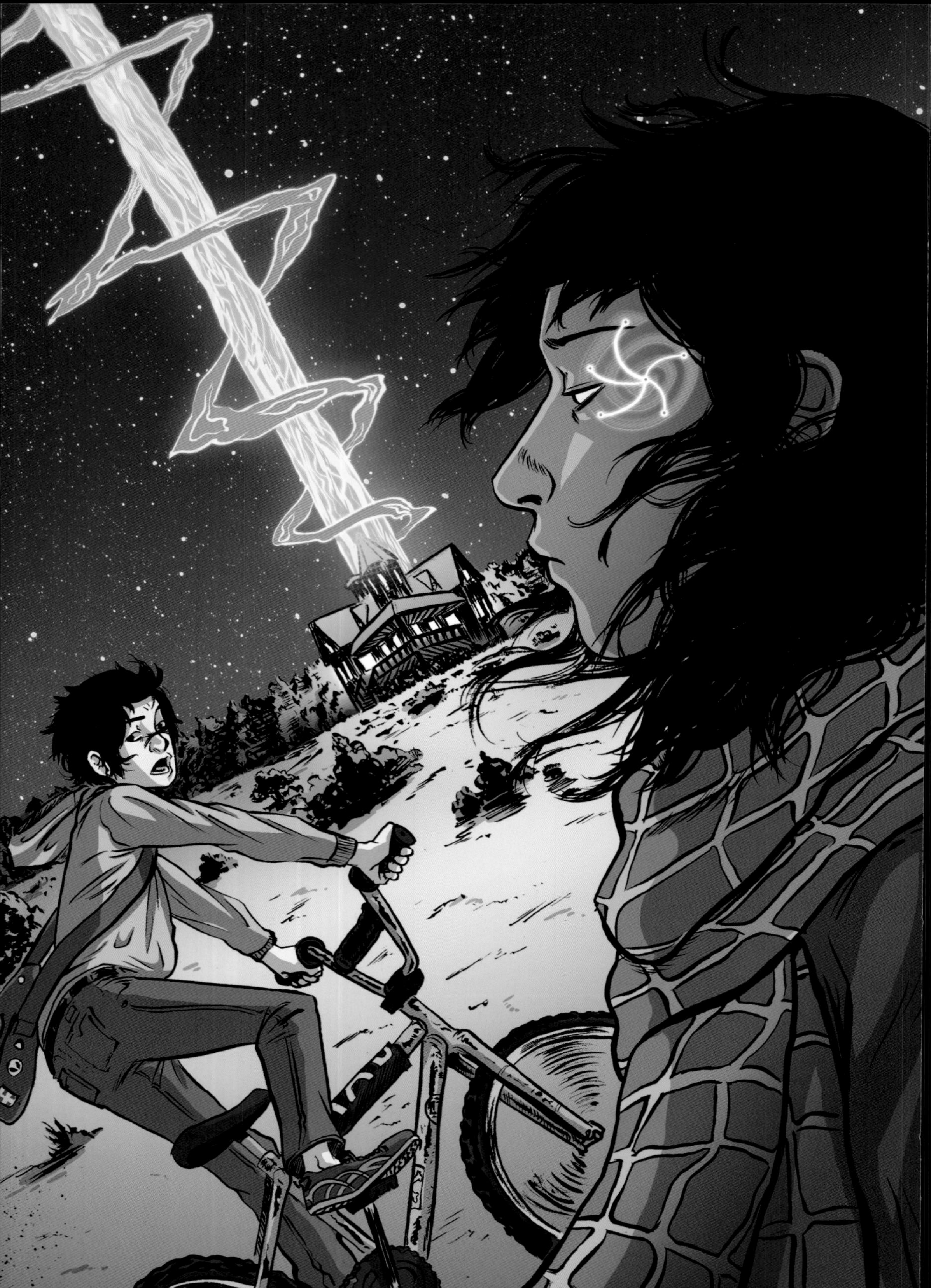

issue one
matthew fox

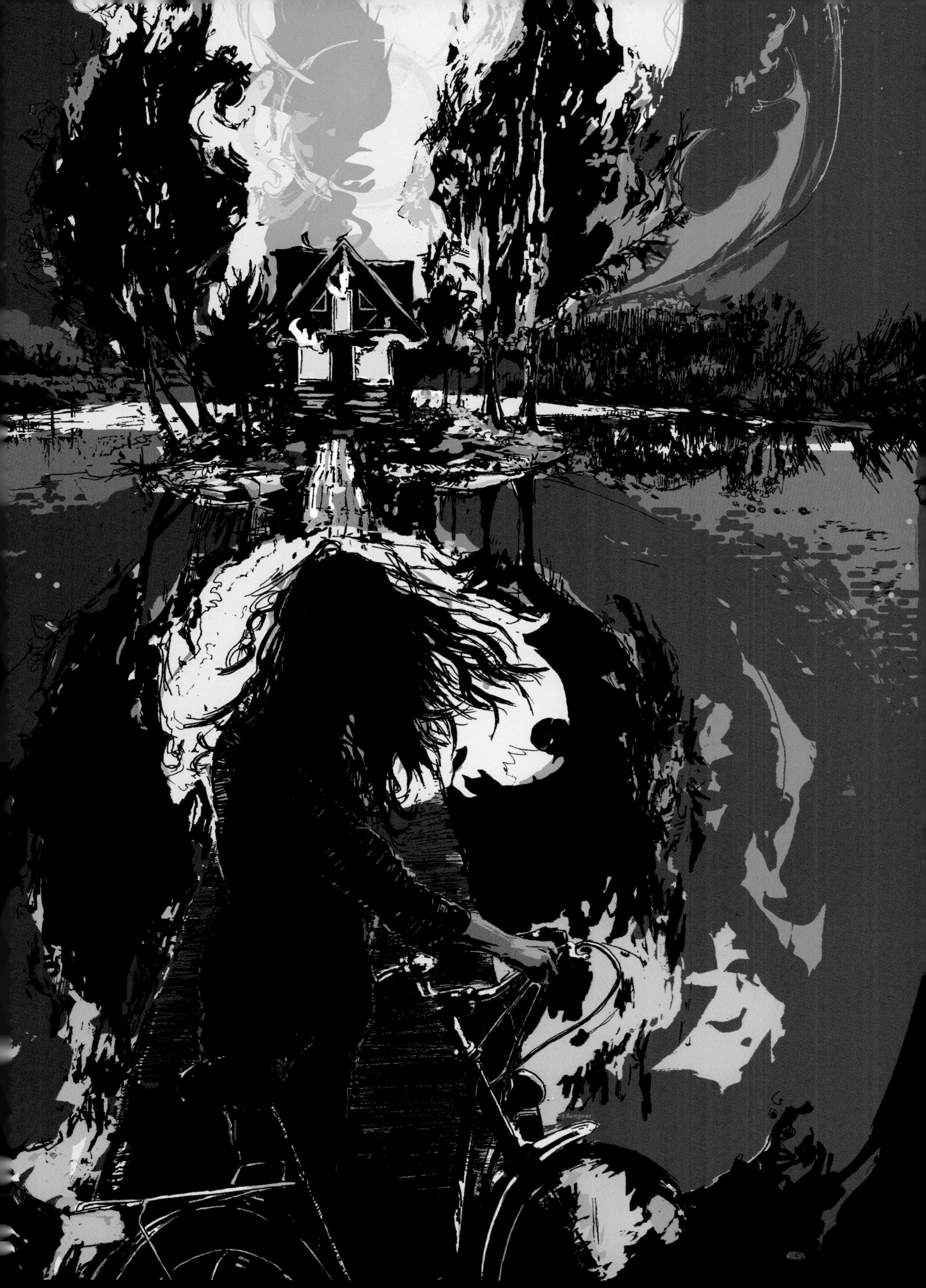

issue one jackpot variant
alison sampson

issue one BOOM! ten years variant
frazer irving

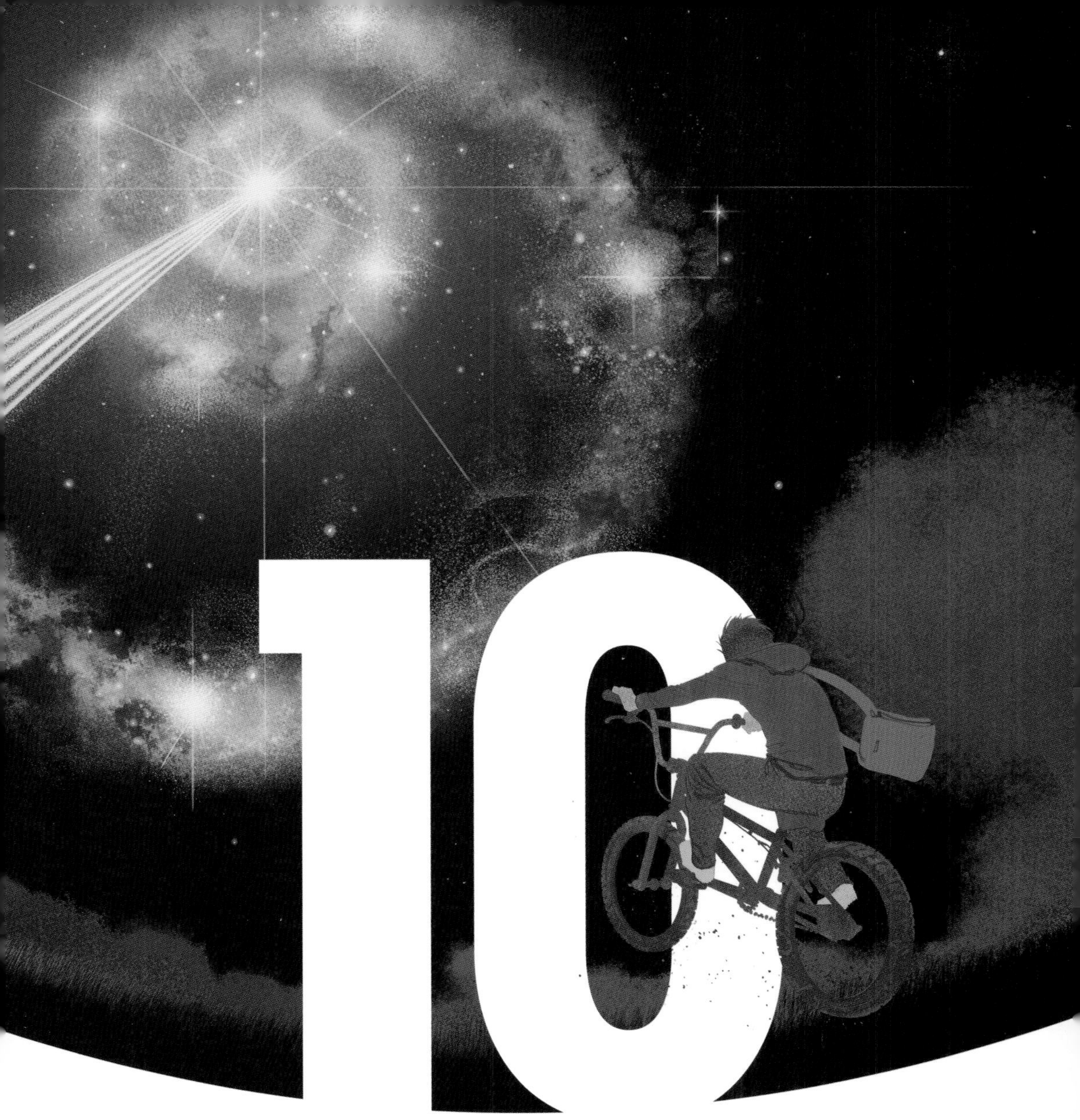
10

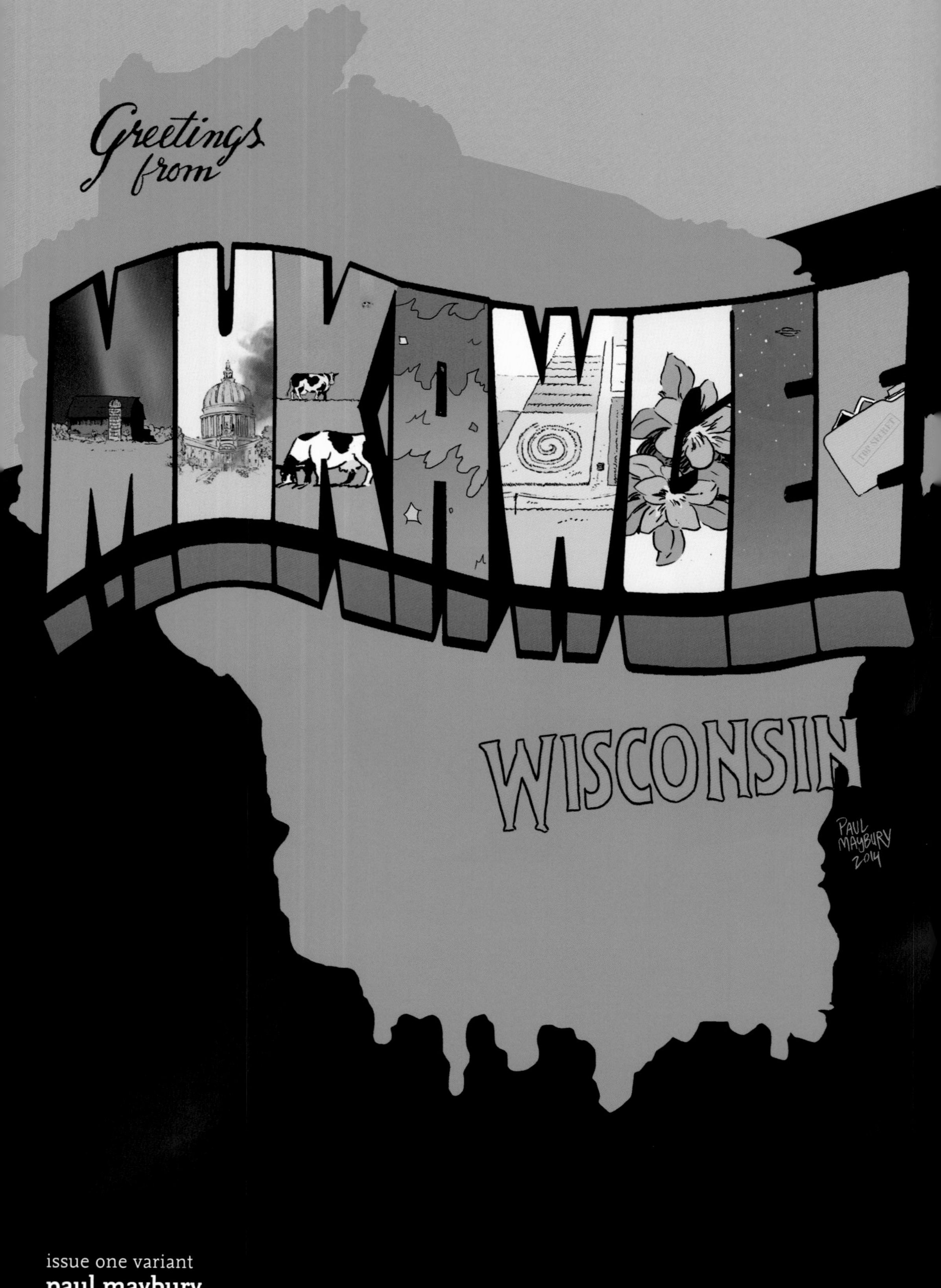
Greetings from
WISCONSIN
PAUL MAYBURY 2014

issue one variant
paul maybury

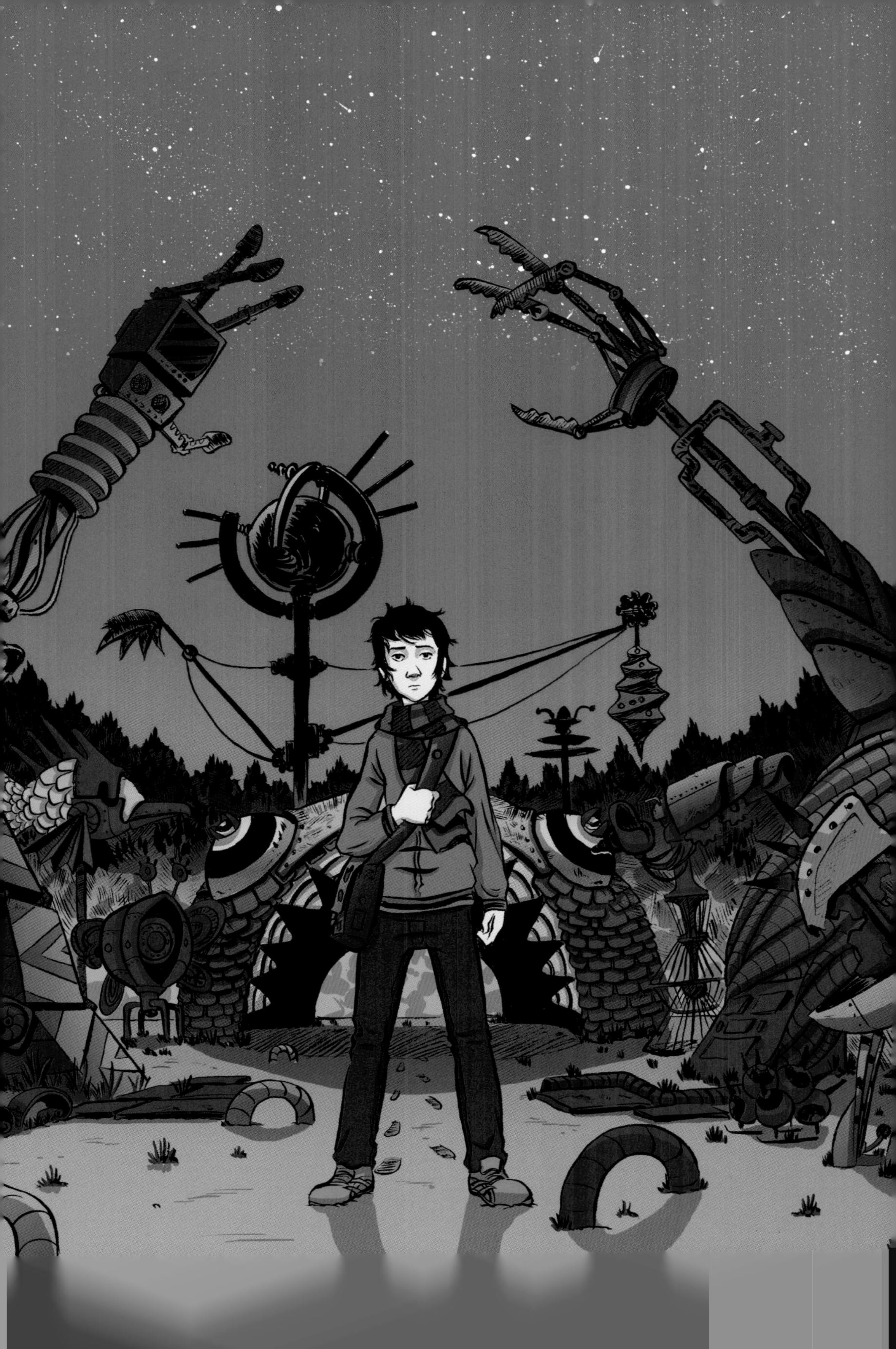

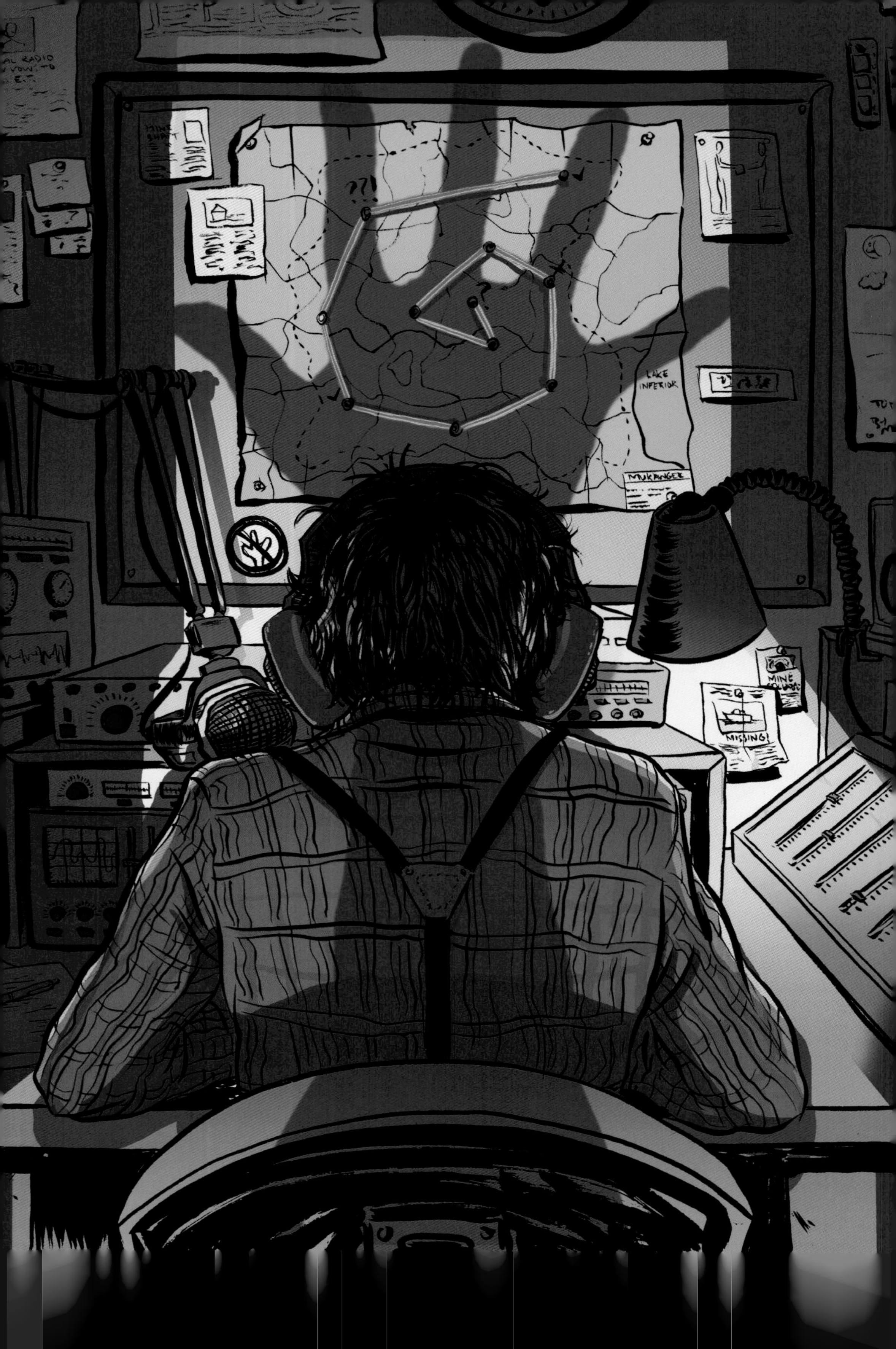
LAKE INFERIOR
MISSING!

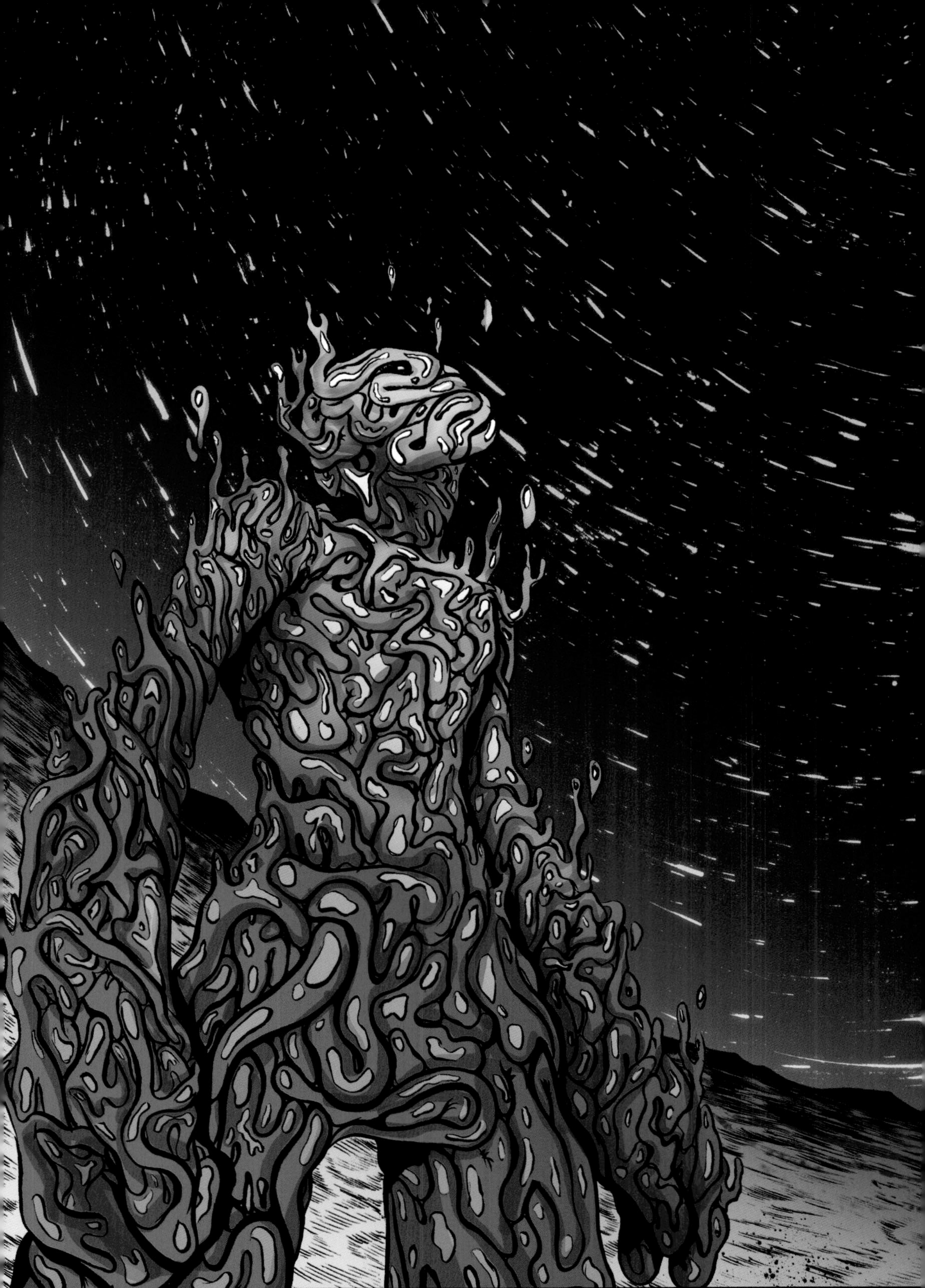

issue four
matthew fox

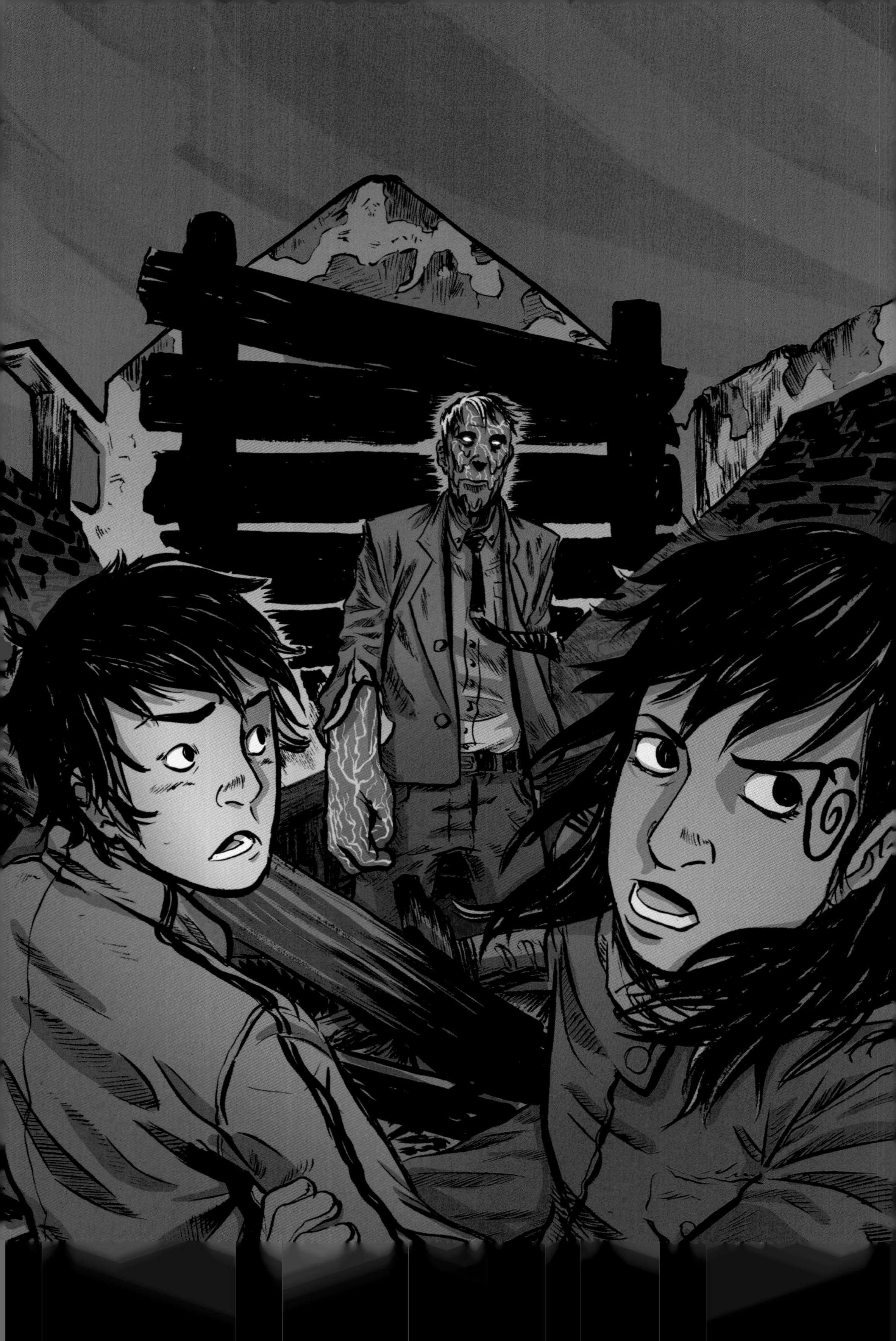

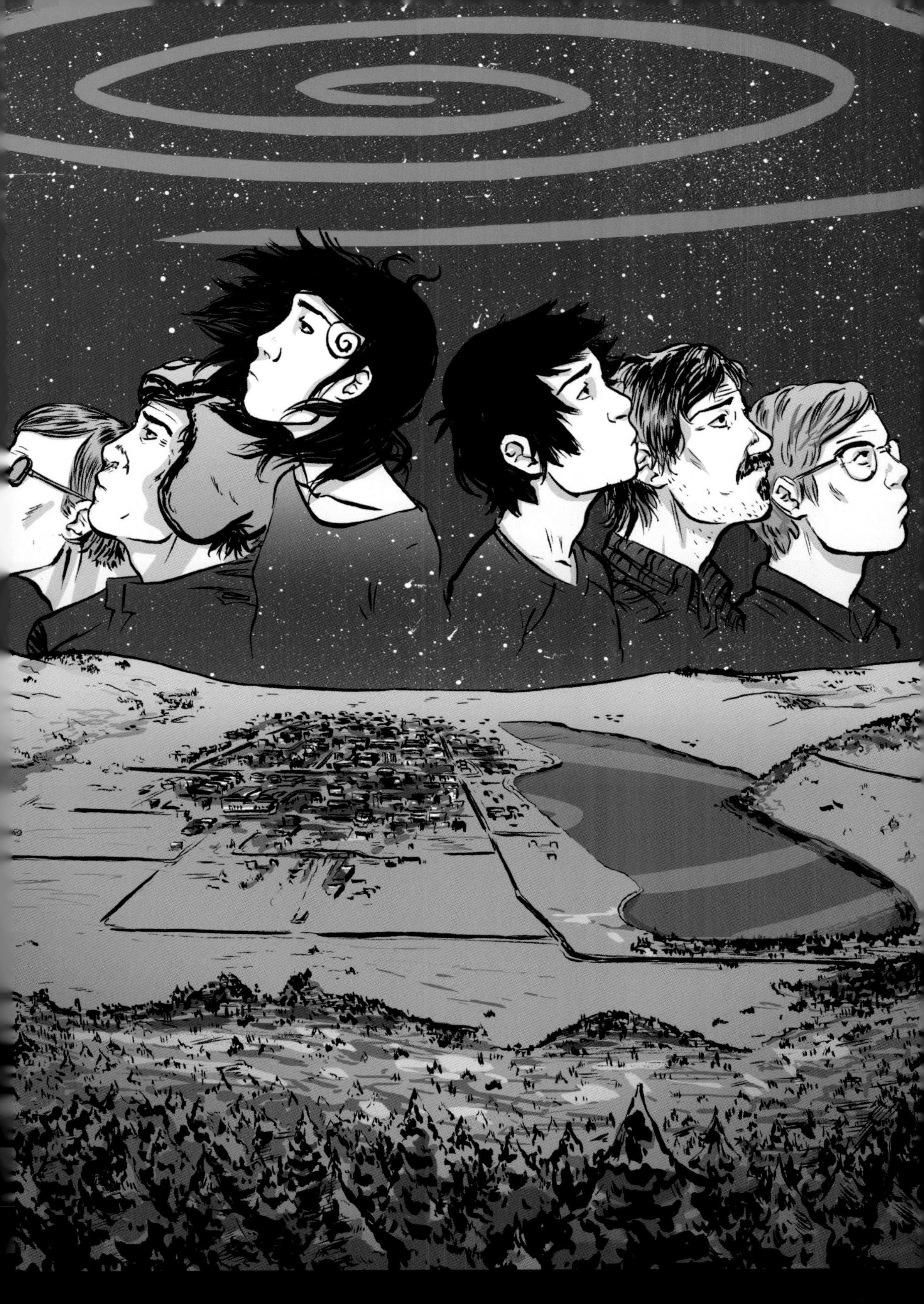

issue six
matthew fox